UNITED IRISHMEN, UNITED STATES

UNITED IRISHMEN, UNITED STATES

Immigrant Radicals in the Early Republic

DAVID A. WILSON

Cornell University Press

Ithaca and London

First published 1998 by Cornell University Press

Printed in the United States of America

Cornell University Press strives to use environmentally responsible suppliers and materials to the fullest extent possible in the publishing of its books. Such materials include vegetable-based, low-VOC inks and acid-free papers that are also recycled, totally chlorine-free, or party composed of nonwood fibers.

Library of Congress Cataloging-in-Publication Data

Wilson, David A., 1950–
United Irishmen, United States : immigrant radicals in the early republic / David A. Wilson.
p. cm.
Includes bibliographical references (p.) and index.
ISBN 0-8014-3175-1 (cloth : alk. paper)
1. Irish Americans—Politics and government. 2. United States—Politics and government—1783–1809. 3. Radicalism—United States—History—18th century. 4. Ireland—Politics and government—1760–1820. 5. United Irishmen. I. Title.
E184.I6W47 1998 98-10377
973′.049162—dc21

Cloth printing 10 9 8 7 6 5 4 3 2 1

No hero hang'd, no hamlet burn'd
No peasant robb'd and a that
No spitefu spy, no coward turned
We never dream't o a that.
The neighbours soon combin'd we saw
In union, love and a that
But love wa[illegible] the law
And so we p[a]ied for a that.
    And a that, and a that
    And twice as mickle's a that
    The blessings o America
    Will make amends for a that.

—Andrew Parks, "Emigration to America," 1798.

"[I do] not wish to invite hordes of wild Irishmen, nor the turbulent and disorderly of all parts of the world, to come here with a view to disturb our tranquillity."

—Harrison Gray Otis,
Debates and Proceedings of Congress, 1797.

For Liam Kennedy,

and for the memory of Gwyn A. Williams

Ni welir ei debyg byth eto

Contents

Acknowledgments ix

Introduction
The Most God-Provoking Democrats on This Side of Hell 1

Chapter 1
A Green Bough 12

Chapter 2
Hordes of Wild Irishmen 36

Chapter 3
The Land of Liberty 58

Chapter 4
Humbling the British Tyrant 77

Chapter 5
Marching to Irish Music 96

Chapter 6
Signs of the Times 112

Chapter 7
No Excluded Class 133

Chapter 8
The Cause of Ireland 153

Conclusion
The Tradition of All the Dead Generations 172

Notes 181

Index 213

Acknowledgments

This book brings together two fields that have interested me for many years—transatlantic radicalism during the Age of Revolution, and modern Irish history. My work on transatlantic radicalism was stimulated by Gwyn A. Williams at the University of York, England. He was a brilliant lecturer and a poetic writer. Inspired by his teaching, I wrote my first book on the Anglo-American careers of Thomas Paine and William Cobbett, and later edited a collection of Cobbett's American writings. And it was through Cobbett that I became aware of the importance of the United Irishmen in the United States.

At Queen's University, Kingston, I studied modern Irish history with Donald Akenson, and learned a great deal from his searching critique of received historical wisdom. After teaching in the United States and Canada, I worked in Belfast as a freelance journalist and broadcaster in the mid-1980s, where I spent many hours discussing history and politics with Liam Kennedy. He is not only one of Ireland's leading economic and social historians, but also a courageous, compassionate and open-minded peace activist in the North. His influence on this book appears not so much on particular arguments (although it is sometimes there) as on the general approach that I have taken.

Thanks also go to Roger Haydon, my editor at Cornell University Press. He not only initiated the project, but also provided much good-humored encouragement in the race against a very tight deadline. Without him, this book would not have been written. His colleagues at Cornell, Terence McKiernan and Grey Osterud, helped to fine-tune the manuscript with skill and grace. I also thank the Social Sciences and Humanities Research Council of Canada for the research grants that enabled me to visit archives in Philadelphia, Washington, Belfast and Dublin. The interlibrary loan department at the University of Toronto's Robarts Library responded with remarkable efficiency to my apparently inexhaustible requests for books, pamphlets and newspapers. In particular, I thank Jane Lynch and Candy Cheung for all their help.

Ann Dooley, Máirín Nic Dhiarmada and Jean Talman of the Celtic Studies Programme at St. Michael's College, the University of Toronto, have been extremely supportive throughout the research and writing; I could not ask for better friends and colleagues. Martha Smith, Assistant Professor of American history at the University of Saskatoon, prompted me to move from a biographical to a thematic organizational structure; the result is a more analytical approach than would otherwise have been the case. Among the people who helped me to track down various sources, I thank Joseph Jones, Kyla Madden, Seán McAnulla, John McCabe and Andrew Shields. Professor Kerby Miller of the University of Missouri generously provided me with information from his forthcoming book on the letters of Irish immigrants to the United States. Seán McKay cheerfully checked the grammar and hunted down typographical errors, and Bruce Rolston compiled the index with his customary efficiency.

I thank Professor James S. Donnelly, Jr., of the University of Wisconsin at Madison, for his helpful remarks about the chapter on Thomas Ledlie Birch, and Dr. Ian McBride of Durham University for his insights about Ulster Presbyterianism. Professor A.T.Q. Stewart of Queen's University at Belfast, and Professor Richard Twomey of St. Mary's University in Halifax, Nova Scotia, both read the manuscript in its entirety. I benefited immensely from their depth of knowledge and generosity of spirit; their perceptive comments are very much appreciated, and have contributed significantly to the final version of the book.

Throughout the writing of this book, Zsuzsa Balogh has reminded me of the relationship between personalities and politics, and has helped me to keep my priorities in perspective. For her encouragement, and above all for her love, there can never be thanks enough.

None of the above, it must be added, should be considered guilty by association.

David A. Wilson

Toronto, Ontario, Canada

P.S. Since writing this, I have had the pleasure of reading Michael Durey's magnificent *Transatlantic Radicals* (Lawrence, Kansas, 1997). I hope that readers will enjoy the similarities and differences between our books, and that both works will generate still more research on the British and Irish influences on American politics.

UNITED IRISHMEN, UNITED STATES

INTRODUCTION

The Most God-Provoking Democrats on This Side of Hell

In the summer of 1800, shortly before the election campaign that would sweep Thomas Jefferson to the Presidency and inaugurate the "second American Revolution," the Federalist Congressman Uriah Tracy traveled around Pennsylvania to take the political pulse of the state. He did not like what he found. The previous year, the Pennsylvania Republicans had elected Thomas McKean as Governor, with the result, in Tracy's view, that "the few remaining honest men and Federali[s]ts" were now being elbowed out of office by "every scoundrel who could read and write." His mood soured by a "bilious fever," Tracy had no difficulty identifying the people responsible for turning the political world upside down. "In my very lengthy journey through this State," he wrote, "I have seen many, very many Irishmen, and with a very few exceptions, they are United Irishmen, Free Masons, and the most God-provoking Democrats on this side of Hell."[1]

Uriah Tracy was far from being the only American politician who feared the effects of democracy in general and the United Irishmen in particular on the American way of life. Across the Atlantic in London, the American Minister Rufus King had been appalled when in 1798 he learned that the British government was striking a deal with the imprisoned leaders of the United Irishmen. In return for providing information about their revolutionary activities and their attempts to bring about a French invasion of Ireland, the leaders would be allowed to emigrate to any neutral country upon which they and the government could agree. King moved quickly to prevent them from coming to America. The United States was in an undeclared war with revolutionary France; the Federalist administration of John Adams viewed the opposition party, the Jeffersonian Republicans, as factious, destabilizing, pro-French, and potentially subversive. Among the strongest supporters of the

Jeffersonians were many of the Irish immigrants who had arrived in the country earlier in the decade. From King's viewpoint, it was imperative that United Irish leaders, who had close political and ideological links with France and a ready-made radical constituency in America, be kept out of his country. "I certainly do not think that they will be a desirable acquisition to any Nation," he wrote the British Home Secretary, the Duke of Portland, "but in none would they be likely to prove more mischievous than in mine, where from the sameness of language and similarity of Laws and Institutions they have greater opportunities of propagating their principles than in any other country." He was successful in his efforts, at least in the short run; the United Irish leaders would stay in prison for another four years, until the Peace of Amiens in 1802.[2]

Apart from anything else, the views of Tracy and King serve as a powerful negative indicator of the impact of the United Irish émigrés on American politics during the Age of Revolution. There are plenty of positive indicators as well. Throughout the country, Republican politicians quickly recognized the political potential of United Irish support; Jefferson established close contacts with radical Irish immigrants, and owed his victory in 1800 at least in part to their organizational and propagandistic skills. At the state level, radical politicians who formed alliances with the United Irishmen reaped the benefits; the political fortunes of people like Pennsylvania's Simon Snyder and New York's De Witt Clinton became closely tied to their ability to bring out the radical Irish vote. Rufus King's fears were not misplaced; the United Irishmen did indeed contribute significantly to the democratization of American life.

In part, this was a matter of numbers, of sheer political presence. During the 1790s, over 60,000 Irish emigrants arrived in the United States, many of whom left their homeland for political as well as economic reasons.[3] With each crackdown on radicalism in their own country, a new wave of United Irishmen swept across the Atlantic. By 1797 and 1798, when the repression was at its peak, the boats were crammed with political refugees. "We had a set of Steerage Passengers ripe for every Species of Disorder particularly while their Whiskey lasted," wrote one alarmed cabin passenger on his way to New York in 1797, "most of them being United Irishmen who had fled."[4] Ulster Presbyterians predominated, but there was a growing Catholic component as well; according to one estimate, Catholics constituted 20 percent of the Irish immigrant flow between 1797 and 1800.[5] Contrary to the myth that originated with the United Irish immigrants themselves and that has been echoed by their historians, the majority settled in the countryside rather than the seaboard cities; travelers routinely stumbled across "colonies of Irish" throughout the length and breadth of the United States.[6] Nevertheless, it was in such places as New York, Philadelphia, Washington, Baltimore and Charleston that they were most visible and reached the critical mass necessary for concerted political action. The urban Irish may not have been typical, but they provided the United Irish leaders with vitally important radical constituencies.

Following well-established Irish-American trade and migration routes, the United Irishmen moved through social networks that had been built up by earlier immigrants, and formed their own political communities in the New World. In the process, they effectively took over Irish America, and remodeled it according to their own revolutionary democratic republican image. Where the United Irishmen belonged to pre-existing radical transatlantic groups with close family, business or religious ties, this transformation was relatively easy to accomplish. Elsewhere, however, it was fraught with tension. Many of the older immigrants, including a good number of Catholics, were aligned with the Federalist Party, and they resented the way in which in the United Irishmen arrogated to themselves the right to speak for all of the Irish people, whether at home or abroad. Irish Federalists condemned the United Irishmen as dangerous demagogues who had brought the horrors of civil war into their own country and were now employing the same “disorganizing principles” in the United States. For their part, the United Irishmen caricatured their opponents as “un-Irish” Orangemen and “pro-British” Federalists, [illegible] them as double traitors whose political voice should be silenced in the name of Liberty. And this was the view that ultimately triumphed.

Given the importance of the United Irishmen in redefining Irish America and helping to push the United States in more democratic directions, it is surprising that they have received so little attention from historians. The best studies are those of Richard Twomey and Michael Durey, both of which view the United Irishmen as a subgroup within the larger phenomenon of transatlantic republicanism. Emphasizing the sheer heterogeneity of the movement, Twomey argues that the émigrés were divided between middle-class and plebeian elements, and shows that their political radicalism often went hand-in-hand with social conservatism; thus he writes of the “ambivalent” and “limited” nature of Anglo-American radicalism. Durey, on the other hand, is more concerned with identifying common features within transatlantic patriotism; from this perspective, he maintains that most radicals were “marginal men” from the professional middle classes in Britain and Ireland, who attempted to realize their “quasi-millennial” vision of a just and meritocratic society in their new American home.[7]

Ultimately, the similarities between Twomey's and Durey's analyses are more striking than the differences. Both historians place the émigrés firmly within the Paineite democratic republican tradition, with its emphasis on political liberty and economic opportunity. They point out that the patriots emerged at the forefront of American economic nationalism, and trace the trajectory through which many of the leading figures came to embrace protective tariffs, manufacturing, a central bank and internal improvements as a means of establishing the Empire of Liberty. And they agree that the influence of the transatlantic radicals was much greater than their numbers alone would suggest.

The work of Twomey and Durey cannot fail to benefit all subsequent scholars in the field, and many of their conclusions about transatlantic patriotism in general can be applied to Irish-American radicalism in particular. Nevertheless, Durey's view of the political refugees as middle-class professionals requires some comment, as does Twomey's description of the radicals as "Jacobins." Moreover, the subsumption of the United Irishmen within the general category of transatlantic radicalism not only reduces their political significance but also blurs the distinctive relationship between their Irish and American experiences.

It is certainly true that most Irish émigrés who left written records were from the professional middle class. Indeed, their writings form the principal source for this book, which can be read as a collective study of the leading United Irishmen in the United States embedded in a general analysis of early Irish-American history. But precisely because of this focus, it is important to remember that our sources are skewed; most United Irishmen in the United States did not record their experiences in writing, and the social composition of the leadership was quite different from that of the rank-and-file. For every United Irishman who crossed the Atlantic as a cabin passenger, there were scores who traveled by steerage. And along with the radical Irish journalists, lawyers and doctors who captured public attention in the United States, there were many more men lower down in the social scale who supported the Republican cause in the Irish districts of the seaboard cities and the expanding frontier regions of the West. Such people have largely vanished from the historical record. Without their elusive but important presence, however, the political influence of the leaders would have been considerably diminished.

Every so often, we catch glimpses of people who would otherwise have remained invisible. In the summer of 1800, an American traveler found himself on a stagecoach with "two Jacobin foreigners just arrived from Ireland." They asked him if he knew how far it was to Duane's quarter or Callender's district; William Duane was a self-proclaimed United Irishman and newspaper editor, and James Callender was a leading Scottish radical in the United States. When the American said that he knew of no such quarters or districts, one of the Irishmen

> turned to me and with a sneer said we should all be taught to know things *by their proper names,* within a short time, and then proceeded to talk Irish only for the rest of the Journey during which they seemed to vaunt of their own exploits in Battle displaying great heat and energy, sometimes in the attitude of firing a Musket, at other times as if thrusting a pike or cutting a throat, to the *great* terror of the women who were fellow passengers.[8]

This account should probably be taken with a few grains of salt, but there were many veterans from the Rising of 1798 who sought sanctuary in America. Among them were a man who had fought at the Battle of Carnew, one of the bloodiest conflicts in the civil war that raged through County Wexford, and another who had participated in the Battle of Ballynahinch in County Down and had escaped to America after jumping from the third-story window of the inn where he was being held prisoner. John Driscoll from County Cork, who had been badly wounded in the Rising, made his way to Connecticut and died from his wounds in 1817, "after years of suffering."[9]

The social origins of such men remain unclear, although it would not be surprising if they were indeed from the professional middle class; it cost money to travel by stagecoach, and John Driscoll was described as being "very respectably connected in his native land." But there were also people like Peter Rodgers, an artisan from Cork City who was banished from Ireland at the age of seventy and wound up in Washington, where he displayed a sign-board on his shop which read: "Peter Rodgers, sadler, from the green fields of Erin and tyranny, to the green streets of Washington and liberty."[10] In rural western Pennsylvania, whole groups of United Irish Presbyterians from County Down, one of the storm-zones of the revolution in the north, transplanted themselves lock, stock and barrel onto farms at the edge of the wilderness. Many of these settlers became involved in politics at the local level, and remained radicals for the rest of their lives. Thus in 1823, the obscure but not atypical Jeremiah Menin could announce with pride: "In Ireland I was what was called a 'UNITED MAN;' and have been a DEMOCRATIC REPUBLICAN, without deviation, since my arrival in this country, *and am one now.* I am a friend to liberty and equality; and suffered persecution for my principles in Ireland."[11]

As Twomey and Durey have argued, the United Irish definition of "liberty and equality" assumed a liberal-republican character; the radicals believed in the rights of man, freedom of thought, equality of opportunity and economic expansion. But there were also traces in their thought of an earlier classical republican tradition, which regarded commercial growth with suspicion or hostility. According to this worldview, the survival of republicanism depended on the spirit of virtue, which was defined as the willingness of citizens to sacrifice narrow personal interests on behalf of the common good. Commerce, it was believed, was a corrosive, corrupting force, which promoted the values of selfishness, luxury and vice, and undermined public virtue; in the final analysis, the rise of commerce would culminate in the fall of republicanism.[12]

Such views had been commonplace on both sides of the Atlantic, and had been voiced in Ireland during the debate on the American Revolution; it was not surprising that they would be carried across the Atlantic by some of the émigrés of the 1790s.[13] Before he arrived in the United States, the Dublin bookseller and United Irishman John Chambers expressed deep fears that Americans were putting private gain above republican principles. "If it becomes the fashion of America to be influenced by Mercenary Motives," he wrote in 1795, "her people will lose the virtue of republicanism, & her government will be despised—she will become a Nation of Shopkeepers with all their groveling vices." Fifteen years after he emigrated to the United States, Chambers continued to sound the alarm; the "feverish itch for Manufactures," he argued, threatened to produce in America the same "baneful moral & political mischief" that was occurring in English cities like Manchester and Birmingham.[14] Other United Irish exiles agreed; the Belfast radical George Cuming even welcomed the post-Napoleonic War economic slump in America on the grounds that less commerce meant more liberty and would check the growth of an aristocracy of wealth. Similarly, Archibald Hamilton Rowan associated commercial growth with class conflict, and the Presbyterian licentiate and political revolutionary David Bailie Warden argued for the moral supremacy of an agrarian rather than an urban way of life.[15]

And yet, the practical significance of this classical republican outlook can easily be exaggerated; there was a wide gap between idealized notions of political philosophy and actual behavior in everyday life. Chambers may have condemned the commercial values of shopkeepers, but he continued to operate his own bookshop without any consciousness of irony. Rowan's hostility to commercialism did not stop him from opening up a calico business in America during the 1790s. And for all Warden's comments about the "social virtues" and "primitive purity" of rural society, he actually spent most of his life in Paris. Indeed, Warden's writings combine a theoretical preference for agrarianism with the practical recognition that large-scale manufactures were the way of the future. Although he "regretted" this reality, he wrote in glowing terms about the growth of industry in America during and after the War of 1812: "It not only proves the great extent of our resources," he remarked, "but shows a degree of enterprise, inventiveness, and versatility of talent, in our citizens, which is altogether unparalleled."[16] In late eighteenth- and early nineteenth-century America, faith in economic progress and the creative potential of free individuals appeared more relevant to the new realities than did the receding tide of classical republicanism.

It was precisely this liberal-republican outlook, along with their commitment to political democracy and support for the French Revolution, that prompted Twomey to describe the transatlantic radicals as Jacobins. There is much truth in this; in social and ideological terms, the United Irishmen can indeed be placed within an eighteenth-century Jacobin International. But in the specific context of America, the United Irishmen themselves were deeply troubled by the label of Jacobinism, since it was used by their enemies to tar them with the brush of French Revolutionary terror. A minority, it is true, adopted the term with pride. The radical Irish newspaper editor James Carey printed an article that called upon republicans to reclaim and redefine the word in a positive sense: "It is easy to blunt the edge of slanderous appellations," it ran, “by adopting that in a *good sense,* which was intended in a *bad one*—it is thus that epithets applied with the most degrading intention, have been rendered the most honourable—therefore, with the most cordial detestation of tyranny and slavery, I subscribe myself, A JACOBIN.”[17] For the most part, however, the leading United Irishmen in the United States wished to dissociate themselves from the charge of Jacobinism.

Even the most militant Irish democrats in America rejected the label. John Daly Burk, who had organized secret revolutionary cells in Dublin, maintained that Jacobinism began in France as a “holy spirit of Insurrection founded on reason and justice” but had subsequently degenerated into an “enthusiastic spirit pushed beyond the limits of reason into the regions of inhumanity.” He described himself as “a republican from principle, a despiser of royalty and Aristocracy; he is neither Jacobin nor Royalist, the latter of which he contemns, and the other execrates.” John Binns, one of the leading Irish revolutionaries in London during the 1790s, criticized Jacobinism after he arrived in America as an attempt “to array the Poorer, against the Richer, portions of our population.” And David Bailie Warden was incensed by the Federalist accusation that he was “at heart a bitter Jacobin.” [illegible] such a “[illegible] attack,” he decided to make his position absolutely clear: “I am not,” he declared, “and never was, a jacobin.”[18]

This repudiation of Jacobinism is highly revealing. The Federalists knew that they could strike a sensitive nerve among the United Irishmen by depicting them as rebels and Jacobins, and thus making them appear as a foreign, undesirable and un-American element in society. But the émigrés identified themselves primarily with the American, rather than the French, Revolution. The Irish democrats, they argued, had fought the same struggle against British tyranny that the American patriots had waged during the War of Independence, adding for good measure that because the weight of oppression was much heavier in Ireland than in America, the Irish Rising was correspondingly easier to justify. By aligning themselves with the American republican tradition, the United Irishmen could present themselves as being even more patriotic than their Federalist opponents, who seemed suspiciously sympathetic to the aristocratic values of the old imperial enemy. By jettisoning Jacobinism, the United Irishmen were assuming the mantle of Americanism and respectability, both of which were central to their self-image in the New World.[19]

But in the process of becoming Americans, the United Irishmen helped to change the very concept of Americanism. During the 1790s, when the United Irishmen began arriving in the United States, the “friends of government” regarded democracy as a threat to the American way of life. By the War of 1812, in contrast, democracy was increasingly seen as a positive element of the American political character. The United Irishmen participated in this transformation not so much through injecting fresh or original ideas into American political discourse as by adding extra momentum to pre-existing radical movements and encouraging earlier egalitarian and Anglophobic tendencies within the United States. With their large constituency, their sophisticated organizational skills, and their influential position within the American newspaper industry, they were exceptionally well placed to become a powerful presence on the radical edge of American republicanism.

To understand fully the contribution of the United Irishmen to the radicalization of American politics, it is essential to locate their attitudes and actions within a specifically Irish context. This is a crucial point, because America served a powerful symbolic and psychological function for the United Irishmen; it was a place of wish-fulfillment, where the broken dreams of the failed Irish revolution could actually be realized. As they crossed the Atlantic, the United Irishmen brought with them political, economic, cultural and religious forms of thought that would rapidly be filled with American content. Both the symbolic role of America as a place of wish-fulfillment, and the combination of Irish form with American content, provide the keys to explaining the activities and attitudes of the United Irishmen in the United States.

With this in mind, I begin by discussing the origins, nature and development of the United Irish movement during the 1790s, paying special attention to the careers of those radicals who eventually wound up in the United States. From this basis, the book examines the political experiences of the émigrés in America, especially in the crucial period between 1795 and 1815. There were, in effect, two main phases of radical Irish immigration. The first occurred between 1795 and early 1798, in response to the repression of the emerging revolutionary movement in Ireland; it included some who saw America as a temporary base in their continuing struggle for Irish independence, and others who regarded the United States as their new home. Moving through a sequence of utopianism, disillusionment and struggle, they organized themselves into the American Society of United Irishmen, weathered the storm of the Alien and Sedition Acts, and regrouped to fight for the Republican Party in 1800. By this time, the second phase of immigration had already made its presence felt; it began after the failure of the Rising in 1798, when the boats were packed with political refugees, and continued right up to 1805 and 1806, when the last of the state prisoners originally kept out by Rufus King eventually crossed the Atlantic.

In the new context of Jeffersonian America, the United Irish immigrants attempted to implement the kind of political program that they had been unable to achieve in Ireland. Among other things, they demanded the wholesale removal of their Federalist opponents from office, pushed for a broader political franchise (including liberalized naturalization laws), pressed for constitutional reform at the state level, worked to make the legal system more equitable and accessible, and supported freedom of religious belief. At the same time, the comprehensive defeat of Federalism after 1800 reduced the need for Republican unity, and opened the way for deepening divisions within the democratic camp. Clashes of personality, competition over the division of the patronage spoils, and power struggles for the control of the Irish vote meant that the United Irishmen were far from being united. On the contrary, there were severe tensions among them, which sometimes resulted in verbal or even physical violence. To some extent, though, these fissures were counter-balanced by a shared Anglophobia that focused on breaking America's neo-colonial relationship with Britain and culminated in a common commitment to the War of 1812. And these very divisions, operating as they did within a specifically American frame of reference, actually helped to integrate the United Irishmen into their new political environment.

After addressing these issues, the book considers the impact of the United Irishmen on American cultural, religious and social life. Again, the connecting thread is the relationship between Irish aspirations and American activities. In the fields of literature, historical writing, education, theater and music, the United Irish immigrants drew on their earlier experiences in an attempt not only to achieve cultural emancipation from Britain but also to create a new kind of citizen who would internalize and act upon democratic republican values. My discussion of religion examines the Irish [illegible] Presbyterian network in general, and the powerful millenarian impulse in particular, by focusing on the career of a remarkable but neglected United Irish minister who settled in western Pennsylvania, Thomas Ledlie Birch. The question of United Irish social values is also examined within a transatlantic context. In Ireland, the radicals failed to develop a consistent or coherent social program; they had a stronger sense of what they were against than what they were for. The same lack of consensus appeared in America, particularly on the question of race and slavery, which became a practical rather than a theoretical issue. Some of the radicals remained firm opponents of slavery, but many others, including a number of the most militant democrats, supported the institution and became slaveowners themselves. The radical egalitarianism of the United Irishmen would not be extended to African Americans or Native Americans; nor, for that matter, would it encompass women or the emerging trade union movement.[20]

As well as examining the way in which the radicals' Irish background helped to shape the character of their democratic republicanism in America, the book also discusses the origins of Irish-American nationalism. In contrast to the customary view that such nationalism began with the Famine, or at the very earliest with the mass migration at the end of the Napoleonic Wars, I argue that the modern, secular, republican form of Irish-American nationalism originated with the United Irishmen who arrived between 1795 and 1806. And, in what would become a familiar pattern, the Irish-American variety of nationalism was from its inception much more radical than that of Ireland. In the Old Country, the defeat of the Rising of 1798, together with the failure of Robert Emmet's attempted coup in 1803, discredited revolutionary nationalism for a generation. Although the United Irishmen in the United States supported, with reservations, the constitutional nationalism of Daniel O'Connell, they were closer in spirit to the more radical variant that found expression in the Young Ireland movement of the 1840s.

In approaching the subject, I have tried to understand the United Irishmen on their own terms, while critically examining their ideas and impact on Irish and American politics. Many of their historians have supported or identified themselves with the United Irish side; the most obvious example is Richard R. Madden's useful but uncritical *The United Irishmen: Their Lives and Times.*[21] My own verdict is more mixed. The United Irishmen's anger and frustration about the state of Irish politics is, in my view, both understandable and justifiable; similarly, their emphasis on human rights, freedom of religion and equality before the law can only be admired. But they seriously underestimated the breadth and depth of communal tensions in Ireland, and pinned their faith on an ahistorical and simplistic approach to change that paid insufficient attention to the probable consequences of their actions.

Convinced that their principles would liberate humanity from political and economic oppression, the United Irishmen frequently exhibited a moral self-righteousness bordering on the insufferable, a sometimes disturbing sense that the ends justified the means, and a deeply held but ultimately parochial belief that Britain was the primary source of evil in the world. In the United States, paradoxically, they were much more at home with their ideas than had ever been the case in Ireland. There was not, in America, the same history of deep-rooted ethnic antagonism that the United Irishmen had unwittingly summoned to the surface during the 1790s in their own country. On the other hand, the United States had within its own tradition a strong emphasis on rights, a distrust of power, a sense of destiny, an increasing degree of socio-economic fluidity, and a significant strand of Anglophobia, all of which corresponded closely to United Irish views of the world. Even here, though, the United Irish émigrés often displayed an intolerant streak, which was directed first against the Federalists and less radical Irish immigrants, and which was increasingly turned inwards as the Republican movement triumphed. The positive contribution of the United Irishmen to the development of American democracy should not blind us to the less attractive features of their political theory and practice.

Finally, a word is needed about my definition of the United Irishmen. During the late eighteenth century, the term was used in a variety of different ways. The Federalists, particularly between 1797 and 1799, adopted a broad construction, and cheerfully denounced any radical democrat who opposed their policies as a United Irishman; the idea was to make the description as repugnant as that other all-purpose term of abuse, Jacobinism. At the other pole, a strict construction applied the expression only to those who had actually been sworn into the organization and attended its meetings.

Steering between these positions, I have employed the term to incorporate three types of Irish radicals. First, and most obviously, there were those who took the United Irish oath. Some did this openly; in an act of considerable courage, Thomas Addis Emmet swore public allegiance to the organization while defending prisoners who had been charged with that very offense.[22] Later in the 1790s, though, when the movement went underground, the oath was taken secretly; this practice was also followed by the American Society of United Irishmen after its foundation in 1797.

Second, my definition includes people who actively supported the principles and practices of the United Irishmen but did not actually become members of the Society. William Sampson, for example, had an aversion to "joining" organizations, and never took the oath.[23] But in Ireland, he defended United Irishmen in court, wrote radical newspaper articles and pamphlets, and made speeches supporting the movement. In America, he became a central figure in New York's Irish community, continued to support Catholic emancipation and Irish independence, and produced a lengthy justification of the Irish revolutionary movement. For all practical purposes, he can safely be counted as a United Irishman.

And third, there were those radicals who had been born or brought up in Ireland, but were out of the country during most or all of the crucial period between 1791 and 1798, and backed the organization from afar. This category includes John Binns, the Dublin-born radical who moved to London in 1794, joined the democratic London Corresponding Society, and became a pivotal figure in the city's network of United Irish clubs before moving to America. "John Binns," he wrote of himself in 1807, "is an Irishman by birth, an American by choice, and an United Irishman from principle."[24] William Duane, who was born in America but raised in Ireland, is another example; after returning to the United States following a turbulent career as a radical writer in India and England, he proudly announced that he was a United Irishman. The Carey brothers, Mathew and James, had emigrated to the United States before the Society of United Irishmen was founded in 1791, but became strong supporters of the movement. Despite their denials, which were made during the hue and cry of the Alien and Sedition Acts, they were both up to their necks in the American Society of United Irishmen.

These, then, were among the men who were regarded by their allies as America's strongest advocates of liberty and by their enemies as the most God-provoking democrats the country had ever seen. Their story remains to be told.

CHAPTER ONE

A Green Bough

At one level, the central characteristics of the United Irishmen appear fairly clear. Formed by middle-class radicals in Belfast in 1791, spreading outward to Dublin and other towns, and attracting significant grass-roots support, the Society of United Irishmen attempted to break with the patterns of the past, and establish a new political order based on the rights of man. They believed that the root cause of human misery lay in oppressive institutions of government rather than within human nature itself; from this perspective, they presented themselves as radical reformers who were eventually forced into revolution and separatist republicanism by the intransigence of their opponents. Convinced that the ruling powers had deliberately fomented sectarian prejudices in a divide-and-rule strategy, the United Irishmen demanded religious liberty, and called for a union of all creeds against British dominance. Their eyes had been opened, they argued, by the French Revolution, the "brightest, and yet the bloodiest, page in the annals of man," which politicized an entire generation. "There is scarcely an OLD WIFE in the province," reported one newspaper, "that does not see the absurdity of triumphing in the progress of liberty abroad, and, at the same time, hesitating whether we shall aid in unshackling three-fourths of our COUNTRYMEN at home."[1]

This picture is deceptively simple. For one thing, the notion that the United Irishmen only became revolutionary republicans under the pressure of events overlooks the fact that a significant minority wanted to break the connection with Britain right from the start.[2] William Drennan, one of the founders of the movement, had long intended to create an "interior circle" of revolutionaries who would secretly work for a "total separation from Britain" behind the facade of demands for reform. Wolfe Tone, by far the best-known United Irish leader, adopted a similar position. In public, he argued during 1791 and 1792 that some link with Britain was acceptable as long as it was consistent with "the honor, the interests, and the happiness of Ireland"; his private correspondence, however, reveals a very different picture. "My unalterable opinion," he told Thomas Russell in July 1791, "is that the Bane of Irish prosperity is the influence of England: I believe that influence will ever be exerted while the connexion between the Countries continues: Nevertheless, as I know that opinion is, *for the present,* too hardy, tho' a very little time may establish it universally, I have not made it a part of the resolutions." As Tone's comments indicate, most of the people who would join the United Irishmen later in the year were not separatists; nor, for that matter, were they all in favor of universal male suffrage. But the existence of a "benevolent conspiracy" for an independent republic significantly qualifies the United Irishmen's later insistence that they only became revolutionaries when reform failed.[3]

Just as the United Irishmen were divided between reformers and revolutionaries, they were also deeply ambivalent about the question of religious liberty. Many of the leading Protestants in the organization approached Catholic emancipation with considerable doubts and misgivings. Drennan, caricatured by a recent historian as "bigotedly anti-Catholic," provides a classic example. After learning of an atrocity in Forkhill, he labeled the Catholics in general as "savages," while adding that their savagery was the product of their oppressed condition. "I can see, though shortsighted, as far into the Catholic mind as others," he later wrote; "I do not like it. It is a churlish soil, but it is the soil of Ireland and must be cultivated or we must emigrate." Other revolutionaries, such as John Daly Burk, equated Catholicism with superstition, idolatry and political tyranny; in his view, the Glorious Revolution of 1688 had delivered an "enlightened nation" from "popery and arbitrary power." The tension runs like a fault-line through Protestant radicalism. Thus the Presbyterian radical John Caldwell could sympathize in one breath with the Ulster Catholics who had been "evicted, slaughtered, driven to the mountains, or compelled to flee by their ruthless invaders the Saxons," and comment with pride in the next about "the gallant deeds of our forefathers" who withstood the siege of Derry at "the zenith of its glory in 1688–89." Such people may have thought like radicals, but they felt like settlers.[4]

The objective, then, was to "enlighten" the Catholics and educate them in the principles of the rights of man. And in this respect, the French Revolution was of central importance. What struck many Protestant United Irishmen about events in France was not only the general assault on hereditary privilege but also the particular attack on the power of the Catholic church. The French Revolution demonstrated to them that Catholics could indeed embrace democracy, despite the authoritarian nature of their religion. There was, it appeared, a lesson here for Ireland; it was entirely possible that once Catholics were admitted to full citizenship, once they were touched by the rays of the

Enlightenment, they would actually cease to be Catholics. In Drennan's view, the principles of civil liberty would "necessarily terminate in the pure principles of protestantism and of religious freedom," and "bring on another & a purer *reformation*." Similarly, Wolfe Tone and Archibald Hamilton Rowan had long believed that religious liberty would culminate in the decline of priestly power. Catholic emancipation, from this viewpoint, really meant emancipation *from* Catholicism.[5]

There is no doubt that the French Revolution transformed the terms of political debate in Ireland, not only by encouraging radical Protestants to rethink their relationship to Irish Catholics, but also by turning the question of reform into an immediate practical issue. Yet many of the ideas that were discussed during the 1790s had already been developed during the American Revolution; the towering presence of France can easily blind us to the important influence of America on Irish politics. A revolutionary catechism circulating later in the decade caught the sequence:

What have you got in your hand?
A green bough.
Where did it first grow?
In America.
Where did it bud?
In France.
Where are you going to plant it?
In the crown of Great Britain.[6]

The fact that the American and French Revolutions were actually very different was hidden by what appeared to be common ideological imperatives, expressed in the common language of the rights of man. But the point remains that many of the United Irishmen who became émigrés in the United States had received their political education during the American, rather than the French, Revolution; when they crossed the Atlantic, a circle was being completed.

"A voice from America shouted to liberty," proclaimed the Irish Patriot Henry Flood during the War of Independence; "the echo of it caught your people as it passed along the Atlantic, and they re-echoed the voice till it reverberated here." The reverberations were felt most deeply in the Presbyterian north-east, where large-scale migration had produced a transatlantic network of political, religious, intellectual, economic and familial connections through which that voice could echo. In America, the Ulster Scots had been in the revolutionary vanguard; one Hessian officer even believed, wrongly but understandably, that he was fighting "nothing more or less than a Scotch Irish Presbyterian rebellion." The folks back home seem to have agreed; bonfires lit the Antrim skies to celebrate the Battle of Bunker Hill, Presbyterian ministers denounced the government's "mad crusade" against American liberty, and fast-days were held to hasten the humiliation of the British army. "Presbyterians in the North," commented Lord Harcourt in 1775, " . . . in their hearts, are Americans." "I regretted that I was not an American," recalled Archibald Hamilton Rowan, "but I was determined, if ever I was able, to play the same role in Ireland."[7]

Such sentiments were strongest in the Presbyterian north-east; the further one moves from this base, the weaker was the sense of commitment to the American cause. Many Church of Ireland Protestants who sympathized with American colonial grievances, and a fair number of Presbyterians as well, began to pull back after the Declaration of Independence in 1776. In the "little club" in Ballymoney that supported the American Patriots, the members who belonged to the Church of Ireland stormed out when they learned of American independence and joined in "the hue and cry against the rebels"; the entire village split on the question, in a feud that lasted throughout the war and beyond. Even within Presbyterian circles, on both sides of the Atlantic, there was a significant loyalist strand of opinion whose importance can easily be underestimated.[8]

Independence, for most Irish Protestants, was something that could not be countenanced. The primary objective of the Irish Patriots was to secure the maximum degree of autonomy within the British Empire, rather than to break with it altogether; they were colonial nationalists, who depended on Britain for support against the external threat of Catholic France and Spain and the perceived internal danger posed by the overwhelming Catholic majority in Ireland. In these circumstances, complete separation appeared to them as a form of political, religious and cultural suicide.[9]

Irish Catholic reactions to the American Revolution are much more difficult to gauge. The very fact that many of their traditional Protestant enemies sympathized with the American cause prompted the leadership to take precisely the opposite position and express loyalty to the British government. The entire rationale of the Penal Laws that had operated against the Catholics during the eighteenth century was based on the assumption of Catholic disloyalty. In the view of many leading Catholics, the best way to undermine the penal system was to demonstrate that they were in fact more loyal subjects than the Protestants. In 1774, the aristocratic Catholic Committee had explicitly rejected the political power of the Papacy. During the War of Independence, it came out unequivocally against the "unnatural rebellion" in the Thirteen Colonies; this was standing the language of radical pro-American Presbyterian ministers on its head.[10]

It should not be assumed, however, that the position of the leaders reflected that of the rank-and-file. Bitter memories of dispossession were deeply embedded in Catholic culture, and popular discontent found direct and immediate expression through agrarian secret societies such as the Whiteboys, an economically driven movement that tapped into traditional notions of communalism, custom and justice within Irish society.[11] In this prepolitical culture, "America" and the strategy of the Catholic Committee must have seemed totally irrelevant. But at other levels of Catholic society, particularly in the increasingly important middle class, there are signs that the American Revolution struck a responsive chord. Catholic merchants occupied a prominent place in the transatlantic carrying trade; they had formed close connections with the American colonists, and signed petitions against the war. Reports from Cork and Limerick spoke of widespread Catholic support for the Americans.[12] In Dublin, a new generation of middle-class Catholics were strongly attracted to pro-American radical ideas; they included such people as Patrick Byrne and Mathew Carey, whose revolutionary politics would eventually force them to leave Ireland for the United States.

Nevertheless, it remains clear that the main thrust of support for the American Patriots came from within the Protestant, rather than the Catholic, community. And if the ideological revolution in America supplied Irish radicals with the vocabulary of liberty, the War of Independence provided the opportunity for action. The key year was 1778, when France entered the war. With the British army stretched across the Atlantic, and with Ireland apparently wide open to a Catholic French invasion, thousands of Protestants formed themselves into Volunteer Companies as a line of defense against foreign attack. People who had been shut out from the "political nation," and who had long resented the power of an aristocratic and oligarchic Irish Parliament, were now acting together in what the radical Presbyterian minister William Steel Dickson called a "self-created, self-arrayed, and self-supported, army," with its own leaders and chains of command.[13] Becoming increasingly aware of their power, the Volunteers transformed themselves into the armed expression of Protestant colonial nationalism; before long, they linked up with the Patriot Party in the Irish Parliament, and pushed for radical reform.

The results appeared impressive. In 1779, they won a significant measure of free trade for Ireland, and followed this up in 1782 with the repeal of legislation that had subordinated the Irish Parliament to that of Britain. "Ireland is now a nation," exulted the Patriot leader Henry Grattan, amid Volunteer celebrations of victory; the Irish, he proclaimed, had at last become a "free people."[14] But in fact, the settlement of 1782 was profoundly ambiguous. The Irish Parliament did not, as it turned out, achieve parity with Westminster under a common allegiance to the Crown; the British government retained significant political and financial control over Irish affairs. Nor was there any broadening of the polity within Ireland; the Irish Parliament remained an exclusive club for wealthy Protestants. The middle-class Protestants who formed the backbone of the Volunteers were kept out; the vast Catholic majority in the country were still beyond the political pale. In many respects, this was an illusory independence for an imaginary people.

Under these circumstances, a radical minority of Volunteers continued to press for the democratization of Irish politics; some even began to argue in favor of Catholic emancipation. But the questions of parliamentary reform and enfranchisement of Catholics proved divisive, at precisely the time that troops were returning home after the American war. With 20,000 soldiers at its back, and with no further need for the Volunteers, the Irish government stood firm against reform. The crucial confrontation came in 1783, when the Volunteer Convention in Dublin directly challenged the power of the Irish House of Commons and was stopped in its tracks. All the momentum went out of the movement. Volunteer companies kept on meeting in the north, and individual radicals kept up demands for wide-ranging reforms, but they increasingly sounded like voices in the political wilderness.

During this agitation, with all its frustration of rising expectations, many subsequent United Irish émigrés acquired their political experience and established their reputation for radicalism. Napper Tandy, who would wind up in Philadelphia and Paris in the 1790s, became a Dublin folk hero during the Volunteer days. As captain of the city's artillery train, he had brought out the cannons in a decisive free trade demonstration in 1779; one cannon carried a placard reading "Free Trade—or else." Hamilton Rowan, who had been living in France, rushed to join the Volunteer movement, and soon became known as a "man of the people." In County Down, Presbyterian ministers Thomas Ledlie Birch and William Sinclair rose to local prominence as active Volunteers; both men ended their days as political refugees in the United States. Further north, in County Antrim, the "notoriously disaffected" Caldwell family prided themselves that their Volunteer Company in Ballymoney had been the first in Ulster to enlist a Catholic; after the Rising of 1798, they all sought sanctuary in New York.[15]

The most significant figure among the Volunteers, in terms of the Irish-American connection, was the radical journalist Mathew Carey.[16] He burst onto the political scene during the free trade campaign of 1779, when he was nineteen years old. In a revolutionary pamphlet, he demanded "the Immediate Repeal of the Whole Penal Code," and suggested that failure to do so might well result in rebellion. The advertisement of the pamphlet alone was enough to bring down the roof on him. Members of the Irish Parliament seized on it as "proof of the seditious and treasonable views of the Roman Catholics." The Catholic Committee was furious, since its strategy of demonstrating Catholic loyalty was now in danger of being discredited. Faced with the wrath of both the government and the Catholic Committee, which he denounced as a "cringing body" with a "servile spirit," Carey sought temporary refuge in France—where he found employment, appropriately enough, in Benjamin Franklin's printing office.[17]

By 1781, he was back in Dublin, where he resurfaced as an editor of the *Freeman's Journal;* two years later, he established the *Volunteers Journal,* the most radical newspaper in the country. All the evils that Ireland experienced,

Carey argued, came "FROM OUR BLASTING CONNECTION WITH BRITAIN!" In a series of articles that served as dress rehearsals for the United Irish movement, he demanded political democracy, religious equality, economic independence and cultural self-determination for Ireland. And when reforms were not forthcoming, he drew on the example of America to argue in 1784 for armed revolution. Against the background of food riots among Dublin's "STARVING MANUFACTURERS," he called for the tarring and feathering of John Foster, the Speaker of the Irish House of Commons; on one occasion, he suggested that Foster should be hanged as a traitor. The government immediately cracked down on the paper, and Foster sued for libel. With the police on his trail, Carey went into hiding, and published an impassioned article predicting that fifteen thousand Volunteers would link up with a French invasion fleet to break Britain's hold on Ireland and recommending that the Lord Lieutenant be held as hostage for the behavior of the British army. When the authorities caught up with him, he was kept under close guard and committed to Newgate prison. Temporarily released when Parliament adjourned, Carey disguised himself as a woman (thus setting a trend for other radical refugees) and took the first boat that he could get for America; by November 1784, he was safely in Philadelphia.[18]

Back in Ireland, the revival of radicalism after the French Revolution made Carey's confrontational style of politics appear increasingly relevant to more and more people. In the Catholic Committee, middle-class militants successfully challenged the aristocratic leaders who had counseled caution, pragmatism and patience. "Our Catholic brethren," commented the radical bookseller John Chambers, who had printed Carey's pro-emancipation pamphlet in 1779, "have ventured to put their heads out of their hiding holes, & have shaken off a little of that accursed timidity that has been more their Enemy than all the penal Statutes." Linking up with the United Irishmen, the radicals in the Committee ousted the moderates, shed the politics of deference, and demanded immediate political equality. Among the new militants was William James MacNeven, a Catholic physician from County Galway who had been educated in Europe. In 1792, he played a leading role in the Catholic Committee's petition to the throne for the extension of the suffrage to Catholics on the same basis as Protestants. Later in the decade, MacNeven would join the United Irishmen and work for a French invasion of Ireland; he eventually became a prominent figure in the Irish community in New York. One of his closest allies in the campaign for Catholic emancipation was the Protestant lawyer Thomas Addis Emmet, who joined the United Irishmen in 1792; Emmet also wound up in New York, where he became the most respected Irish American of his generation.[19]

Within the Dublin Society of United Irishmen, Hamilton Rowan and Napper Tandy rapidly emerged as central figures. They had become good friends during the 1780s, when they worked together on a variety of libertarian causes. Rowan cut a striking and eccentric figure in the streets of Dublin; tall, and wearing a conspicuously patriotic green uniform, he would make barking sounds to communicate with the large Newfoundland dog that he took with him to political meetings. Tandy was nothing if not controversial; Drennan regarded him as a coward, Tone could not stand him, and one twentieth-century writer described him as "this ugly, loquacious, drunken and wholly absurd little man." But Tandy had a powerful base of support among Dublin's artisans, tradesmen and shopkeepers, and brought many of them into the United movement. Rowan and Tandy were among the radicals who drew up plans in late 1792 to remodel the Dublin Volunteers along the lines of the revolutionary French National Guard. Another United Irishman who wound up in the United States, the ironfounder Henry Jackson, was deputed to supply the Volunteers with cannons from his Dublin factory. Faced with the militarization of the movement, the government launched a preemptive strike that December, and prohibited the Volunteers from assembling in arms. Drennan rushed into print with an "Address to the Volunteers of Ireland," urging them to defy the ban, and called for a National Convention—at a time when a similar body in France was trying its king for treason. When Rowan and Tandy helped to distribute the address, they were arrested and charged with sedition. In Rowan's case, the trial was deferred until January 1794, when he was sentenced to two years in prison; by that time, Tandy had jumped bail and escaped to England, en route for America.[20]

It is clear that Tandy had been following a revolutionary trajectory in the winter of 1792–93; shortly after the crackdown on the Dublin Volunteers, he began probing the possibility of linking up with the increasingly important Catholic Defender movement based in County Armagh. Arising out of fierce sectarian conflict over issues of land and work in the linen industry, the Defenders combined traditional anti-Protestant resentments with the modern language of liberty, equality and fraternity. As they spread southwards into County Louth, they raided Protestant homes for arms, and talked about settling old scores; the idea, one of them said, was "to knock the Protestants on the head, and . . . take their places." Believing that the movement could be harnessed to the United Irish cause, Tandy met the Defenders and took their oath himself. When the authorities found out, he was a marked man; he had little alternative but to flee the country.[21]

The government's response to the growing radical movement was a characteristic combination of reform and repression; the outbreak of war between Britain and France in February 1793 meant that Irish affairs could not be allowed to drift out of control. In an attempt to detach middle-class Catholics from the United Irishmen, Britain persuaded the Irish Parliament to pass a Catholic Relief Bill that April. Among other things, Catholics could now vote on the same terms as Protestants; they were still excluded, however, from actually sitting in Parliament. In what became a classic pattern, which has persisted right up to our own time, this policy only succeeded in alienating most Protestants without securing the support of most Catholics. Within the Protestant community, there were complaints that the government had gone too far, that Britain could no longer be trusted to protect their interests, and that concessions to Catholics would only result in more demands; fears of the reversal of the seventeenth-century land settlements bubbled to the surface. Within the Catholic community, there were complaints that the government had not gone far enough, and that their exclusion from Parliament was a humiliating confirmation of their subordinate status, imposed upon them by Protestant bigotry. Far from stabilizing the situation, the Catholic Relief Act intensified the Protestant siege mentality and increased the militancy of Catholic middle-class leaders, many of whom now formed closer ties with the United Irishmen.[22]

In fact, the Relief Act of 1793 constituted the *ne plus ultra* of reform; from then on, repression would be the order of the day. As part of the crackdown on the Defenders, a Secret Committee of the Irish House of Lords met to investigate the situation in County Louth. One of the people they examined was James Reynolds, a physician from County Tyrone who was active in the Dublin Society of United Irishmen. He refused to testify, challenged the Committee's constitutional and judicial authority, and demanded that he either be liberated or imprisoned. "He has put them into a nonplus," reported Drennan. "They know not what to do, but hope that a system of intimidation will do, as he is of a nervous habit; hence his treatment is rather harsh. . . . They think they will terrify this very young man, but they are mistaken." He spent the next five months in jail, where if anything his radicalism became more entrenched. Upon his release, he lodged with Hamilton Rowan and his wife Sarah, who were becoming notorious for their violent shouting matches over politics; Sarah Rowan was convinced that the United Irishmen were leading the country in general and her family in particular to disaster. Neither man would listen; within eighteen months, they would be sharing accommodation again, this time as political refugees in Philadelphia.[23]

The limits of reform were underlined by the decisive defeat of Henry Grattan's Reform Bill in March 1794, and by the failure of the new Viceroy, the Earl of Fitzwilliam, to complete the process of Catholic emancipation in 1795. Fitzwilliam's recall, after he spent less than two months in Ireland, has often been seen as the turning point in the transition of the United Irishmen from a reformist to a revolutionary organization. Such a view, however, seriously underestimates the extent to which revolutionary sentiments had already been building up within the movement. Thomas Emmet, for example, never expected anything from Fitzwilliam in the first place; with the recall, he argued, "the fallacy of ill-founded hopes had been . . . speedily exposed."[24] And long before Fitzwilliam's appointment, a significant minority of United Irishmen had already developed a daring new strategy; they were forming contacts with secret agents from Paris, and concocting plans to liberate Ireland with French guns, ammunition and soldiers.[25]

Preliminary soundings were made in early 1793, when the French government sent the American Eleazor Oswald on a fact-finding mission to Dublin. Meeting the United Irish leadership, Oswald floated the idea of French financial assistance for an Irish revolution, only to find that the organization was unprepared for such action. But a radical minority, including Rowan, saw greater possibilities here, and informed Oswald that money was not enough; what was needed, they insisted, was full-scale military assistance. A French invasion in conjunction with an Irish rising would, they were convinced, break the back of British power and pave the way for an independent republic.[26]

For the moment, nothing happened. The idea resurfaced in 1794, however, when another agent from France, William Jackson, arrived in Ireland. Against the opposition of the moderates in the movement, Rowan, Tone and Reynolds set out to convince Jackson that an Irish revolution would succeed with French military help. By this time, Rowan was in Newgate Prison, serving his sentence for seditious libel; after being visited by Jackson, he persuaded Tone to draw up a memorandum for the Committee of Public Safety on the state of Irish opinion. "There seems to be little doubt," wrote Tone, "but an invasion in sufficient force would be supported by the people." Other sources bear him out, at least in relation to nationalist opinion; Martha McTier, for example, reported from the north that there existed among the lower orders "an almost general wish (of what I think would occasion ruin in *our time* to this country), a visit from the French." To strengthen the ties between France and Ireland, Reynolds was chosen to become the United Irish representative in Paris. A coherent revolutionary strategy appeared to be emerging.[27]

And then, everything collapsed. The government had its finger on the pulse of Jackson's mission right from the start; Jackson's traveling companion, John Cockayne, was actually an English spy. Tone's memorandum was intercepted in the mail, and Jackson was arrested for treason. Immediately afterwards, Reynolds, Tone and Emmet visited Rowan at Newgate, almost certainly with emergency plans for his escape. Telling his jailer that it was his twelfth wedding anniversary and offering a large bribe into the bargain, Rowan was allowed home to sleep with his wife. Once in the bedroom, with the jailer on guard next door, he disguised himself in butcher's clothes, and slid down a rope to freedom. In a state of extreme anxiety, and carrying a razor to commit suicide if he were captured, Rowan was smuggled out of the country to France, from whence he eventually traveled to the United States. On May 4, the day before his escape, the government suppressed the Dublin Society of United Irishmen, and moved against the revolutionaries. A warrant was out for Reynolds on the charge of treason; he made it onto a boat for America before the authorities could catch up with him, and took symbolic revenge on his enemies by hanging an effigy of George III from the ship's yardarm.[28]

Meanwhile, Tone tried to save himself by making a deal with the government. In an arrangement that anticipated the pact between the state prisoners and the government in 1798, he agreed to tell the authorities about his own involvement in the attempt to get French aid, without incriminating others; in return, he would be allowed to leave the country. Tone's confession was purely pragmatic, and implied no weakening of his revolutionary will. Shortly before his departure for the United States in 1795, he walked up Cave Hill outside Belfast with his fellow radicals Thomas Russell, Robert Simms, Samuel Neilson and Henry Joy McCracken. From McArt's Fort, with its sweeping view of the northern countryside, they made a "solemn obligation" never to rest until Ireland had been liberated from British rule. In America and then in France, Tone would continue the struggle.[29]

Jackson's trial came up in April 1795. His defense team included William Sampson, a brilliant young lawyer from Londonderry; as a fellow traveler with the United Irishmen, he would eventually join the Irish émigré community in New York. The chief counsel for the defense was John Curran, one of the greatest orators in the country. But the case against Jackson was too strong; on April 30, at the same time that Hamilton Rowan was setting out on his voyage to America, Jackson was found guilty of treason. Rather than suffer the horrors of being hanged, drawn and quartered, he took arsenic that his wife had smuggled to him, and died in the dock.[30]

The Jackson mission not only brought about the flight of United Irish leaders such as Rowan, Reynolds and Tone to the United States; it also accelerated the process of radicalization within Ireland. Given the reality of internal repression and the hope of external support, the United Irishmen began in 1794 and 1795 to reconstitute themselves as a secret revolutionary society, and attempted to broaden their base by forming an alliance with the Defenders; in this sense, they were picking up the threads of what had been Tandy's strategy during the winter of 1792–93. By the summer of 1795, continuing Protestant-Catholic clashes in and around Armagh had escalated into a species of civil war. Protestant weavers and farmers linked up with the local gentry to form the militantly anti-Catholic Orange Order. Gaining the upper hand in a conflict characterized on both sides by intimidation and terror, they drove thousands of Catholics out of their homes, and scattered them throughout the land. As they traveled, the Defenders carried with them bitter memories of Protestant violence, sanctioned by local landlords who were acting in the name of loyalty to the state. The dispersal of the Defenders meant the spread of their ideology and organization across the country; they became a powerful and pervasive force at the grass-roots level. Just as the Jacobins in France had formed an alliance with the sans-culottes, the United Irishmen decided to join forces with the Defenders.[31]

One of the central figures in the creation of a revolutionary underground with links to the Defenders was John Daly Burk, a deist and democrat who was related to Edmund Burke, and who had arrived in Dublin from Cork as a student at Trinity College in 1792. Vain, histrionic, and given to bouts of excessive self-dramatization, Burk had mixed in radical circles in Cork; among his friends was Denis Driscol, a former Catholic priest who had moved through a brief period as a loyalist Protestant curate before being reborn as a Paineite. In Dublin, Burk rubbed shoulders with Rowan and Reynolds, wrote democratic articles for the *Dublin Evening Post,* and attempted to convert his fellow students to deism. All this was too much for the Board of the University, which expelled him from Trinity in the course of a general crackdown on student radicalism in the spring of 1794. Likening the Board to the Inquisition and comparing himself to figures like Demosthenes and Newton, Burk based his defense on the grounds of freedom of enquiry and freedom of speech. His tone was truculent, indignant, angry and hyperbolic. "My father has travelled a hundred and twenty miles to see me," he wrote, only to see his son "dragg'd by the fiends to their execrable altars and given into the hands of the sanguinary high priests. Great God! what must be his despair when he sees the bloody knife lifted up and his child immolated before his eyes? Such has been the state of my circumstances." Here, clearly, was [illegible] who [illegible] and [illegible] in [illegible].[illegible]

Before his expulsion from Trinity, Burk joined a group known as the Strugglers, named after the tavern where they met. Founded by James Reynolds, whom Burk greatly admired, the society operated as a revolutionary cell within the United Irish movement. Among its members were Oliver Bond, Bagenal Harvey, and the Sheares brothers (also from Cork), none of whom would survive the Rising of 1798; the tavernkeeper himself, Luke Daignan, fought with Robert Emmet in the failed insurrection of 1803. It was probably in the Strugglers that Burk learned the pike exercise and decided to establish a clandestine revolutionary network of his own. At the end of 1794, he formed the Philanthropic and Telegraphic Societies, which operated under the cover of reading clubs; they disseminated the principles of deism, recruited Defenders in the city, and plotted insurrection. One of their members, a tambour maker called LeBlanc who had come down from Belfast, drew up plans to kidnap or assassinate John Cockayne, the chief prosecution witness in the Jackson trial.[33]

Burk's secret societies were organized into units of ten; each member was expected to bring in ten friends, until the force was strong enough to seize Dublin Castle, the center of the administration. This plan, he later wrote, was "adopted as the model for the new military organization of the United Irishmen." But, for all the attempts at secrecy, Burk's societies were vulnerable to government infiltration; on the evidence of a spy in the movement, William Lawler, several of its members were hanged for High Treason. When he learned that Lawler had been assassinated by United men in Belfast, Burk rejoiced that vengeance had been served. By that time, though, the government knew that he was at the center of a revolutionary conspiracy, and was trying to track him down. He hid at a bookseller's shop in Dublin, dressed himself in female attire, and embarked on a brig for Boston in the spring of 1796. It was at this point that he added "Daly" to his name, in honor of the woman who had supplied him with her clothes.[34]

When Burk left the country, the United Irishmen were beginning to enlist more and more Defenders in their organization; by the end of the summer, tens of thousands of Defenders had taken the United Irish oath. In adopting this strategy, though, the United Irishmen were opening up a wide and potentially disastrous gap between means and ends. The Defenders, as one government report put it, were primarily interested in "Restoring Popery" and "Equalizing Property"; the United Irishmen stood for a non-sectarian republic characterized by political democracy and economic liberalism. Yet without the grass-roots support that the Defenders could supply, the United Irishmen believed, a democratic revolution in Ireland would remain impossible. The stakes, after all, were high. "Aristocracy is a heavy clog," John Chambers had written to Mathew Carey earlier in the decade, "& if not tumbled and crushed for ever, a la mode de Paris, will keep the yoke another Century about their Necks." Besides, the United Irish leaders managed to convince themselves that they could control or even change the Defenders. "As the remnants of religious animosity were still chiefly to be found in the lower orders," recalled Thomas Emmet, "it was hoped that by bringing together those of that description, though of different sects, they might soon learn the identity of their views and interests, and as ardently love, as for centuries past they and their ancestors had feared, one another." But the process of control and change could work both ways. In the end, the verdict of the government spy Thomas Reynolds proved more accurate than that of Emmet. Because the Defenders now formed the majority in the movement, he wrote, "instead of becoming United Irishmen, they induced the mass of the United Irishmen to become Defenders in principle, in practice, in short, in everything except name."[35]

A similar tension between means and ends characterized United Irish efforts to liberate Ireland through a military alliance with France. From one perspective, the prospect of French aid appeared to counterbalance the risk of linking up with the Defenders; some leading United Irishmen believed that the presence of a French army on Irish soil would enable them to suppress any outbreaks of populist social violence. But the strategy of the French alliance was itself extremely dangerous; armies of liberation had a strange habit of becoming armies of occupation, and the "sister republics" that France established on the continent looked suspiciously like satellite states. When challenged on these points, Emmet and MacNeven argued that the French had promised to help them in the same way that Rochambeau had helped America back in 1778; besides, added MacNeven, any French army that overstayed its welcome would itself be resisted by patriotic Irishmen.[36] Such a position, however, seriously misread French war aims, as both men eventually came to realize. France was quite prepared to use Ireland as a pawn in peace talks with England, or if necessary to establish an Irish Catholic monarchy on Britain's western flank. And the notion that French troops could be dislodged at will flew in the face of all subsequent experience in Europe. In retrospect, the United Irishmen appear to have been following different routes to disaster. If dependence on the Defenders threatened to engulf the country in a sectarian civil war, dependence on the French threatened to replace one form of imperialism with another.

By the end of 1796, though, it seemed that the twin strategy of enlisting the Defenders and working with the French was about to pay dividends. In December, a large French invasion fleet broke through the British blockade at Brest, and headed toward Bantry Bay in the south-west of Ireland. On board one of the ships was Wolfe Tone, who had worked in Philadelphia and Paris for precisely such a moment. For a full day, in calm seas, the fleet anchored just off the coast, waiting for the arrival of their military commander whose ship had become separated from the rest of the expedition. Then the weather changed. Had the fleet not been battered by a ferocious east wind, the French army of 15,000 would have been able to land unopposed, and could probably have taken the entire south of Ireland within a week. It had been, as both the republicans and loyalists fully realized, a very close call; radical hopes and conservative fears were raised to a new pitch of intensity.[37]

Inspired by the prospect of further French help, the United Irishmen intensified their revolutionary activities. In Ulster, where the next invasion attempt was expected to occur, membership doubled during the first three months of 1797. A new spirit of subversion was in the air; the servants of one local aristocrat even taught her favorite parrot to repeat revolutionary slogans.[38] Pikes were manufactured, and arms and ammunition were stored for future use; from his iron foundry in Dublin, Henry Jackson began to calibrate cannon balls that met French artillery specifications. At the same time, Protestant loyalists became increasingly determined to crush the revolution before it crushed them. Martial law was proclaimed in Ulster; republicans were purged from the militia, the presses of the radical *Northern Star* newspaper were destroyed, suspects were arrested, and their houses were burnt down. The emigration of United Irishmen to America was actively encouraged; it not only got rid of "mischievous Agents," argued one magistrate, but also saved "expense, trouble & the chance of Juries acting corruptly."[39] But the policy of repression cut both ways; the sheer ferocity of the loyalist backlash drove many people, especially the Catholics who bore the brunt of the counter-revolutionary campaign, straight into the arms of the United Irishmen. And as the best-known leaders were arrested, the initiative passed to younger militants who were ready for action. The pressure for action, with or without French help, began to build.

But the question of whether or not to wait for the French proved deeply divisive. On the one hand, people like Emmet and MacNeven believed that the risks of a French invasion were fewer than the risks of a Defender-driven revolution from below. As a member of the Leinster Directory of the United Irishmen from January 1797, Emmet worked to prevent a rising until the French landed. "I was certain," he explained, "that an invasion would succeed speedily, and without much struggle." For much the same reason, MacNeven traveled to France later in the year to speed up invasion plans. "The [United Irish] executive . . . wished through the co-operation of a respectable French force, to exclude the barbarity of a purely civil war," he wrote.[40] On the other hand, a rival faction led by Arthur O'Connor and Edward Fitzgerald believed that the United Irishmen should go it alone. The difference between O'Connor and his rivals, reported Leonard McNally, the government mole within the organization, "is merely on two points—The time to act—and the manner of acting—He [O'Connor] was for an immediate exertion without waiting the event of an invasion—and severity that would strike terror—They [Emmet and MacNeven] are for patiently waiting the result of the French preparation—and securing life and property—He is for immediate execution—They are for—[a] form of trial."[41]

With the French nowhere to be seen, and with the continuing government crackdown on the United Irish movement during 1797, a growing minority began to move toward O'Connor's position. At a meeting in June, amid "much altercation and dispute," the militants accused the moderates of cowardice, and threatened to go ahead without them. In December, O'Connor tried to persuade the leadership to launch a coup at Dublin Castle that Christmas. He planned to spread rumors of an impending Orange massacre of Catholics to bring his supporters onto the streets—in effect, to whip up sectarian animosities for the greater good of a non-sectarian republic. This was too much for the moderates, who moved quickly to block the scheme. Furious at being overruled, O'Connor left for England in early 1798, where he tried to strengthen his position by linking up with the Irish revolutionary underground that was emerging in London. Here, he contacted John Binns, who had arrived in the city from Dublin in 1794 and risen to prominence in the English popular democratic movement; Binns would become one of the leading journalists in America during the early nineteenth century.[42]

There were no doubts about Binns's revolutionary credentials. Coming from a radical family background (his grand-uncle had worked with Napper Tandy on the Dublin Council), he developed both his republicanism and his formidable rhetorical skills in Ireland, and applied them to great effect in London. He mixed with the growing numbers of radical Irishmen who came into the city in the wake of Orange violence and military repression, and fought with them—sometimes literally—against the "violent royalists" in the city. In 1795, at the age of twenty-three, he chaired the mass democratic meeting at Copenhagen Fields, and electrified an audience of over 100,000 people with his oratory. Binns knew in advance of the attack on George III that occurred three days after the meeting, and regretted that the king had not been trampled to death; the event, he believed, might have "overthrown the Government; caused the establishment of a Republic; led to a peace with France, and affected the condition of all the governments and people in Europe." After the repression that followed, he went on the road with John Gale Jones, giving "seditious and inflammatory lectures," and even taking the struggle directly to the heart of the Church-and-King party in Birmingham, in their tavern with the words "*No Jacobins admitted here*" on the door. He was arrested—and eventually acquitted—in the summer of 1796 for his lectures; this was the first of many encounters with the prison system. "We have been in more jails," said his fellow radical Horne Tooke at the end of the decade, "than any two horse-thieves in England."[43]

Increasingly involving himself in Irish affairs, John Binns, together with his brother Benjamin, played a central role in the formation of the London branch of the United Irishmen. In 1797, Benjamin introduced John to James Coigly, a Catholic priest from Armagh who was on the O'Connorite wing of the movement. Coigly was passing through London on his way to France, and helped to coordinate a joint Irish-English revolutionary strategy; in the event of a French invasion of Ireland, the London republicans would launch a diversionary action by seizing members of the Privy Council, paralyzing the government, and pinning down troops in England. Benjamin wrote a memorandum on English radicalism that Coigly took with him to Paris; John began giving lectures on revolutionary tactics to small conspiratorial groups in such London public houses as the Black Horse and Furnival's Inn Cellars. One informer noted that John Binns

> Talked about Pikes, and said it was the most useful Instrument in a field against Horse as the Horse could not advance against it if used in a proper manner—that was to thrust it in the Horses Nostrils which would occasion him to rear up and throw his Rider, which was better than placing it against the Horse's Shoulders, as by that means the man using it might be overpowered.

In later life, Binns would downplay and occasionally deny his role in physical force republicanism; in 1797 and 1798, however, he and his brother clearly meant business.[44]

To strengthen the revolutionary movement in England, the United Irishmen in the capital linked up with the militant wing of the popular radical London Corresponding Society, forming the United Britons; the Binns brothers were on the central committee. When Coigly returned from his mission to Paris, Benjamin accompanied him to Ireland in January 1798, carrying an "Address of the United Britons to the United Irishmen" that promised to "promote the Emancipation of both Countries." The idea was to boost the position of the O'Connorites in Ireland by showing that the revolutionaries were now sufficiently organized and powerful to launch a rising before the French arrived. "A formidable—yes a formidable Diversion would have occurred in London, &c.—in favor of Ireland," Benjamin recalled, "and the manner and direction of which was known only to a few of the 'National Comm[itt]ee.'" In February, Coigly was in London again, with instructions to join O'Connor on another mission to France. Later in the month, John Binns headed for the south coast to hire a boat that would take O'Connor and Coigly across the channel; they assembled at Margate, ready to sail the next day. But that was as far as the three of them would get. Right from the start, they were being shadowed by the police. Not that they were hard to find; they traveled to Margate with an "immense quantity of baggage, mahogany cases, swords, pistols, military accoutrements of all sorts," along with two servants. And Coigly was carrying a letter from the United Britons to the French Directory, which looked forward to a combined English, Scottish and Irish revolution with French help. When the police caught up with them, the "treasonable address" was found in his greatcoat pocket.[45]

Binns, O'Connor and Coigly were taken back to London, and brought before the Privy Council. Following his own advice at the London lectures on how to resist interrogation, Binns simply refused to answer any questions. After solitary confinement in the Tower of London (where Binns wore a yellow neckerchief, the color of the O'Connorites, as a gesture of defiance and solidarity), they were tried for treason at Maidstone that May. The government had enough evidence from its informers to convict all three men, but held it back to keep its spy network intact. O'Connor and Binns were acquitted, but Coigly was executed as a traitor; during the trial, O'Connor tried to shift all the blame onto Coigly's shoulders, in a show of selfishness that surprised even the judge. Meanwhile, the government had already moved against other radicals associated with the United Irishmen in England; in April, it arrested revolutionaries in and around Manchester, and swooped down on the General Committee of the London Corresponding Society. Benjamin Binns was among those who were caught in the net; he wound up in solitary confinement for three years, and suffered from severe mental anxieties, including agoraphobia, for the rest of his life. The government's action, together with Napoleon's decision to invade Egypt rather than Ireland, meant that the entire revolutionary strategy of concerted British and Irish action collapsed before it got off the ground.[46]

A parallel but much more intense pattern of repression was occurring in Ireland, where the revolutionary organization had spread throughout much of the country. From the south and the east, reports were coming in to Dublin Castle of pike-manufacturing, arms raids on gentlemen's houses, intimidation and assassination. The Protestant gentry, isolated and vulnerable, demanded immediate action to protect their lives and property; unless something were done, they argued, the revolutionary momentum would become unstoppable. By the spring of 1798, the government answered their calls; the counter-insurgency methods that had been applied in Ulster were now to be extended to other disaffected areas.[47]

The crackdown in Dublin began in March, when the police moved against the Leinster Directory of the United Irishmen and imprisoned almost the entire leadership of the organization. Thomas Emmet and William MacNeven were among those who were arrested; so too was Henry Jackson, one of O'Connor's principal supporters in the city. A few leaders, most notably Edward Fitzgerald, slipped through the net. He continued to direct revolutionary operations until May, when the police finally caught up with him; he attacked the arresting officers with a dagger, and eventually died from a wound he received in the struggle.[48] The search was also on for William Sampson, who was wanted for treason on the strength of reports that he was a leading military figure in the movement. The reports were almost certainly untrue, but Sampson had long been a source of trouble to the government; he had written radical pamphlets, defended United Irish prisoners, and chaired a committee that publicized military atrocities in the country. Narrowly avoiding arrest when the army searched his house, he lay low for three weeks before making the break for freedom on a coal barge going to England. But he was tracked down in Carlisle, brought back to Dublin, and locked up "in dismal solitude for many months"; his servant was tortured in an unsuccessful attempt to extract incriminating information.[49]

As well as attempting to decapitate the organization by arresting its leaders, the authorities conducted a purge of student radicalism at Trinity College. In a "College visitation" that April, Lord Clare presided over an examination of the students that was designed to root out the disaffected. The Historical Society had a strong radical component, and as many as four committees of the United Irishmen were active in the university. By the time the purge was over, nineteen students were expelled, and their career prospects in Ireland lay in ruins. Not surprisingly, some of them decided to begin their lives over again in America. Among them was Thomas Robinson, who managed to establish himself as "a gentleman, a scholar, and a physician" in Virginia, where he emerged as a prominent figure in Irish-American cultural circles.[50]

Outside Dublin, the juggernaut of repression continued to roll through the south. County Kildare came first, followed by County Wicklow; the whole panoply of free quarters, floggings, half-hangings and house-burnings was used to terrify the population into giving up their weapons. Under these circumstances, and with the entire country under martial law, the reconstituted United Irish executive felt that they had no choice but to launch a rising immediately, before the movement was totally crushed. Even then, there were major splits in tactics; some favored a coup in Dublin, while others wanted to rally the United Irish forces in the surrounding counties and march in strength on the capital. After much debate, the latter strategy prevailed. The rising was timed for May 23; the signal would be the stopping of the mail coaches that left Dublin for the countryside.[51]

In the event, the rising began in confusion and chaos; it was more like a desperate reflex response to repression than a well-organized and tightly controlled United Irish revolutionary movement. Shaped by local conditions, conflicts and personalities, the rising unleashed traditional communal antagonisms that had already been growing in intensity. Atrocities on one side were used to justify atrocities on the other, in a vicious circle of violence that pulled down everyone caught in its path. Protestant loyalist prisoners were massacred at Scullabogue, and taken out to be piked to death on Wexford bridge; some had tried to save themselves by last-minute conversions to Catholicism. Catholic rebels were slaughtered in their camps at the Curragh and at Vinegar Hill. It was, in the words of Roy Foster, "probably the most concentrated episode of violence in Irish history." By the time it was over, at least 30,000 people had been killed; that was more than the entire death toll of the French revolutionary Reign of Terror, which lasted for three years in a population almost six times that of Ireland. The vast majority of the dead were on the rebel side.[52]

There were, in effect, three separate but related risings in Ireland that summer. The first, in the south-east counties of Kildare, Wicklow, Carlow and Wexford, was driven from below with a force that frequently overwhelmed the United Irishmen who were supposedly in charge; it lasted for a month, was bloody and brutal, and was put down with vindictive ruthlessness.[53] The second took place in the north-east counties of Antrim and Down in early June. This was very much a Presbyterian affair; the Catholics, distrusting the motives and intentions of the leaders, generally held back. The northern rising was not fueled by the same sense of social anger that characterized events in the south; the leaders were more enthusiastic than the rank-and-file, and enough discipline was imposed to prevent the massacre of prisoners. The military, however, did not show the same restraint; after initial United Irish successes, the rebels were defeated at the battles of Antrim and Ballynahinch, and the rising was totally defeated.[54]

The third rising occurred over two months later in the west of Ireland, when the French landed a small invasion force in County Mayo, a deeply traditional and Catholic region where the United Irishmen were very thin on the ground and secular democratic republican ideas had little or no popular appeal. French revolutionary soldiers were greeted by peasants who were ready to "take arms for France and the Blessed Virgin." "God help these simpletons," remarked one French officer with contempt; "if they knew how little we cared for the Pope or his religion, they would not be so hot in expecting help from us."[55] The French expected help from them, however, and used their strength to inflict a surprise defeat on the garrison at Castlebar before moving into the midlands. But Lord Cornwallis, who had surrendered to the Americans at Yorktown seventeen years earlier, possessed overwhelming numerical superiority in Ireland; the decisive battle took place at Ballinamuck, "the place of the pig," on September 8. After putting up a token resistance, the French surrendered; in accordance with the rules of war, they were treated as prisoners and taken into custody. The Irish who had fought with them were regarded as traitors-in-arms, and given no mercy; somewhere around 2,000 of them were massacred after the surrender.[56]

Throughout these events, the United Irish leaders who had been arrested in March watched with hope and then horror from their prison cells in Dublin. It was in July, when the treason trials and executions were proceeding, that the state prisoners, including Emmet, MacNeven, and the former editor of the radical *Northern Star,* Samuel Neilson, approached the authorities with an offer of negotiations. The prisoners agreed to supply "detailed information of every transaction that has passed between the United Irishmen and Foreign states," without actually naming any of the participants. In return, they would "emigrate to such Country as shall be agreed between them and Government," and promised "not to pass into an Enemy's Country." From the government's viewpoint, the advantages were readily apparent: the revolutionary conspiracy behind the constitutional cloak would be revealed, and the repressive measures would appear fully justified. From the prisoners' perspective, the agreement had the equally obvious advantage of saving their own lives and enabling them to move to neutral territory.[57]

For many, the most suitable destination was Germany rather than America; MacNeven sought permission "to go to the Continent," and Emmet told the authorities that his preference was "decidedly not America."[58] The United States had just passed the Alien Friends Law, which enabled the president to deport anyone whom he considered undesirable; knowing that they were included in that category, the prisoners feared that they would be sent straight back again. But the British government, for its part, decided that it was too risky to let the prisoners go to Germany, since there would be nothing to stop them from renewing their close contacts with revolutionary France. America appeared less dangerous, but Rufus King's intervention had ruled that out. In September, Sampson was given permission to leave for Portugal, on health grounds; the following month, all the others were informed that they were would be kept in jail for the duration of the war. The news was devastating. Accusing the government of bargaining in bad faith, Emmet insisted that the prisoners had been told that "we should be at liberty to go to whatever Country we pleased, not at war with Great Britain." This was not true; the pact had stipulated that both parties must agree on the choice of country. The government wanted the prisoners out of Europe, but could not send them to the United States without damaging Anglo-American relations; under these circumstances, agreement was impossible.[59]

While the state prisoners languished in jail, hundreds of less prominent United Irishmen who had participated in the Rising of 1798 were making their way to America, banished under pain of death from Ireland. One of them was Richard Caldwell, from north Antrim. A United Irish general at the age of eighteen, he rallied a large contingent of men at Ballymoney, armed with pikes, guns, pitchforks and "Scythes tied upon sticks." Making every effort to prevent them from harming civilians, he marched his troops to Ballymena, where they joined the patriots who had captured the town. When the tide turned after the battle of Antrim, Caldwell crossed the glens to Cushendall and escaped to Scotland, from whence he hoped to reach America. But there was a fifty-guinea price on his head, and his description had been circulated; on information supplied by the man who had taken them across the sea, he was arrested, brought back to Ireland, and tried for treason at a court martial in Coleraine. He was found guilty, and ordered to be "hanged in the town of Ballymena by the Neck untill dead[,] his head to be severed from his Body & placed upon a spike on the Market House in the town of Ballymoney"; afterwards, all his property was to be forfeited to the Crown. His family had already been singled out for revenge. Two days after the battle of Antrim, the army arrived with orders to burn the Caldwells' house to the ground; they were given five minutes to get out, and lost almost all their possessions. In a state of desperation, Richard's relatives did everything they could to save him. James Parks, his brother-in-law, visited Dublin Castle ten times in one day, secured an audience with Lord Castlereagh, and urged John Caldwell, Richard's father, to petition Lord Cornwallis. "Great Moderation must be used," Parks advised; "a shew of humility" might produce a pardon. And, in the event, it did. Richard was spared on condition that he spend the rest of his life in the United States; he was, after all, smaller fry than the state prisoners who had concerned Rufus King. Before long, not only Richard but the entire Caldwell family moved from Ballymoney to start a new life in New York.[60]

Another local leader in the north who followed a similar path was David Bailie Warden, a Presbyterian licentiate from County Down. As a student at Glasgow University, he had been strongly influenced by the radical philosophy of John Millar; in Ireland, he had studied with the Reverend James Porter, the radical minister who would be hanged in front of his own meeting house after a show trial in 1798. When the colonels of the County Down United Irishmen decided at the end of May to rise in support of the insurrection in the south, Warden quickly emerged as one of their most active and enthusiastic members. With the organization reeling from arrests, and in the face of considerable reluctance from the rank-and-file, he took it upon himself to rally the Newtownards Peninsula to the cause. Initial efforts proved fruitless; at Scrabo Hill, where his troops were supposed to gather, Warden was the only one who showed up. But when news came through that a United Irish army under

Henry Munro was assembling at Saintfield, he rode through the night until he had raised three hundred men "armed with Guns & Pikes." Linking up with Munro's forces, they marched into Ballynahinch, and prepared for battle. Even then, the desertion rate was high; Warden repeatedly complained about "the mutinous Disposition of our Troops," and tried to check the "spirit of Insubordination" within the rebel camp. In the end, a divided, demoralized and undisciplined United Irish army proved no match for the British troops who were converging on the town. Warden was among those who managed to escape; after going into hiding, he surrendered to the authorities, and was jailed in Belfast.[61]

Among his fellow prisoners were many who, like Warden himself, would be exiled to America. One of his closest friends, John Caldwell, Richard's older brother, had also been brought to a Belfast jail after being arrested for treason while visiting Dublin in May, just before the rising broke out. John Caldwell had organized lotteries to finance the United Irish movement in County Down, and was a colonel in the organization. His journey back to Belfast had been a harrowing one; as his coach entered the city, he could see "the terrific sights of the heads of our countrymen, who had been decapitated after being hanged by the sentence of court martial." To avoid a similar fate, the Belfast prisoners followed the lead of their counterparts in Dublin, and petitioned the authorities to leave for a neutral country.[62]

While they were waiting for a reply, the prisoners were moved from Belfast to the *Postlethwaite* prison ship anchored in the Lough. John Caldwell recalled the scene as they marched through High Street to the quay: "Many of the inhabitants, out of respect for our feelings, shut their windows and as I passed the houses of some of my old friends I noticed between the nearly closed shutters the moistened eye and the gentle waving of a white handkerchief." For six stinking weeks they endured overcrowded and unsanitary conditions, crammed into decks less than five feet high, on what they called a "floating bastille": Warden, suffering from a dry, hacking cough and loss of appetite, but trying to keep his spirits up through "lively, rational, and entertaining conversation"; Thomas Ledlie Birch, talking non-stop, and preaching to his jailers; Caldwell, driven to distraction by the "incessant querulous lamantation [*sic*]" of a falsely accused inmate.[63] In August, the word came through from Major-General Nugent that the prisoners would be allowed to leave for America. Surprisingly, given the circumstances, only a minority accepted the offer; most hoped that they would be released through lack of evidence.[64] Birch had already been permitted to cross the Atlantic; Warden and Caldwell were among those who followed him to New York. Making the same journey were many other radicals from Antrim and Down who had not been captured but who feared to stay. "*Presbyterians*," commented the Reverend William Campbell, "went in thousands to America. And if ships had been found, thousands more would have sought a peaceful asylum in that land of *Liberty*—a happy refuge from the despotism of England—far removed from the violence of her satellites and legal assassins."[65]

America, from this perspective, held out the prospect of hope in the face of despair. The defeat of the United Irishmen had been total; the consequences of their rising were the very reverse of their intentions. Instead of becoming an independent, democratic republic, Ireland was incorporated into the United Kingdom by the Act of Union in 1800. And instead of bringing Protestants and Catholics together, the revolutionary movement had driven them even further apart. "I begin to fear these people," Martha McTier commented about Catholics, "and think, like the Jews, they will regain their native land."[66]

At the economic, cultural, religious and social levels, United Irish aspirations were crushed. The attempt to establish economic independence lay in pieces, as Ireland became increasingly integrated into the British market system. The confident cultural nationalism that had found its fullest expression in the Belfast Harpers' Festival of 1792, timed to coincide with the Bastille Day celebrations and intended to instill a sense of pride in the past, gave way to a mood of gloom and nostalgia that permeated the poetry of early nineteenth-century Ireland.[67] The powerful religious millenarian impulse, which had supplied radicalism with much of its emotional force, either evaporated or detached itself from United Irish politics. In Protestant Ireland, it gave way to a species of conversionist evangelism characterized by anti-Catholic fulminations against the Whore of Babylon; in Catholic Ireland, it reemerged in the anti-Protestant Rockite movement of the 1820s.[68] And the attempt to establish what Thomas Emmet called "a very different system of political economy," which would revolutionize tenurial relations and recast the social and economic order to benefit the "productive classes," ended in failure, and would not be revived until the Young Ireland movement over forty years later.[69]

The United Irishmen, then, were thoroughly beaten; the decisive defeat of Robert Emmet's insurrection in 1803 only confirmed their collapse. But for those radicals who fled to the United States, there was at least the possibility of redemption; what had been lost in Ireland might yet be won in America. The trouble was that America itself seemed to be hovering between the forces of democracy and conservatism. Under these circumstances, the United Irishmen approached American politics with a strong sense of ambivalence.

On the one hand, the United States represented an asylum of liberty, a country with low taxes and religious freedom, where an industrious man could achieve economic independence, a land free from oppression. "I carry out a great horror of this Country," wrote one radical shortly before he emigrated, "& great love and admiration for the Country I am going to."[70] On the other hand, America was also seen as a land in the grip of the Federalists, a country that had supposedly betrayed its republican roots and formed a corrupt alliance with counter-revolutionary Britain. "If ever the Court of St. James's gets an

Ascendancy in your Councils & that of France should be subjugated," John Chambers had written to Mathew Carey in 1794, " . . . the Sun of Liberty would be set in endless night."[71]

By 1798, when revolution was crushed in Ireland and the Alien and Sedition Acts were passed in America, it appeared to many United Irishmen, including the state prisoners, that the court of St. James did indeed have an ascendancy in American councils, that the republican experiment had gone off the track—an impression that the authorities in Ireland were eager to cultivate.[72] For those United Irishmen who crossed the Atlantic, the central task would be to bring the practice into line with the theory, so that they could realize in America the dreams they had lost in Ireland. In America, they would attempt to transform frustrated aspirations into fulfilled expectations.

CHAPTER TWO

Hordes of Wild Irishmen

"The Country is beautiful but it is like a Beautiful Scene, in a Theatre," wrote Wolfe Tone two days after he arrived in Philadelphia in the summer of 1795; "the effect at a proper distance is admirable but it will not bear a minute inspection." He was even less impressed with the people; "they seem selfish and interested," he commented, "and they do fleece us, Emigres, at a most unmerciful rate." Over the next three months, his negative attitude hardened. The people of Philadelphia, felt Tone, were "a disgusting race, eaten up with all the vice of commerce, and that vilest of all pride, the pride of the purse." In the countryside, the farmers were "extremely ignorant and boorish." Both the Germans and the Quakers came in for severe criticism. But his harshest words were reserved for the Irish in Pennsylvania. "If you meet a confirmed blackguard," he asserted, "you may be sure he is Irish—You will of course observe I speak of the lower orders—They are as boorish and ignorant as the Germans, as uncivil and uncouth as the Quakers, and as they have ten times more animal spirits than both, they are much more actively troublesome."[1]

Nevertheless, Tone was able to fit these unpleasant perceptions into a politically acceptable framework. If the Irish in America appeared obnoxious, rude and unruly, he argued, it was because the British government had made them that way; they had been "corrupted by their own execrable Government at home," and were correspondingly ill-equipped to handle their new-found freedom in the United States. "After all," Tone commented, "I do not wonder at, nor am I angry with them." And although the living and breathing people of Pennsylvania proved deeply disappointing, their government was still "the best under heaven," in which democratic republicanism brought "Affluence and ease" to all the citizens. "These are the things," he concluded, "for which the lives of Thousands and Tens of Thousands are a cheap purchase."[2] The logic was both revealing and chilling. Human imperfections were recognized, explained away, and blamed on Britain, and mass deaths became a small price when weighed in the scale against the creation of utopia.

Other United Irish émigrés who arrived in the mid-1790s displayed similar patterns of idealization and disillusionment. In Philadelphia, Tone was reunited with his "old Friend and Brother exile," James Reynolds, as well as with Archibald Hamilton Rowan; the last time they had been together was in Rowan's cell at Newgate, fourteen months earlier. "It was a singular encounter," Tone recalled, "and our several escapes from an ignominious death, seemed little short of a miracle." They exchanged stories of their "several adventures": Reynolds's flight from charges of high treason, Rowan's experiences in France, near-misses with impressment when crossing the Atlantic.[3] Like Tone, Reynolds expected to find in America a "happier world," with "nature in her noblest scenes," and a new species of man who was "busied in rendering himself worthy of nature"; shortly after his arrival, however, he became convinced that the promise of republicanism was being subverted by a combination of British influence and American corruption.[4] Rowan was also dispirited by American realities; the man who had once wished that he had been an American now found that the manners of a rough and egalitarian society grated against his aristocratic tastes and temperament.[5]

In Rowan's case, direct exposure to the Terror in France had already shaken his attachment to revolutionary politics. After making his escape from Ireland to France, he had been imprisoned as an English spy in Brest, where he witnessed wagon-loads of fellow-prisoners going to the guillotine each day. Upon his release, he traveled to Paris, and arrived just in time for the anti-Jacobin coup of Thermidor; the blood had streamed beneath his feet as he watched the guillotining of sixty Robespierrists in the Place de la Revolution. The experience, he later told his wife, had drastically altered his views of reform and revolution. "I have seen," he wrote, "one faction rising over another and overturning it; each of them in their turn making a stalking-horse of the supreme power of the people, to cover public and private massacre and plunder; while every man of virtue and humanity shuddered and skulked in a disgraceful silence." And yet, such scenes of violence had not in themselves stopped Rowan from seeking French assistance for a revolution in Ireland; his hatred of England continued to outweigh his horror of France. In a memorial to the French government in October 1794, he expressed the desire to "exterminate the English" in Ireland, and presented plans for an invasion; it was only when it became clear that factionalism in France prevented assistance to Ireland that he left in disgust for America.[6]

Rowan's disenchantment with the practice—although not the principles—of republicanism increased during his stay in the United States. After an initial foray into politics, he became increasingly alienated from American life; the youth were too ill-behaved and ill-natured, the adults were too avaricious, and the people in general were too uncouth, he wrote. In addition, the old demon of factionalism that had destroyed the French Revolution was now at work in the United States; Rowan registered with mounting despair the "violence of party" in Philadelphia, and finally left the city to escape its effects. By 1796, he sank into depression, reproaching himself for his "imprudence" and wishing he were back in Ireland. "I dwell too much, perhaps," he wrote his wife, "upon the probable events of times like these, so black, so melancholy!" Sarah Rowan, for her part, had a much more hard-headed approach to life: "As to where we shall meet, you must be the best judge," she informed him toward the end of the decade. "I do not suppose in America; your picture both of that country and its inhabitants is indeed sufficient to deter any person from going thither. But then you did expect to find perfection there; and I do not think it exists any where."[7]

The careers of Rowan, Tone and Reynolds exemplify different responses to a common disillusionment. Just as Rowan became increasingly withdrawn, other émigrés also came to regret their role in the revolutionary movement and dropped out of American politics altogether. Some, including Rowan himself, wound up petitioning the British government for a pardon, and were eventually allowed to return home.[8] Meanwhile, a hard core of exiles steered clear of American issues for precisely the opposite reason; like Tone, they were concerned above all with the emancipation of Ireland, and would not be distracted from the pursuit of that goal. Napper Tandy, for example, believed that "as an alien, it would be ungrateful in me to take any active part in politics" in the United States, and left for France in 1797.[9] Many other émigrés decided to carry on the struggle for democratic republicanism in their new home, and were determined to bring American realities into line with their own political ideals. Among them were not only Reynolds in Philadelphia but his old friend and fellow-conspirator John Daly Burk.

Burk wrote in the first issue of his newspaper, the Boston *Polar Star*, in 1796:

> From the moment the stranger puts his foot on the soil of *America*, his fetters are rent in pieces, and the scales of servitude which he had contracted under *European* tyrannies fall off. . . . He sees a moral, intrepid, and enlightened community, ranged under the banners of equality and justice; and by the natural sympathy that subsists between the mind and every thing that is amiable, he finds his affections irresistibly attracted.

This mythic view of America was fundamental to Burk's outlook; those politicians who appeared to threaten or undermine the ideal were denounced as "gloomy, weak, irritable and . . . wicked beings," who should be made to realize that "the terrible vengeance of the Republic would put an end in the same instant to their lives and their *projects*." Convinced that he spoke for "THE PEOPLE" and that he stood for Reason and Truth, Burk became one of the most partisan, impassioned and intolerant democrats in the country.[10]

The principal targets of émigré anger were the conservatives who dominated American politics through the 1790s. At the beginning of the decade, the unstable coalition that produced the Federal Constitution of 1788 had broken into loosely defined but increasingly powerful political parties, the Federalists and the Republicans. The Federalists, who were in power during the Washington and Adams administrations, were deeply influenced by the political economy of Alexander Hamilton. Believing that the United States had more to fear from excessive liberty than from the accumulation of power, they attempted to build a polity characterized by deference to authority, the rule of the wealthy, educated and respectable, and a government powerful enough to withstand the changing whims of public opinion. Good relations with Britain were central to their political program; the revenues from Anglo-American trade were essential to Hamilton's effort to achieve fiscal stability, and many of the government's strongest supporters were merchants whose livelihood depended on the British connection. In the context of the French Revolution and international war from 1792, the Federalists also saw Britain as a bulwark against a tide of international Jacobinism that threatened to engulf America as well as Europe.[11]

According to the Republicans who were coalescing under the leadership of Thomas Jefferson and James Madison, such policies subverted the spirit of the American Revolution. They believed that the Federalists were attempting to establish an exclusive and aristocratic social elite, instead of creating a more open and dynamic society in which new men on the make could reap the economic and political rewards. The Republicans also accused the Federalists of accepting and indeed embracing America's neo-colonial relationship with Britain, instead of working for economic independence. And they argued that the Federalists were aligning the United States with the sinister forces of the European counter-revolution, instead of supporting America's fellow republicans in France.

In its struggle against the Federalist program, the emerging Republican Party not only commanded considerable support in the southern states and the western grain-growing belt but also established an important base in the seaboard cities. Merchants who traded outside the British Empire, artisans who wanted protection from British imports, and ambitious entrepreneurs who challenged existing elites were drawn toward the Republicans. It was no coincidence that the Republicans were particularly popular in neighborhoods on the rapidly expanding edges of the cities, such as the Northern Liberties and Southwark districts of Philadelphia, Wards Six and Seven in New York, and

Fell's Point in Baltimore—all areas where large numbers of Irish immigrants were settling. Many of these immigrants were immediately attracted to a party that combined anti-British rhetoric with the promise of economic and political opportunity.[12]

Irish immigrants were moving into the Republican camp before the first wave of United Irish refugees arrived in America; men like Burk and Reynolds strengthened an alliance that was already in the making. In 1793, many Irish immigrants had joined the Democratic Societies that sprang up to express solidarity with revolutionary France and to combat what were regarded as aristocratic, monarchical and pro-British tendencies in America. When the French minister Edmund Genet attempted to organize anti-British privateering expeditions from American ports, he made a special appeal to the "generous and intrepid natives of Ireland," and invoked folk memories of the "Wild Geese" who had flown to France after the Treaty of Limerick in 1691. (Quite what the predominantly Protestant Irish population in America made of this remains unknown). And although Genet's plans collapsed in chaos, Irish democrats registered their presence in American politics the following year by contributing to the victory of Republicans Edward Livingston in New York and John Swanwick in Philadelphia during the Congressional elections of 1794. Significantly, the defeated candidate in Philadelphia was Thomas Fitzsimons, a prominent Irish Catholic Federalist who had worked for the "equal rights of citizenship" for his co-religionists during and after the American Revolution. But for the Irish who voted against him, most of whom were almost certainly Protestant, the key point was that Fitzsimons supported Hamilton's fiscal program and foreign policy and must therefore be "pro-British."[13]

What brought the United Irishmen, earlier Irish immigrants and American Republicans together was their common opposition to Jay's Treaty, which arose from the Federalist government's attempt to defuse the growing crisis in Anglo-American relations in 1794. In the Atlantic, the Royal Navy had been seizing American ships that were trading with France; in the Northwest, British forces occupied strategic military posts and worked to establish a Native American buffer state against American expansion. From the Federalist perspective, war with Britain would be disastrous for the United States; rather than risk further confrontation, they sent John Jay to London for negotiations. In return for peace and the British evacuation of the Northwest, the United States agreed to give up the principle of freedom of the seas, and to conduct its trade according to British conditions. When, in the summer of 1795, the terms were leaked to the American press, the Republicans reacted with fury. Not only did the treaty perpetuate America's neo-colonial status, in their view; by bringing the country into the British sphere of influence, they argued, it betrayed the "sister republic" of France and endangered liberty at home. Over the course of the next year, they fought a hard but unsuccessful battle to block its ratification.[14]

The first United Irishman to participate in the protest movement against Jay's Treaty was Hamilton Rowan. Only a few days after he arrived in Philadelphia, Rowan attended a mass meeting at which leading Republicans denounced the treaty's terms; possibly as many as one-fifth of the crowd were of Irish origin. One of the speakers was Blair McClenachan, a populist democrat and wealthy merchant from Londonderry who had made his fortune in the flaxseed trade, and who had been described back in 1788 as the "most violent anti-foederalist [*sic*] in America." At the end of his speech, McClenachan whipped up anti-British emotions by requesting "*three cheers for the persecuted patriot, Hamilton Rowan,*" throwing a copy of the treaty into the crowd, and recommending that they "kick this damn treaty to hell." He then directed a stone-throwing crowd of three hundred people to the windows of the British minister, George Hammond, and a Federalist senator, William Bingham. It was one of many protests against what Mathew Carey described as "that baleful compact"; John Jay himself remarked that he could find his way across the country by the light of his burning effigies.[15]

By far the most vociferous United Irish opponents of Jay's Treaty were James Reynolds and, from the spring of 1796, William Duane. Duane had been born of Irish parents in New York in 1760; in 1771, after the death of his father, he and his mother returned to Ireland. Displaying an anti-authoritarian temperament from an early age, he rebelled against the Franciscans who educated him by becoming a deist, and against his mother by marrying a Protestant. (She took her revenge by promptly disinheriting him). Duane left Ireland in 1782, and became a radical journalist first in England and then in India; after a series of escalating conflicts with the British authorities in Calcutta, he was deported from the colony without trial in 1794, and returned to England a deeply embittered man. Duane became active in the revolutionary wing of the London Corresponding Society, and after the British government's crackdown on radicalism he departed for his native land in May 1796. With his "wild hair, long beard and fierce expression," he soon acquired a reputation as an extreme democrat; by 1798, he had become the editor of the *Aurora,* the leading Republican newspaper in the country. In his own words, he "both was, and was not, an Irishman"; although he had been away from Ireland during the 1790s, he identified emotionally and intellectually with the United Irish movement. "If to be ready, at any time that my slender efforts could in the least tend to the emancipation of Ireland from the horrid yoke of Britain, to embark in her cause, and to sacrifice my life for that country as readily as I should for this which gave me birth," he wrote, "—then am I as very an United Irishman as any tyrant could abhor."[16]

In the summer of 1796, Duane and Reynolds were among the leaders of a new political club in Philadelphia that decided to attack President Washington for his role in signing the Treaty. Arguing that pro-British elements in the administration were exploiting the president's prestige and concluding that Washington himself was betraying the principles of the Revolution, they set out to destroy his political reputation by assassinating his character. In this campaign, they worked closely with Benjamin Franklin Bache, the editor of the *Aurora*, who opened his columns to Washington's critics, published forged letters to discredit the president, and poured out plenty of invective on his own account. Under the pseudonym of Jasper Dwight, Duane wrote a pamphlet that attacked Washington as an enemy to liberty at home and abroad, denounced him as a hypocrite for owning slaves, and suggested that his "attachment to the revolution was not the result of a love of republican freedom, but of disappointed ambition." Reynolds went further still. "If ever there was a period for rejoicing," he wrote in the *Aurora* when Washington left office, "this is the moment—every heart, in unison with the freedom and happiness of the people ought to beat high with exultation, that the name of WASHINGTON from this day ceases to give a currency to political iniquity; and to legalize corruption."[17]

Such a confrontational style was both daring and dangerous. On the one hand, the attempt to break through the wall of respect for Washington was intended to clear the path for democratic republicanism; on the other, there was a strong possibility that the strategy would produce an anti-democratic backlash. This risk was particularly pronounced within the Irish community in America, which was steeped in pro-Washington sentiment. During the War of Independence, Irish patriots had treated Washington as a revolutionary hero who could do no wrong; such attitudes were carried across the Atlantic, and remained deeply embedded within the Irish-American consciousness. In Mathew Carey's view, the "coarse and vulgar" attacks on the president "did more to injure the cause of Democracy than all the efforts of its enemies could have done in five years." As far as Carey was concerned, Reynolds was a walking disaster, who destroyed everything he touched. "So convinced was I of the fatality of his efforts," Carey recalled, "that I once told him, half jest, half earnest, that if I were a leading federalist, I would give him 500 dollars a year to take an active part in the affairs of the Democrats, for so surely as he did, so surely would they be utterly blasted."[18]

Despite these differences, the United Irishmen continued to work together against the Federalists. During the 1796 Congressional elections, they helped to secure Blair McClenachan's victory in Philadelphia County, and loosened the hold of the Federalists in New York City's artisan community. In the presidential election of that year, they attempted to mobilize the Irish vote behind Jefferson's campaign against John Adams. No one threw himself into this task with greater energy than Mathew Carey. Over the previous decade, he had worked through immigrant aid organizations such as the Hibernian Society to bring the Irish into the democratic fold. Now his Philadelphia bookstore became a nerve center of the Republican organization, and his grassroots work with the Irish constituency contributed to Jefferson's victory in Pennsylvania. Reynolds and Duane were also among Jefferson's strongest supporters; strange to say, the issue of slaveowning was passed over in silence. From the heart of Adams country in Boston, Burk feigned impartiality while clearly favoring Jefferson. The next president, he wrote, must be a "hater of monarchy," a lover of science, liberty and revolutions, and a supporter of close Franco-American relations. Despite his claim of neutrality (which no one took seriously), there was only one man who fitted that particular bill. In the end, it was a close call; Adams won the presidency by three votes, and the Federalists remained in power.[19]

Against the background of deteriorating Franco-American relations and intensifying Federalist-Republican tensions, the United Irishmen continued their struggle for democracy. Their numbers were boosted in 1797, when governmental repression in Ulster drove hundreds of radicals to the boats. "One of my Companions," reported a passenger who had just arrived in New York, "unexpectedly met his Brother in law a Presbyterian Clergyman from the North of Ireland, neither of whom knew that the other had left Ireland so precipitate was their flight." Such immigrants could not yet vote in American elections, although that did not stop many of them from trying anyway; the election of the democratic republican Israel Israel to the Pennsylvania state senate, for example, was invalidated on the grounds that non-citizens from the Irish strongholds of Southwark and the Northern Liberties had illegally cast ballots. But they quickly gravitated to a new organization that effectively combined Irish concerns with American politics, the American Society of United Irishmen.[20]

Formed in the summer of 1797, and growing out of earlier radical coteries grouped around Reynolds, Duane and Burk, the society began in Philadelphia, and quickly established branches from New York to South Carolina. The extent of its membership is difficult to determine, given the climate of denunciations and denials in which it operated. Duane argued that it "never amounted at any one time to more than about 60 or 70 members," but he had good political reasons to play down its size, on the grounds that he could more easily accuse his opponents of hysterical overreaction. According to William Cobbett, who had equally good political reasons for exaggerating the society's significance, there were 1,500 members in Philadelphia and its environs alone.[21]

In 1798, the Federalist journalist John Ward Fenno published a list of seventeen leaders of the organization. It included long-standing Irish-American radicals such as Mathew Carey and his brother James, comparatively recent arrivals from Ulster such as John Black, and fellow-travelers such as the Scottish democrat James Thomson Callender and the Irish-born Republican

Congressman Matthew Lyon. There were teachers, journalists and shopkeepers; one of the central figures, Daniel Clark, was a shoemaker. The accuracy of the list, however, is problematic. Mathew Carey, along with James, angrily denied that he had anything to do with the society; his private correspondence, however, tells a very different story. "The accusation made by John Ward Fenno," concluded Edward Carter, "was probably correct. Carey was a leader of the American Society of United Irishmen." Similar denials by the schoolteachers John Black and Samuel Wylie must also be taken with a grain of salt; both men were clearly supporters of the movement, but could have put their careers in jeopardy by admitting to membership in the hostile atmosphere of 1798.[22]

Like the Strugglers and the Philanthropic and Telegraphic Societies that Reynolds and Burk had formed in Dublin, the American Society of United Irishmen was a secret, oath-bound organization divided into close-knit and compact cells. In the cities and large towns, each section contained no more than eight people, who met each week, read and discussed political works, and formed committees of secrecy and correspondence. The sections sent delegates to the state committee, which in turn elected members to the general executive committee in Philadelphia. All offices were rotated regularly to keep the structure as democratic as possible. In Cobbett's view, "the ceremonies of the compact are essentially the same as those of freemasonry," and there is little doubt that Reynolds drew on masonic models for the society. As president of the General Masonic Committee of his native County Tyrone in 1793, he had praised the "masons of America" as the "first founders of the Temple of Liberty," applauded the "rapid progress of liberty in France," and called for radical reform in Ireland. Earlier still, William Drennan had called for "the secrecy and somewhat of the ceremonial of Freemasonry" in the organization of what became the United Irishmen. And radicals such as Mathew Carey, Hamilton Rowan, William MacNeven and John Caldwell were part of a broader masonic network that provided a conduit for democratic ideology and organization. One does not have to accept the wilder Federalist conspiratorial claims that the Age of Revolution was the work of the Society of the Illuminati to recognize that freemasonry deeply influenced the form and content of the United Irish movement on both sides of the Atlantic.[23]

The central aim of the American Society of United Irishmen was to "*promote the emancipation of Ireland from the tyranny of the British government.*" It also operated as a support group for political refugees, some of whom had crossed the Atlantic as indentured servants; among other things, the society raised funds to release them from servitude.[24] But there was an American dimension to the organization that alarmed Tories like Cobbett and High Federalists like Fenno. The formation of the society coincided with French seizures of American ships trading with Britain and the diplomatic crisis precipitated in 1798 by the so-called XYZ affair. This crisis arose from the treatment of the American envoys whom Adams had sent to Paris in an effort to reestablish good relations with France. The envoys had been approached by three French agents, known in Adams's report to Congress as "X," "Y," and "Z," and were told that the French foreign minister, Talleyrand, would only open negotiations if he were paid $250,000, the United States would lend France $12 million, and the president would publicly retract his earlier criticisms of France. When the story reached America, there was a popular outcry against such "insulting" behavior; during the summer of 1798, the two countries moved into a state of undeclared war.[25] In the event of hostilities, believed many Federalists, the United Irish émigrés would be more likely to support France than to defend America; the Irish radicals, after all, had seen France rather than the United States as the key to Irish emancipation. Cobbett and Fenno, in particular, were convinced that the society was plotting to link up with a French invasion force that would revolutionize the American republic.

Cobbett's fears centered on the fact that the society was open to all democrats, whether or not they were Irish, and that each member swore to work for "the attainment of LIBERTY, and EQUALITY TO MANKIND, IN WHATEVER NATION I RESIDE." Since the members actually resided in America, and were thus not in a position to do anything about British rule in Ireland, he argued, it was clear that their real purpose was to promote democratic republicanism in the United States. And the secrecy of the organization, he continued, demonstrated that its members were prepared to use conspiratorial and revolutionary means to realize that end. Most disturbing of all, in his view, was the provision in the society's constitution for collective action in the event of "*cases of urgency*." Cobbett believed that this was a code phrase for a French invasion, at which point the Irish conspirators, in league with their American allies, would spring into action. "Thus has it proved in every country," he added, "which the infamous sans-culottes have invaded with success." Fenno took substantially the same position, arguing that Irish democrats were using the Republicans as a front for their nefarious designs to Jacobinize the United States. There was only one solution, he wrote; "every United Irishman ought to be hunted from the country, as much as a wolf or a tyger."[26]

It is customary to accuse Cobbett and Fenno of deliberate distortion and fear-mongering, and there is indeed much substance to the charge. But it is not enough to dismiss their arguments as "hysterical" and "paranoid" and simply leave it at that. In the context of the time, Cobbett's and Fenno's views appeared quite plausible; nor, for that matter, were they entirely detached from historical realities. The United Irishmen in the United States were among the most dedicated revolutionaries in the western world, and enjoyed significant support within the growing Irish community in America. Moreover, the Federalists had good reason to suspect that the public statements of the United Irishmen could not be taken at face value. In Ireland, it is clear, a militant minority had concealed revolutionary intentions beneath public declarations of reform. Benjamin Binns, who would eventually come to America in 1817, happily cited Plutarch to justify the smokescreen sent out by the United Irishmen in London: "To deceive a friend is impious—But to outwit an Enemy is not only just and glorious—but profitable and sweet." When Cobbett compared the United Irishmen to the French Jacobins, quoting William Playfair's observation that they had "*two creeds*, one to *amuse the public*, and another that, for [a] long time, never was known but to the members," he was very close to the mark.[27]

Given the evidence coming out of Ireland about the secret dealings between the United Irishmen and the French government, it was not surprising that most Federalists, including Secretary of State Timothy Pickering, feared that the pattern could repeat itself in America. If the French attacked an American government that the Irish radicals believed was betraying the cause of liberty, it seemed probable that the United Irishmen would welcome the troops as liberators. Under these circumstances, the formation of Irish militia companies at the height of the crisis appeared particularly alarming. In Baltimore, the Catholic Corps opened its ranks to Protestants in 1798, and changed its name to the Baltimore Irish Brigade; according to one report, it was "composed to a man of United Irishmen," who wore French uniforms. When Duane organized an Irish volunteer company of Republican Greens in Philadelphia the following summer, Pickering's reaction was understandable: "He is doubtless a United Irishman, and the company is probably formed to oppose the authority of the government; and in case of war and invasion by the French, to join them."[28]

The fear of Irish sedition in America was heightened by the fact of revolutionary violence in Ireland. Cobbett's and Fenno's columns were full of lurid pictures of the United Irishmen as a dangerous gang of "cut-throats" and "assassins"; the "United Dagger men," as they became known, were said to be "actuated by the same infamous principles, and actuated by that same thirst for blood and plunder, which has reduced France to a vast slaughter-house." Such images were clearly a gross caricature of reality, and are best understood as a Federalist attempt to demonize the democratic enemy. But although the United Irishmen may not have been personally bloodthirsty, men like Burk fully supported, and in Ireland may well have planned, the assassination of hostile witnesses and informers for the greater good of liberty. Burk's friend and colleague Denis Driscol publicly approved of plans to assassinate a member of the royal family, and John Binns regretted that George III had not been killed by the crowd that attacked his carriage in 1795. Wolfe Tone may have written an entertaining diary and doubtless had an engaging personality, but he could write with disturbing ease about sacrificing tens of thousands of lives in the name of democratic republicanism. There was, in short, a recognizable reality beneath the caricature, which helps to explain the sheer intensity of Federalist reactions to the United Irishmen.[29]

In attempting to isolate the United Irishmen from the rest of the population, the Federalists condemned not only their politics but also their putative national character. Earlier in the century, Irish immigrants had been associated with crime, drink and poverty. During the 1790s, the old image of the "wild Irish" increasingly became politicized, and was applied to the new immigrants. Cobbett opened the attack in 1795, when he maintained that a people with "such confused ideas of *mine* and *thine*" would naturally support leaders who wanted to plunder the rich and line their pockets with the proceeds. By 1798, the air was thick with such denunciations. Fenno's *Gazette of the United States,* in particular, carried numerous columns that presented the United Irishmen as being fundamentally un-American. One such article ran:

> The genius of an American soars to every thing noble; of a seditious Irishman to meanness. The American disposition delights in uprightness and every species of ingeniousness; the out-cast Irishman in injustice and every species of low deception. The [illegible] country, and especially to support the laws and constituted authorities; the abandoned Irishman's chief pride, is to destroy his country's dearest rights, to trample down her laws, and overturn all legal power.

"As well might we attempt to tame the Hyena," the writer concluded, "as to Americanize an Irishman."[30]

This was extreme meeting extreme, with the closed-mindedness of a chauvinistic and exclusivist American nationalism running up against the absolute moral certainty of United Irish radicalism. But it was not simply a conflict between conservative Americans and radical Irishmen; the Irish in America were themselves divided between supporters and opponents of the democratic republican movement. "Too many United Irishmen arrived here within a few Days," sniffed Hugh Gaine into his diary in October 1798; as an Irish Presbyterian and former vice-president of the New York St. Patrick Society, he had supported the loyalist side during the American War of Independence, and he completely rejected the politics of the newcomers.[31] So too did the Irish Catholic supporters of Thomas Fitzsimons, the Philadelphia Federalist whose defeat in 1794 registered the growing strength of Republicanism in the city. Some of the fiercest attacks on the United Irishmen in the United States came from recently arrived Irish loyalists who had emigrated to escape the incipient revolution at home. Such people regarded themselves as authorities on United Irish tactics and goals, and found a ready audience for their views in the American Federalist press.

Among other things, Irish loyalist sources of information fed directly into

Federalist forebodings about the "secret, close and unfathomable" conspiratorial intentions of the radical émigrés. Drawing on Irish newspaper reports, one of Fenno's correspondents repeated the Orange myth that "the United Irishmen of Europe used as a pass-word the mystical term *Eliphismatis*, containing the very horrible oath:—

E very
L oyal
I rish
P rotestant
H eretic
I
S hall
M urder
A nd
T his
I
S wear."[32]

This appeared to validate what "A Loyal Irishman" told Fenno's readers about the strange language that was being used by the American Society of United Irishmen. At the head of a notice advertising a meeting of the society in Philadelphia in November 1798 were the words CODROMAGHT and SAOIRSEAUGHT. The "mystical meaning" could be deciphered, he wrote, once it was realized that these words actually constituted an anagram: "The Parole is ROOM AHOA! Countersign, THIS DAGGER CUTS. It was originally intended for Dublin, where most of the *United Irishmen* were armed with *Daggers* only, owing to the difficulty of concealing their pikes and muskets from the general search by government,—but this is the first time I have met with it in this country." In fact, the words were actually Gaelic for Equality and Liberty, but no good conspiracy theorist worth his salt would be deterred by such minor details.[33]

Along with this storm of vituperation in Federalist newspapers, the United Irishmen were also faced with a hostile Congress. Both the Naturalization Law and the Alien Friends Law of 1798 were passed with the Irish very much in mind. In the course of his argument for tighter naturalization laws, the Federalist Congressman Harrison Gray Otis declared that he "did not wish to invite hordes of wild Irishmen, nor the turbulent and disorderly of all parts of the world, to come here with a view to disturb our tranquillity." Partly as a result of his efforts, the new legislation of June 1798 increased the waiting period for citizenship from five to fourteen years, and put a five-pound tax on certificates of naturalization; the intention, and to some extent the effect, was to check the growing power of the radical Irish vote. Even more alarming and offensive to the Irish and British émigrés was the Alien Friends Law, which gave the president the power to deport any alien whom he believed was "dangerous to the peace and safety of the United States." There was to be no trial and no appeal; the United Irishmen, like their fellow radicals from Britain, were subject to arbitrary arrest through the exercise of an emergency measure. For the two years of the act's official duration, the threat of expulsion would hang over their heads.[34]

In the event, the bark was worse than the bite; indeed, one of the reasons behind Cobbett's offensive against the radical Irish was his desire to have the legislation implemented much more vigorously.[35] The only United Irishman who came close to being pushed out was John Daly Burk, who had left Boston in 1797 for the more fertile republican soil of New York. Under the patronage of Aaron Burr, and in partnership with Doctor James Smith (who had been involved in the anti-Catholic Gordon Riots of 1780 in London), Burk became the editor of the *Time-Piece,* by far the most radical newspaper in the city. In the tense political atmosphere of New York, when Federalists and Republicans were fighting each other in the streets during the summer of 1798, Burk organized a small army of seventy men to protect his presses, and sometimes got into fist fights himself. The paper provided a key link between the city's Irish constituency and the Burr and Livingston Republicans; under Burk's control, it not only increased in circulation but also launched a series of scathing attacks on the Adams administration.[36]

Much of Burk's anger had been directed toward the Alien and Sedition Bills as they were being debated in Congress. He believed that the legislation was intended to muzzle opposition while the Federalists reversed the American Revolution and transformed the United States into a pro-British, aristocratic state. In reaction to this perceived plot, his language became increasingly extreme. He regarded the legislation as the American equivalent of Robespierre's reign of terror, saw spies and informers everywhere, and demanded that the "*coward traitors*" who were betraying the Republic should be tarred and feathered. No one in the government could be trusted, he believed; Timothy Pickering was implicitly accused of murdering Cobbett's Irish clerk, and John Adams was explicitly described as a "mock Monarch" and charged with transmitting forged documents to Congress to bolster his warmongering strategy.[37]

In addition to these public attacks, there were also reports that Burk privately hoped for a French invasion of the United States. "He believed the French would come here," it was said, "and he wished to God they would, when every scoundrel in favor of this government would be put to the guillotine—that they had hinted that he would be sent away as an alien—but then he would let them know who was the strongest party." For Pickering, this was the last straw; in July, before the Alien and Sedition Bills came into effect, Burk and his co-editor were charged with seditious libel under the common law.

New York's Republicans raised $2000 to pay his bail, and Burk strenuously denied that he had supported a French landing.[38]

Historians of the Alien and Sedition Acts have generally accepted Burk's position that he was, above all, an American patriot. In his defense, James Morton Smith has pointed out that Burk drank a toast at the United Irishmen's Fourth of July dinner to "The Day; may Americans never be ashamed to celebrate this glorious anniversary, unless they permit their constitution to be *violated*." But this view ignores the fact that Burk did indeed feel that the constitution was being violated; the qualification was large enough to drive an army through. Looking back on this period, Burk argued that the Alien and Sedition Acts "openly violated the constitution" and that the "advocates of royalty became the masters of the Republic." Even at the time, he began to suggest that the Federalists should be purged from Congress. Immediately after his release from prison, he reproduced Cromwell's speech at the dissolution of the Long Parliament, entitling it "A LESSON FOR VENAL ASSEMBLIES"; the relevance to America's situation was unstated but obvious. The same message appeared in one of his poems, based on Swift's "The Inquirer and the Echo," which argued that the only way to gain reform was through force. On balance, Burk's denials appear less than convincing.[39]

At any rate, the government's prosecution soon caused the *Time-Piece* to self-destruct. While Burk continued to condemn the government, his co-editor, James Smith, preferred a more prudent approach. The crunch came in mid-July, when Smith refused to publish one of Burk's attacks on Adams on the grounds that it went too far and broke the conditions of bail. Burk was furious. Calling Smith "a paltry old woman" and "a driveling old p—s Doctor," he demanded that his piece be published; Smith responded by picking up the type and flinging it into Burk's face. Despite the efforts of leading New York Republicans to patch things up, the paper collapsed in a welter of mutual recriminations. In the face of this defeat, Burk tried to strike a deal with the government; if the charges against him were dropped, he would leave the country. Pickering agreed, adding that this "turbulent mischievous person" must be banned not only from the United States but from the entire western hemisphere. Burk's initial plan was to reach France, and work for another invasion of Ireland. But, fearing that he was about to be seized by British spies, he broke his part of the bargain, went into hiding, and resurfaced in the relative safety of Jefferson's Virginia.[40]

Just as Burk had been forced into a tactical retreat, the Alien and Sedition Acts and the Federalist newspaper offensive pushed the Irish radicals in general onto the defensive. James Carey, whose *United States Recorder* conducted a continuous guerrilla campaign against Cobbett during the summer of 1798, insisted that the American Society of United Irishmen was "a respectable society, innocent in its intentions, as they regard the United States." One of his correspondents, who signed himself "Montgomery," argued that the society's emphasis on secrecy was necessary to shelter it from British agents; the American United Irishmen, he declared, "possess no secrets but what regard their own country." The choice of pseudonym was significant. Richard Montgomery was an Irish-born general who had been killed during the American siege of Quebec in 1775. He became a cult figure second only to Washington among the United Irishmen in the United States, and was seen to exhibit the Irish qualities of courage, sacrifice, respectability and patriotism in the service of America. While the Federalists portrayed them as foreign troublemakers, the United Irishmen placed themselves firmly within the American revolutionary tradition; they were fighting the same struggle against the same enemy. "It is not a little flattering to be denominated rebels," ran an article in the *Aurora* when news of the Irish Rising reached America, "by those who set a price upon the head of Washington, and exempted Samuel Adams and John Hancock from an amnesty, for being rebels!"[41]

From this perspective, it became possible to present the Federalists as the real threat to American liberty and equality; the United Irishmen, it was argued, were "true republicans," while Cobbett and his crew were selling the country out to Britain. While the Federalists believed that the United Irishmen were part of an international revolutionary conspiracy, the United Irishmen were equally convinced that they were facing a British-based counter-revolutionary plot. The British, in this view, had insinuated themselves into the highest echelons of government, and their supporters in the press were spreading wild tales about the United Irishmen to terrify the population into accepting draconian measures such as the suppression of free speech and the establishment of a standing army.[42]

The United Irishmen were not, of course, the only people who felt this way; their interpretation of events was shared by most American Republicans. But the Irish had actually seen and felt the results of the counter-revolution in their own country, and were acutely sensitive to any of its apparent manifestations in America. Viewing American politics through Irish lenses, they equated the Federalists with Irish loyalists, and believed that both groups were in league with a British government that specialized in whipping up anti-democratic hysteria to justify aristocratic repression. In addition, the Irish radicals had obvious personal reasons to fear the consequences of conservatism; if the Alien Friends Law was put into effect, they could well be forced back to Ireland, where they would face imprisonment or death. Hamilton Rowan wrote anxiously to Pickering for clarification about the destination of anyone who might be deported, but he never received a reply. What made matters even worse for someone with his aristocratic background was that his fate was in the hands of American *parvenus*. He wrote his wife: "Over and over again do I say, if I am to live under the lash of arbitrary power, at least let the whip be in the hands of those accustomed to use it, not picked up by a foot-passenger, who, unaccustomed to ride, keeps flogging every post and rail he comes near, pleased to hear how he can smack the whip. O upstart aristocracy, what a fiend art thou!"[43]

Along with feelings of political betrayal and personal insecurity went a strong sense of anger. Daniel McCurtin asked Mathew Carey in June 1798:

> What think you of the Alien and Sedition Bills? Such rapid strides towards Despotism are unexampled. Heavens! what a return to the generous efforts of the Irish in favour of America both in Europe and in this Country during the American war. Never had this Country more sincere friends. Ireland considered it's [*sic*] emancipation inseparably connected with American Independence. This development of the American character must be singularly pleasing to the friends of tyranny all over the world. A Gov't founded on the rights of man—a Representative Republican Government brands with every opprobrious term every nation attempting to imitate their example. The naturalization law crowns the Climax. Were I near the press I should conceive myself bound to caution aliens against enlisting in the army or navy of the U.S. What! fight in defence of the rights of others, when absolutely deprived of them myself? I am d——d if I would.[44]

Similar sentiments were expressed throughout the radical Irish community in the United States; there were sarcastic references in republican newspapers to the "land of liberty," and suggestions that the immigrants would be better treated by the Hottentots of Africa than the citizens of America. It is not surprising that emotions boiled over when Fenno published his list of United Irishmen at the end of the year. Shortly afterward, two men paid him a nocturnal visit, took him by surprise, and bludgeoned him on the head. Meanwhile, Mathew Carey called Cobbett "the most tremendous scourge that hell ever vomited forth to curse a people," incited his fellow countrymen to assault him with a shillelagh, and publicly fantasized about skinning him to death.[45]

Early in 1799, Reynolds and Duane prepared a memorial to Congress urging the repeal of the Alien Friends Law. The legislation, they maintained, contradicted the presumption of innocence, gave the president arbitrary power, and denied the right of due process to the accused. Moreover, they argued, it was based on the false assumption of Irish disloyalty to the Republic; to counter this image, the memorial underlined the contribution of Irish immigrants to the War of Independence. "We glory in the belief," it stated, "that of the Irish residents in the United States, a greater *proportion* partook of the hazards of the field and of the duties of your independent republican councils, than of the native Americans"; the Montgomery syndrome was at work again.[46]

Having implied that the Irish were actually more American than the Americans, the memorial pointedly reminded Congress of John Adams's *Address . . . to the People of Ireland* of 1775, which had invited Ireland to share in the struggle against British oppression. And that, it continued, was precisely what the Irish democrats were doing. Like the Americans, the United Irishmen believed in the principle that "all men are created equal" and stood for religious liberty. Like the Americans, they had only turned to revolution when petitions for redress had failed. And like the Americans, they realized the importance of "foreign assistance in wars of emancipation." The main difference, the memorialists argued, was that Ireland experienced a much greater degree of tyranny than had the Thirteen Colonies. "If America was alarmed by a violation of important principles, and a little oppressed in fact," they wrote, "all principle has been outraged towards Ireland, and oppression there exceeds the conceptions of the Americans." The Irish, in short, were still fighting for the freedom that the Americans had already won. "Suffer *us* then to enjoy among you," they concluded, "the peace, liberty, and safety, which our gallant countrymen have helped to establish."[47]

On Sunday, February 9, just before the memorial was to be presented to Congress, Reynolds and Duane, along with fellow radicals Robert Moore and Samuel Cuming, visited Philadelphia's churches to gather Irish support. At St. Mary's, one of the Catholic churches in the city, they put up notices asking the parishioners to sign their petition, only to run into the objections of the more conservative members of the congregation. As the Federalists tried to eject the radicals from the churchyard, Reynolds pulled out a pistol and was immediately hauled to the ground and kicked before he had the chance to use it. The four radicals were promptly marched to the mayor's office, where they were charged with riot and assault; Reynolds faced a second indictment for assault with intent to kill. Bail was set at $4000 each; thanks to chief justice Thomas McKean, who was running as the Republican candidate for state governor and who quickly came up with the cash, all except Cuming were released later that day.[48]

In the high-profile trial that followed, defense counsel Alexander Dallas argued for freedom of speech, and attempted to clear his clients from the "malicious rumours" that they were Jacobinical revolutionaries. Reynolds carried a pistol after hearing stories that he was to be assassinated, Dallas said, and only produced it to protect himself from an angry crowd. For the prosecution, Francis Hopkinson took a hard anti-immigrant line, and insisted that as noncitizens they had "no right whatever to petition, or to interfere in any respect with the government of this country." If they did not like the laws of the United States, he added, they could always take the boat back home. He declared:

> I will say that the greatest evils this country has ever endured have arisen from the ready admission of foreigners to a participation in the government and internal arrangements of the country. . . . This has been the bane of the country: had the Americans been left to themselves, we should not this day have been divided and rent into parties; it would not have been necessary that one party should carry

> pistols and dirks for defence against the other . . . and that this conduct should be justified by a public advocate in a court of justice.[49]

Meanwhile, Federalist newspapers cheered Hopkinson on, calling the affair the most "daring and flagitious riot" that had occurred in the city over the last forty years, and arguing that all their warnings about the United Irishmen were now amply vindicated. "That there is such a banditti, organized for the subversion of government, and the establishment of a system of terror and anarchy, cannot longer be doubted by the most incredulous," it was asserted. "'*The United Irishmen*' have at length broken out into acts, which render them no longer the objects of uncertain suspicion." If the petitioners were really Americans, argued Fenno, they would not concern themselves with "the grievances, real or pretended, of Ireland"; if they were really Irishmen, then "*they have no voice here.*" But neither the hostile press nor Hopkinson's arguments cut any ice with the jury, which wound up acquitting the accused on all counts.[50]

The Federalist outrage over the St. Mary's Riot was entirely predictable; the script had been written many months in advance. More striking, in many respects, was the division within the Irish Catholic community. It is clear that the petition against the Alien Friends Law had a measure of support at St. Mary's; some of the parishioners had helped to choose the committee that gathered signatures, and others were ready and willing to sign. Most, however, were not; "the majority of the congregation," observed Mathew Carey, "were federalists, and hostile to the object of Dr. Reynolds." And it was the Irish parishioners who were most hostile of all. As one of Fenno's correspondents pointed out, the "*good old Irish names of Gallagher, O'Connor, Ryan, &c. were most prompt witnesses against the conduct of their alienated countrymen.*" Such people had generally arrived in America earlier, and for them the United Irishmen were indeed alien beings; they had no wish to be tarred with the brush of revolutionary Irish politics. But there was more to it than politics. It was bad enough that Duane, Reynolds, Moore and Cuming were democrats; what really stung was the fact that they were Protestant democrats. "I felt myself hurt," commented James Gallagher, the man at whom Reynolds had pointed his pistol, "by the injury and insult done to my religion, making that a place of political meetings; and more so because I did not observe a single Catholic among them."[51]

The St. Mary's Riot was the most visible of several angry confrontations between the United Irishmen and their Federalist opponents that year. In March, Andrew Brown, the editor of the *Philadelphia Gazette,* was beaten up for writing an article that contrasted the United Irishmen's praise for the "independence of the Bar" in America with their assassination of jurors and witnesses in Ireland. Two months later, the boot was on the other foot. After Duane attacked the militia that suppressed Fries Rebellion in southeastern Pennsylvania for abusing the local population, several outraged officers went round to his office and flogged him. It was all he deserved, commented Fenno, who had no trouble distinguishing between "good" violence and "bad" violence. Duane, he wrote, "was not an American but a foreigner, and not merely a foreigner, but an United Irishmen, and not merely an United Irishman, but a public convict and fugitive from justice."[52]

Organizing his own militia, the Republican Greens, and enjoying considerable support from the Irish in Southwark and the Northern Liberties, Duane continued his unrelenting attack on the Federalists. Accusations flew from his pen. The British government had spent $800,000 of secret service money in 1798 to keep the Adams administration in its pocket, he asserted without producing a shred of evidence. The Federalist senator James Ross was plotting to manipulate the system of vote-counting in the forthcoming presidential election to prevent a Republican victory, he wrote; in this case, there was substance to the charge. Duane displayed a remarkable capacity for political survival. When Adams and Pickering decided to charge him with seditious libel, Duane let it be known that he possessed a letter written by Adams in 1792 complaining about British influence in American affairs; under these circumstances, the prosecution was postponed indefinitely. When the Senate attempted to arrest him for contempt, he fought a skillful rearguard action that generated considerable popular support and strengthened his reputation as the scourge of arbitrary power. For the Federalists, this was frustrating in the extreme; it is no wonder that Adams included Duane among the "foreigners and . . . degraded characters" whom he blamed for his government's downfall.[53]

In many respects, the Federalists were responsible for their own defeat in 1800. The party had split when Adams decided in early 1799 to reopen negotiations with France; hardliners such as Hamilton and Pickering, who wanted an Anglo-American alliance against French republicanism, were appalled. At the same time, the measures that were occasioned by the war crisis of 1798 were beginning to rebound on the government: higher taxes, the growth of the military establishment, and the Alien and Sedition Acts all heightened popular fears that power was encroaching on liberty. This could only benefit the Republicans, with their sophisticated electoral machine and their growing support in the politically crucial mid-Atlantic states. In New York, where the rival Republican factions formed a common front against the Federalists, Aaron Burr's cultivation of the Irish vote helped to win the state for the Republicans. And in Pennsylvania, an emerging Irish-German alliance contributed to the Republican triumph in the gubernatorial and congressional elections of 1799; this paved the way for the state's support of Jefferson the next year.[54]

More generally, the Republicans planned to saturate Irish communities with anti-British propaganda. In July 1800, Tench Coxe, a key Republican organizer, sent Mathew Carey a broadside that accused the Federalists of contributing to the British suppression of the 1798 Rising. The broadside had already been used in the Pennsylvania elections, he told Carey, where it had produced "satisfactory, violent, sudden" results. Given such success, Coxe continued, thousands of copies should be circulated among the Irish in every state; this would "answer the general purpose of opening their eyes regarding the Case of Ireland and the Party opposing the interest of the people here."[55] Just as the Federalists attempted to associate the Republicans with the revolutionary violence of the United Irishmen, the Republicans attempted to associate the Federalists with the counter-revolutionary violence of the British government. But in 1800, it was clearly the Republicans who had the better of the argument.

For the first wave of United Irish émigrés in the United States, Jefferson's victory represented the culmination of their campaign against Federalist apostasy, the reward for years of struggle. Their early activities in the United States, as in Ireland, had been conditioned by their opposition status; after recovering from the shock of disillusionment about American politics and society, most of them carried the attack to their new enemy. The United Irishmen strengthened the emerging alliance between the Republican Party and a significant section of the Irish immigrant community. Before the leading figures arrived in 1795, many of their compatriots had already joined the Democratic Societies, cheered Edmund Genet, voiced their opposition to Jay's Treaty, and contributed to Republican Congressional victories in New York and Philadelphia. During the second half of the decade, the United Irishmen assumed the leadership of the democratic republican wing of Irish America, and effectively eclipsed the moderate and conservative elements within the community; the Irish Catholics at St. Mary's church who objected to the radical Protestant Irish agitators were fighting a losing battle.

The United Irishmen made their presence felt at every level of popular politics. They formed some of the most militant clubs in the country; the anti-Washington society in Philadelphia sent shock-waves through the political nation, and the American Society of United Irishmen almost certainly contained some members who wanted to revolutionize the American government. They organized militias in the eastern seaboard cities, bringing Irish immigrants into radical political organizations with shared social values. They wrote anti-Federalist pamphlets, and they edited leading Republican newspapers; the government was sufficiently scared of Burk's *Time-Piece* and Duane's *Aurora* to try to shut them both down. And they worked to bring out the radical Irish vote during Congressional and presidential elections; the Republicans owed their victories in the politically crucial mid-Atlantic states at least in part to the increasingly sophisticated Irish political machines that were emerging in Philadelphia and New York.

Although their critique of Federalism was by no means original, the United Irishmen brought a sharper edge to the attack, a more radical rhetoric of opposition that manifested itself in Reynolds's character assassination of Washington and Burk's excoriation of Adams. In the black-and-white world of the most militant figures, the Federalists in general were repeatedly described as wicked, vicious, corrupt men, and were routinely denounced as enemies of liberty, traitors to their country, and pro-British aristocrats. The Federalists, of course, gave as good as they got, in a political atmosphere that was not conducive to compromise. By 1798, it seemed that the United Irishmen had overreached themselves; in the context of the Quasi-War between the United States and France, they faced a ferocious backlash that had them reeling against the ropes. It was, in fact, their bleakest year; in Ireland, the revolution had been ruthlessly suppressed, and in America, they were confronted with the Alien and Sedition Acts and a Federalist newspaper offensive that branded them as un-American.

In response, they reasserted their own identity with the American revolutionary tradition, and attempted to invert the nativist image by constructing a counter syllogism. To be American, they argued, was to support the principles of democratic republicanism, to align oneself with the "spirit of 1776." The United Irishmen were the most democratic republicans [illegible]; therefore, the United Irishmen were the most American people on the planet—far more American, in fact, than the Federalists who merely happened to be born in the country. As they regrouped in 1799 and 1800, benefited from the Federalist split, and mobilized for the presidential election, the United Irishmen were attempting to align American realities with their collective self-definition. And with Jefferson's victory, it seemed, aspirations and actualities had finally converged. For the first time in their lives, the United Irishmen found themselves on the winning side, as they moved from opposition into the republican mainstream. How would they respond to this new reality?

CHAPTER THREE

The Land of Liberty

"Here is your old friend arrived in the land of Liberty," wrote the Dublin bookseller and United Irish leader John Chambers to Mathew Carey in 1805, three years after his release from Fort George prison in Scotland. "I have undergone, since you & I parted (now, I believe 20 years) great difficulties and sorrows, & personal hardships, & have now sought in your happy land, an oblivion, or Solace for them all." Chambers settled in New York, and despite some problems of adjustment—including the "very bad" climate, the "very dangerous state of the roads," and the even more dangerous "habits of dissipation which our Countrymen in this Quarter of the Continent lead their friends into"—he eventually found the solace that he sought. Within a few years, Chambers was described by a fellow radical as "happy and prosperous" in his new environment.[1]

The Republican victory of 1800 had not only vindicated the principles and perseverance of the first wave of United Irish émigrés; it also made the United States increasingly attractive to those radicals who were now coming out of British jails. Among Chambers's fellow prisoners at Fort George were Thomas Emmet, William MacNeven and Samuel Neilson, all of whom crossed the Atlantic to make a new start in Jefferson's America. Emmet and MacNeven had originally gone to France, in the hopes of persuading Napoleon to reactivate his plans for the invasion of Ireland. Before long, however, they came to realize that such a course of action would be disastrous for their country. Repudiating his earlier position, Emmet now felt that "if a French force ever landed in Ireland, its influence & strength would be employed to eradicate every vestige of republicanism.., to establish a Government *which should be modelled after that of the protecting Country* . . . & in order the better to support that fabric, to prop it up by *a Catholic Establishment*." At the same time, his opinion of the United States began to rise; it was, he believed, a "happy country, where Liberty is triumphant and cherished, & where the principles, to which I have sacrificed so much, would be a kind of portion to my children." In 1804, Emmet arrived in New York, where he was warmly welcomed by his fellow United Irishmen and the Clintonian Republicans, and rapidly established himself as a leading lawyer in the state. A year later, on the "wonderfully appropriate" date of July 4, MacNeven joined him, and began an equally successful career as a physician and professor. Samuel Neilson died shortly after his arrival in the United States.[2]

In 1806, Chambers, Emmet and MacNeven were reunited with their old friend William Sampson, who reached New York after being dogged by misfortune in Europe. Allowed to leave Ireland for Portugal after the Rising, he had been shipwrecked in North Wales, where he made the mistake of proselytizing the United Irish cause. The government reacted strongly, and used its influence to have him arrested when he finally reached Oporto. Over the next year, he barely survived imprisonment in some of the worst jails in the world. He was eventually sent off to France, survived a second shipwreck, and eked out a precarious existence in Paris. In 1806, Sampson traveled to London, in the hope that the new Whig government would grant him permission to return to Ireland; instead, he was placed under house arrest, and deported to America. This time, at least, there was no shipwreck. Like MacNeven, Sampson landed on Independence Day, and received a warm welcome from the United Irish community in New York. "It is incredible how many friends I meet every where," he wrote his wife shortly after he arrived. After all his vicissitudes, he felt completely at home in the United States. He shared accommodation with MacNeven, enjoyed a reputation for having the most "*sarcastic humor*" at the American bar, and could not think of living anywhere else. "I am here respected, occupied, and I think I may add prosperous," he wrote, "and my malignant and odious persecutors have no power to hurt me."[3]

What we are seeing here, as the second wave of émigrés came into Jefferson's America, is the consolidation of a transplanted United Irish network in the United States, based on the focal points of New York, Philadelphia and Baltimore. Among the old friends who greeted Sampson in New York was John Caldwell, who in 1799 had chartered a ship that brought hundreds of Irish radicals from Belfast. One of them was David Bailie Warden, whose experiences in the Irish revolutionary movement had left him alienated by the government's "reign of horror" and disgusted with the "wild excesses of the people." Arriving in the United States during the 1800 electoral campaign, he was initially dismayed by the factionalism and careerism of American politics. "Some unhappy destiny seems, at present, to torment the nations of the earth," he wrote to a friend back home despondently. But the gloom began to lift after Jefferson's victory, and his writings about the country became increasingly optimistic. Before long, he carved out a successful career for himself as a college professor, and eventually wound up in the diplomatic service, as the American consul in Paris.[4]

Other radicals in New York who came from northern Ireland included George Cuming, who arrived in 1802, having "suffered," as he put it, for the cause at home; it was Cuming who put up Chambers when he landed in the city three years later. Also from Belfast was Thomas Storey, who had worked with Neilson at the *Northern Star*, and who had escaped from prison in 1798 after a secret message was smuggled to him in a roast goose; following the instructions, he hid himself in a barrel and was rolled out of the jail to freedom. The radical Dublin shipbuilder Thomas Trenor (sometimes spelled Traynor) had an even better escape story. After his arrest during the government's March 1798 swoop on the United Irish leadership, he had been thrown into Newgate jail. A master of disguises, Trenor concealed a set of clothes under his coat, and went into the privy that was just inside the prison grounds. Pretending to have a conversation with an imaginary person inside, he changed his clothes, powdered his hair, and coolly walked past the guard through the lower gate to the streets outside.[5]

In Philadelphia, Duane and Reynolds had already established themselves as leaders of the city's radical Irish community; Mathew Carey, with his relatively moderate outlook, also remained an important figure. The most influential of the second-wave émigrés to join them was John Binns, who arrived in America during the summer of 1801, after spending two years without trial at Gloucester jail for his activities with the United Britons. Binns initially moved to Northumberland, Pennsylvania, where he became part of Joseph Priestley's radical transatlantic circle. There he started up his own newspaper, the *Republican Argus*, with the motto that "*persons* not *property* should ever be the basis of *Representation*." Immersing himself in Pennsylvania politics, Binns moved to Philadelphia in 1807, where he launched the *Democratic Press*, "the *first* paper published in the Union, or anywhere else, under the title of DEMOCRATIC," and enjoyed considerable support from recently arrived Irish immigrants.[6]

A number of other leading United Irishmen settled in the rapidly expanding city of Baltimore. When Chambers visited in 1805, he stayed with his old friend and former colleague on the United Irish executive in Dublin, Henry Jackson. With the support of the American consul, Jackson in 1799 had sought Rufus King's permission to settle in the United States and establish an iron foundry business. After thinking it over, King decided that the benefits of attracting someone with Jackson's capital and skill outweighed the risks of allowing a potential "malcontent" into the country; it was a decision he would later regret. Another of Chambers's friends in Baltimore was John Campbell White, who had been a leader of the United movement in Ulster. The most flamboyant Irish radical in the city, though, was John D'Evereux, a "rebel general" from Wexford who had commanded two thousand men at New Ross and only escaped execution because of his powerful social connections. He became a merchant in the South American trade, and increasingly involved himself in the Spanish American Wars of Independence. Combining ambitions for military glory, wealth and fame with an anti-colonial outlook and republican ideology, D'Evereux would eventually return home in 1819 to raise an Irish Legion for Simon Bolivar's army in Venezuela.[7]

Although the United Irish network was strongest in the seaboard cities of the mid-Atlantic states, it also extended to the South and West. Denis Driscol, the revolutionary deist and democrat from County Cork, wound up as a prominent republican newspaper editor in Augusta, Georgia, another center of exiled United Irishmen. Driscol had left Ireland in 1799, and opened up radical newspapers in New York, Philadelphia and Baltimore before moving south in 1804; under his editorship, the *Augusta Chronicle* became one of the most Anglophobic newspapers in the country.[8] There was also a significant radical Irish community in Petersburg, Virginia, clustered around a group of revolutionary ex-students from Trinity College; their numbers included John Daly Burk, who arrived in 1801, the merchant-poet John McCreery, and the radical physician and cultural nationalist Thomas Robinson.[9] The Irish were thick on the ground in western Pennsylvania, where radical Presbyterians such as Thomas Ledlie Birch attempted to assert their peculiar brand of religion and politics in the face of intense local opposition.[10] Another leading United Irishmen in the West, the "Wild and Eccentric" Harman Blennerhassett, resurfaced as a major figure in Aaron Burr's ill-fated expedition in 1805–6 to liberate Mexico from Spanish rule and link it up with a secession state in the trans-Mississippi West.[11]

Inevitably, one comes to feel, the émigrés viewed American politics through Irish lenses. "The Patriot," wrote Driscol, referring to himself in the third person, "has had experience of British tactics, of British perfidy, of British cruelty and of British insolence in Europe, and he expects he shall place them in their *native* colours in America, where the same arts and the same means are employed as at home, to *divide and conquer.*" Just as the British government had pitted Protestants against Catholics in Ireland, ran the argument, it was now fomenting divisions between Federalists and Republicans in America. And the Federalists, from this perspective, were to the United States what the Orangemen were to Ireland: a faction that supported the British interest, spread the virus of monarchism, and subverted the liberty of the people.[12]

Following familiar Irish traditions that viewed politics as a zero-sum game, some United Irishmen demanded extreme measures against the "enemy within." No criticism of the government could be tolerated; dissent was equated with treason, and a degree of repression was demanded that made the Alien and Sedition Acts pale in comparison. Burk, in a mirror-image of Federalism, blamed conservative British immigrants for America's difficulties, while Driscol railed at the "*Irish orange men*" who were coming into the country. People who traduced Jefferson, he declared, should be "*tarred* and *feathered* and *sent off*, as *scapegoats*; and then we may piously hope that the country will be *saved*." Duane, who was equally convinced that British agents were "fomenting and upholding conspiracy in the bosom of our land," went even further. In his milder moods, he wanted all such "foreign spies and incendiaries" to be expelled from the country; in his more extreme moments, he wanted them hanged.[13]

Not surprisingly, the Irish radicals demanded the wholesale removal of Federalists from office, to settle old scores and strengthen the democratic republican presence in government. Although Driscol welcomed the purging of "*reptiles* and *tories*" (synonymous categories, in his view) from office in New York and Pennsylvania, he was frustrated by Jefferson's desire to conciliate rather than crush the Federalist opposition. The president, he complained, was behaving like a naive philosopher rather than a republican general, and was unwittingly throwing the game to the enemy. There should be no more of this nonsense that "We are all Federalists; we are all Republicans"; this was nothing less than a struggle for survival, and the sooner that the president realized it, the better. In the event, however, Jefferson's strategy of winning over the middle ground proved much more effective than United Irish militancy in undermining the power of Federalism.[14]

The revolutionary political culture of Ireland not only influenced the United Irishmen's attitude to Federalism but also lay behind their attempts to democratize American Republicanism. For the most part, this campaign was conducted at the state level, particularly in the political battlegrounds of Pennsylvania and New York. In Pennsylvania, latent tensions within the Republican movement became manifest almost immediately after the Federalists were defeated in 1799 and 1800. On the very day that Jefferson became president, March 4, 1801, the cracks began to show. After the processions in Philadelphia to celebrate Jefferson's victory, the "*better part*" of the Republicans continued the festivities at Francis's Union Hotel, and drank toasts that emphasized moderation and reconciliation with the Federalists; these were the people who aligned themselves with the relatively conservative Republicanism of Governor Thomas McKean. Meanwhile, the radicals congregated at Cordner's tavern, where they were addressed by more militant figures such as James Reynolds and the English democrat Thomas Cooper. According to the hostile *Gazette of the United States*, the gathering at Cordner's consisted "chiefly of *united* Irish fugitives, and anglo-democratic outlaws . . . and lastly of the refuse of our native vulgar"; throughout the evening, the report continued, they "breathed nought but the foul breath of *sedition* and *insurrection*." The Republicans, observed the paper's correspondent, were splitting into two mutually exclusive camps, each of which despised the other.[15] The divisions in Pennsylvania deepened and widened over the next four years, as the radicals attempted to liberalize the naturalization laws, reform the judicial system, and democratize the constitution. Both Duane and Binns were at the forefront of these campaigns. In Philadelphia, Duane brought his Irish supporters into a close alliance with the radical democrat Michael Leib, who commanded much of the city's German vote; developing a sophisticated electoral machine, they established themselves as brilliant and unscrupulous political manipulators. The Leib-Duane faction formed a tactical but tense alliance with the Republicans of rural Pennsylvania, where a similar Irish-German alliance had been formed between Binns and the state congressman Simon Snyder. Duane and Binns had first met in 1795, when the London Corresponding Society was organizing mass protests against Pitt's government; now they continued the struggle for democracy in their new environment.[16]

Significantly, one of the first areas of conflict between conservative and radical Republicans in Pennsylvania arose over the issue of naturalization. In 1803, the state legislature voted that immigrants could participate in politics after two years' residence in Pennsylvania; this appeared to be a major victory for the United Irishmen, who had unsuccessfully pressed for similar legislation at the national level. But Governor McKean vetoed the proposal, on the grounds that immigrants needed more time to be "weaned away from their monarchical prejudices." His position infuriated the Irish radicals, who argued that their countrymen were "republicans from sore experience," complained that governor's veto power contradicted democratic principles, and warned McKean that he would pay a heavy political price for betraying "his best supporters and friends" in the immigrant community.[17]

Anti-McKean sentiment found wider expression over the question of judicial and constitutional reform. To make the legal system more equitable and democratic, the legislature attempted after 1800 to introduce the principle of arbitration for minor property suits. McKean blocked the measure, however, on the grounds that it removed too much power from the judges and juries who were best qualified to decide such cases. Tapping into popular hostility to lawyers, reacting against recent attempts by the state's judges to widen their authority, and arguing that the governor's veto was a clear case of "arbitrary power," the Leib-Duane and Snyder-Binns factions in 1805 called for a constitutional convention that would bring the judiciary under popular control and radicalize the government. Their demands included annual elections, equality of status between the General Assembly and the Senate, and a reduction of the governor's powers of patronage.[18]

Arguing that such reforms would destroy constitutional checks and balances and culminate in the tyranny of the legislature, McKean and his supporters organized themselves into the Society of Constitutional Republicans, or "Quids," to resist the radicals. One of their members was Mathew Carey, who was gradually charting a course toward the middle ground of American politics. The democrats rallied behind Simon Snyder, who ran against McKean in the gubernatorial election of 1805. It was a mean-spirited, mendacious and vicious campaign, even by Pennsylvania standards. Duane disseminated forged documents to discredit McKean, McKean's followers misrepresented the radicals as social levelers, and Binns almost had his eye gouged out after writing a series of articles against the governor. Largely because of an anti-democratic alliance between the Constitutional Republicans and the Federalists, McKean staved off the challenge, and the issue of constitutional revision was shelved. The radical Irish, including Binns, Duane and Reynolds, remained active in opposition, and participated in an unsuccessful attempt to impeach the governor in 1807. Only after McKean retired the following year was Snyder able to take over as governor, and even then on a much more moderate platform than before.[19]

A similar pattern of intra-Republican conflict occurred in New York, where the fragile anti-Federalist alliance among the Clinton, Livingston and Burr factions shattered in 1805 over issues of patronage and personality. The United Irishmen were firmly in the Clintonian camp. In 1802, they had formed the Hibernian Provident Society, which was a continuation of the American Society of United Irishmen in all but name; it found employment for fellow political refugees, supported the cause of Irish independence, opened its doors to democratic republicans of all countries, and worked for "the *freedom and prosperity of their adopted country*." As a Paineite republican with a strong pro-immigrant record, De Witt Clinton easily attracted their support. With the backing of the radical Irish, Clinton could broaden his power base in New York City; through their alliance with Clinton, the radical Irish could assert their own influence on the state's politics. The benefits to both sides were clearly demonstrated in the controversial and heated state elections of 1807, when the Clintonians found themselves fighting on two fronts. In the gubernatorial contest, they ran Daniel Tompkins against the Livingstonian Republican incumbent, Morgan Lewis. And in the elections for the assembly, they faced a Federalist ticket headed by none other than Rufus King. Here, for the United Irishmen, was a golden opportunity for revenge.[20]

Their first intervention in the campaign came at a meeting of the Hibernian Provident Society in early April, when John Caldwell carried a resolution that anyone who voted Federalist should be expelled from the organization; thirty members of the society walked out in disgust, leaving the radicals firmly in control. Shortly afterward, Emmet dropped the political bombshell of the campaign when he published King's 1799 letter to Henry Jackson granting him permission to enter the United States. The letter not only contained condescending remarks about the "indigent and illiterate" Irish; it also reopened the issue of King's attitude to the state prisoners back in 1798. Moving in for the kill, Emmet argued that King's actions had been unauthorized, unconstitutional and illegal, and a betrayal of everything for which the United

States stood. "If so," he asked, "is it fit that you should hereafter be entrusted with any kind of delegated authority?"[21]

The most significant characteristic of Emmet's attack was its tone; the pent-up fury of years had finally found a public outlet.

> The misfortunes which you brought upon the objects of your persecution were incalculable. Almost all of us wasted four of the best years of our lives in prison. As to me, I should have brought along with me my father and his family, including a brother, whose name perhaps even you will not read without emotions of sympathy and respect. Others nearly connected with me would have become partners in my emigration. I have been prevented from saving a brother, from receiving the dying blessings of a father, mother and sister, and from soothing their last agonies by my cares; and this, sir, by your unwarrantable and unfeeling interference.

There was a significant degree of distortion here; Emmet had not, after all, actually wanted to go to America in 1798. Nor were his specific accusations accurate; King had acted with the full support of the government, and there was nothing illegal or unconstitutional about what he had done.[22] But the broader point remained; had it not been for King, the state prisoners would have had the option of seeking sanctuary in America in 1798. As such, he was cordially hated by the radical Irish in the United States, who even blamed him for the execution of Robert Emmet after the attempted coup of 1803. According to one story that began circulating later in the decade and soon found its way into the ballad tradition, Emmet's death sentence had been commuted to voluntary exile in the United States. He was "actually embarking for America," the story ran, when he was called back on King's instructions to be hung, drawn and quartered. King's role as the nemesis of the United Irishmen had assumed the proportions of a gigantic myth.[23]

Although he was stung by Thomas Emmet's attack, which he described as "full of insolence, vanity and malignity," King initially decided not to be drawn into debate. He could not, however, resist the impulse to prepare an "Address to the Public," which was anonymously published in paraphrased form in the *Evening Post*. In his defense, King argued that his actions in 1798 had been justified by the international situation and by the pro-French position of the United Irishmen. Moving to the offensive, he maintained that the émigrés had no business bringing Irish issues into American politics. Emmet's appeal to "national prejudices," King wrote, was an "unworthy attempt to excite discord and hatred between the new and old citizens," which ran the risk of creating "a durable and dangerous feud between the foreign and native inhabitants of this prosperous city."[24]

The anti-Clintonian press backed King up, condemning Emmet for appealing to the narrow sectional concerns of the "*Irish interest*" rather than to the common good. King had been right to keep the United Irishmen out of the United States, went the cry; they were nothing more than "foreign desperadoes," and the pity was that they were able to get into the country at all. Thomas Addis Emmet was nicknamed Thomas Adder Emmet, amid pointed reminders that he was not even an American citizen. His friend and colleague Henry Jackson, commented the Federalist editor William Coleman, had played a despicable role in the affair. "He first solicits a personal favour from Mr. KING," wrote Coleman, "and then makes use of the very instrument by which it is granted, to injure, if it were possible, his benefactor!"[25]

As in the attack on the American Society of United Irishmen in 1798–99, there were strong nativist elements at work in New York in 1807. All the old themes recur: the portrayal of the United Irishmen as un-American, the decoupling of the American and Irish revolutions, the association of the Irish with drink and violence. There were some new ones as well, such as the attempt to exploit popular resentment against Clinton's preferential treatment of the Irish in the labor force; as mayor of New York, he had been "licensing them as cartmen, to the exclusion of respectable and industrious Americans." That there was considerable anti-Irish prejudice is beyond doubt; the Irish were described as "*the worst of Europe's scum*," and their radical leaders were denounced as a "restless, disorganizing set of unprincipled demagogues." But the view of one historian that the Federalists in 1807 "tried to capitalize on public hostility to Irish immigrants" in order to "stage a political resurrection" simplifies what was in fact a much more complex situation.[26]

In fact, the Federalist-nativist versus radical-Irish interpretation requires three significant qualifications. First, it was only after the United Irish intervention in the election campaign that the Federalists played the immigrant card, and even then they distinguished between "good" and "bad" Irish immigrants. The Federalists insisted that they were not opposed to "foreigners as such" but rather to "Jacobinical" foreigners in particular. As proof, they pointed out that the Irish-born Andrew Morris was part of the "American Ticket." This was, commented Coleman, "evidence of the liberality with which the federal party view foreigners of good private characters and correct views." He also reminded his Irish Catholic readers that Morris had helped raise funds for their church in New York, and urged them to "rescue your national character from the foul aspersions to which the *Provident Hibernian Conspiracy* have done . . . all they can to bring upon it."[27]

Second, it was not only the Federalists who denounced the United Irishmen as un-American; the Livingston Republicans were equally prepared to use nativist tactics against the Irish who were aligned with their Clintonian rivals. In the gubernatorial election, Morgan Lewis's Livingstonian supporters described the Irish as the "vagabonds of the community," and played on fears that the "peaceful citizens" of New York were being assailed "by foreign influence, by foreign misrepresentation, by foreign threats and (though heaven forbid) by foreign violence." This pattern was repeated elsewhere in the United States; Republican factions would routinely play the nativist card against Irish radicals who belonged to rival groups.[28]

Third, and most striking of all, much of what appeared as nativism was in fact the transference to America of political and communal divisions from Ireland. The parallels with the situation in Philadelphia over the American Society of United Irishmen are immediately apparent. It is no coincidence that the most extreme attacks on Emmet and the Hibernian Provident Society came from conservative Irish immigrants, who either had fresh memories of civil strife in Ireland or had settled in America before the radical democrats began arriving. Thus one "self-imported Irishman" could write that Emmet should have been hanged back in 1798. Similarly, the Irishman Stephen Cullen Carpenter wrote that the ethnic politics of the radical newcomers was destroying the patient efforts of earlier immigrants to acquire a truly American identity.[29]

When the Federalists went down to defeat and the United Irishmen celebrated by shouting "Emmet and Liberty" outside the houses of King and Morris, Carpenter raged at the result.

> Can America, after this, be said to have a character as a nation? . . . Why what people can it truly be called, but a multifarious heterogeneous compound—a Gallo-Hibernico-Hispanico-Corsicano race, living where once lived Americans. Oh, rare Americans!—A foreigner of three years standing [Emmet] is brayed up to the skies, while your Washington and your Hamilton are forgotten. Let it be remembered, that had Americans alone voted, the result would have been as it ought to be.

It is tempting, but wrong, to put Carpenter's sentiments down to a deep-seated desire for assimilation and acceptance and a corresponding fear of rejection. Carpenter refused to become an American citizen, since this would mean renouncing his loyalty to the king. His protest was really an Irish loyalist attack on the United Irishmen in the guise of Americanism.[30]

With the support of the city's radical Irish community, the Clintonians not only defeated the Federalists in the assembly election but also replaced the Livingston faction's Morgan Lewis with their own candidate, Daniel Tompkins, as state governor. For Emmet and the Hibernian Provident Society, the victory over King was welcomed on both personal and political grounds. "I have enjoyed as much pleasure as I could derive from overthrowing Mr. Rufus King in his country, for his conduct to me and my fellow prisoners in our own," wrote Emmet; "and with that I have had the infinitely higher gratification of having most essentially contributed to the complete and, I hope, conclusive triumph of principle here." King's political career was finished,

Emmet added, "& unless the federalists possess the power of raising the dead, I hope & believe he will never again do much mischief." Nine years later, when King ran for governor of New York, all the old accusations resurfaced, as his Irish enemies circled around him once again. He lost the election.[31]

Within this general attempt to defeat Federalism, democratize the Republic, and present themselves as the authentic voice of Irish America, a minority of radicals insisted upon the need for legal as well as political reform. They noted with dismay that English legal precedents remained an integral part of American law, and believed that the common law should be replaced by a new system based on the principles of liberty, equality and reason. To a large extent, their attack on "judicial tyranny" in America was an outgrowth of their earlier activities and experiences back home. As a lawyer for the United Irishmen and Defenders in Ireland, William Sampson had developed a deep antipathy for common law traditions, and had written a brilliant satire on seditious libel trials which would later be published in America. Similarly, Denis Driscol had first attacked the common law as a newspaper editor in Cork, and continued the fight in the United States; the location changed, but the arguments remained the same. William Duane followed a different pattern; his hostility to the English legal system arose from conflicts with authority in India rather than Ireland. Sampson, Driscol and Duane agreed that the United States must emancipate itself from this vestige of British rule.[32]

Central to their approach was a strong anti-historical and anti-colonial outlook. Just as Paine had ripped through the whole notion of political precedents in the *Rights of Man* and demolished the "Norman yoke" myth of original Saxon freedom, Sampson and Duane applied the same approach to the legal sphere. Against the notion that the common law represented the collected wisdom of ages, they argued that it actually arose from centuries of English barbarity and oppression. The result, in their view, was a set of complex, confusing and contradictory laws that benefited no one but the lawyers. In short, the existing system was "one of the greatest evils" facing the United States, wrote Duane; it contradicted common sense, threatened to subvert American liberty, and perpetuated a colonial mentality. "We should import no more," declared Sampson; "for with every deference due to the learning, wisdom, and integrity of the English judges"—that "*sarcastic humor*" again—"they are not fit persons to legislate for us." The task for Americans, he concluded, was to establish a truly independent and rational judicial code that would complement the country's political system.[33]

Their efforts brought mixed results. In Pennsylvania, the radicals gathered sufficient support to pass a bill in 1810 that abolished the reading of English precedents in the state's courts. New York, however, remained resistant to reform; the dominant argument here was that the common law was central to the Americans' birthright and that the revolution had been intended in part to protect the law from arbitrary and tyrannical British measures. Even the

United Irishmen themselves were divided on the issue; Emmet, for example, believed that the common law could safeguard liberty, and noted that Americans could always make specific exceptions when circumstances warranted. A case in point, he argued, was New York's legislation that established equality of status for all Christian religions. That particular issue was one upon which virtually all the radical émigrés could agree.[34]

In Ireland, the United Irishmen had seen and felt the consequences of religious discrimination, and fought against the privileges of the Anglican church; in the United States, their energies were directed toward celebrating, consolidating and extending the degree of religious freedom that already existed. America, from this perspective, stood as living proof of the United Irish argument that freedom of religion actually strengthened social stability. "In nothing have the United States more to congratulate themselves," wrote David Bailie Warden, "than in their total exemption from the numerous dissentions, jealousies, and oppressions that spring from an exclusive religious system."[35]

Nevertheless, there was still room for improvement; as Warden himself pointed out, some states continued to discriminate against Catholics, Jews and deists. In New York, Sampson rushed to the defense of a Catholic priest who refused to divulge confessional evidence in court, and argued strongly against the prosecution's use of Irish precedents to bolster its case. "If there be any country on the habitable globe, where we should not go for a pure and sound decision, upon the rights of Roman Catholics," he declared, "it is surely that one from which this precedent is brought. . . . For every where else, though there may be madness, superstition, or idolatry, there may be some chance of impartiality; but in Ireland there can be none!" Drawing further on his own experiences in Ireland, Sampson warned that anti-Catholic discrimination would only produce disaffection and disloyalty. "There is but one way to make such persons dangerous," he said; "that is, to put their clergymen in prison for not betraying the most holy of all engagements towards God or man." The jury agreed; Irish precedents were deemed to have "little or no weight" in the state, and Sampson won the case.[36]

Those radicals who traveled beyond Christianity toward deism experienced considerable hostility as they attempted to extend their influence in the Republic. Among them was Driscol, who joined Elihu Palmer's Theophilanthropic Society and established the deist newspaper, *Temple of Reason,* shortly after his arrival in New York; its central aim, he wrote, was to counter the "torrents of illiberal reflections and unqualified abuse poured forth every day, through the channels of bigotry and intolerance, against Deists." In response, the paper ran articles like "JESUS CHRIST A DEIST, AND NO GOD, *Clearly Proved from the Scriptures, especially from his own words,*" serialized the writings of Volney and Paine, and carried stories about Irish patriots who refused to be attended by priests before they were executed in 1798. "This is all the more wonderful," Driscol added, "as the human mind in Ireland had not as yet, the same opportunity of shaking off the yoke of priests and the prejudices of superstition, that the citizens of France had."[37]

The Theophilanthropic Society was closely connected with New York's Clintonian Republicans, and had a strong immigrant component. According to one less-than-flattering account, it consisted of the "imported scum of the Edinburgh Convention" and the "refuse of the banished rebels of Ireland," along with the "Infidels of New York." John Binns became a member during his brief stay in the city in 1801. By that time, Driscol had relocated in Philadelphia, where a sister society had been formed, and continued to publish the paper "under the auspices of the friends of Mr. *William Duane*." It seems likely that one of those friends was James Reynolds, who had earlier organized study groups for Paine's *Age of Reason* in the American Society of United Irishmen. Another deist who traveled between New York and Philadelphia was John Daly Burk; shortly after his escape to Virginia in 1799, he opened up an "Infidel Club" in Amelia County with the Republican Congressman William Branch Giles.[38]

For such people, deism was the logical corollary of republicanism. In much the same way that Drennan had argued in Ireland that civil and religious freedom would result in the triumph of Protestantism, Driscol in America believed that liberty of thought would necessarily culminate in deism. "It would appear to be a contradiction in terms," he wrote, "to find men renouncing *King-craft*, and still remain *enchanted* by Superstition and Priest-craft." In Driscol's view, the enemies of deism were infected by Old World prejudices and Old World despotism, and wanted to "set up an uniform standard for the human mind, and measure every ones [*sic*] faith and capacity by the *same rule!*"[39]

Ironically, though, Driscol fell into exactly the same trap himself, and exhibited the very intolerance that he condemned in his opponents. As an ex-priest, he approached Reason with all the zeal of the convert and all the faith of a missionary; not only would sickness, poverty and war be eradicated, but natural disasters like hurricanes, frosts and fire could be prevented if men "universally taught, studied and practised the religion of nature." And those people who were perverse enough to reject Reason would be swept aside by a revolutionary movement from which the "wise and good" need have nothing to fear. The "wise and good" were easily identifiable; they were the ones who agreed with Driscol.[40]

This was very much a minority sensibility, and one whose radical edge became blunted in the first two decades of the nineteenth century. The Theophilanthropic Society of New York probably numbered around a hundred people, and the *Temple of Reason* did not sustain a sufficient readership to stay in business beyond 1803. In his subsequent career as editor of the *American Patriot* and the *Augusta Chronicle*, Driscol downplayed his deism but did not drop it altogether. In 1810, shortly before his death, he recalled with fondness his meeting with Paine in Baltimore eight years earlier, and announced the publication of Paine's defense of the *Age of Reason* against the criticisms of Bishop Watson. "And the reader will judge," he wrote, "if the Stay-maker has not *whaleboned* the bishop, and all those, who say *Amen* to Established Churches and Tythes."[41]

But, in a sense, that was the problem for Driscol and the deists; hardly anyone in America said Amen to established churches and tithes, and deism did not have the same reactive potential in the New World that it possessed in the Old. Contrary to Driscol's expectations, freedom of religion in America wound up marginalizing deism rather than turning it into the dominant belief system. The fact that the Republicans drew on significant Baptist, Methodist and Presbyterian support was another factor in the equation; it was not in the interests of the Jeffersonians to encourage expressions of support for deism in the press, especially in the context of the religious revival sweeping through America at the turn of the century. Under these circumstances, the "religion of nature" was eclipsed by evangelicalism, and, except for a brief recrudescence in the 1820s and 1830s, had almost withered away by the middle of the century. Only the activities of a new wave of immigrants, mainly from England, prevented it from dying out altogether.[42]

In the course of their political and religious campaigns in the United States, the United Irishmen were bringing extra energy to existing movements rather than creating new ones. The struggle for deism was already under way when radicals such as Driscol and Burk arrived in the country, just as the campaign against the common law had widespread grass-roots American support before Duane and Sampson joined its ranks. Similarly, the Irish radicals in New York provided more fuel for a Clintonian political machine that had already gathered momentum, while their counterparts in Pennsylvania strengthened a democratic-republican outlook that stretched back to the mid-1770s. And in the same way that their attempt to democratize the republic reflected and reinforced broader American trends, the United Irishmen in the United States were also deeply affected by the growing tensions that emerged within Republicanism during the early nineteenth century.

To a large extent, these centrifugal tendencies were the product of Jefferson's success; as the Federalist threat receded, the need for Republican unity became less pressing, and deeper divisions came to the surface. Under these circumstances, many United Irishmen came into conflict with relatively moderate Republicans. If the Federalists were seen as knaves, the ordinary people who stubbornly refused to support the self-evident principles of democratic republicanism were manifestly fools. After 1800, the Federalist knaves had largely been taken care of; only the fools remained. The radicals who thought this way rapidly acquired an ill-concealed contempt for those people who did not share their views.

Drennan had perceived a similar tendency within the United Irish leadership in Ireland. "I saw in most of them," he wrote, "aristocracy in a shabby coat, aristocratic self-sufficiency, aristocratic vengeance, aristocratic intolerance under a Maratism of manners and of language." In America, such attitudes were exemplified by people like Duane, who believed that one-third of the population displayed too much "ignorance, imbecility, instability and hypocrisy" to form political judgments—or at least to form political judgments that corresponded with those of more sensible, sane, stable and sincere figures such as Duane himself. Similarly, Driscol dismissed the people who rejected the truth of deism for the superstitious nonsense of Methodism as "coblers [*sic*], tinkers, pedlars, bellows-blowers, wire-drawers, Scotch cowboys and Irish potatoe [*sic*] diggers, who have the unparalleled impudence to open their mouths, judge and pass sentence on the best philosophers and the most enlightened men of ancient and modern times!!" Edmund Burke's comment about "a swinish multitude" fades into comparative insignificance. Precisely because so many people were so ignorant, in the Duane-Driscol analysis, they could easily be manipulated by malicious men who did not have their "true" interests at heart; High Federalism had been turned upside down.[43]

In addition to this ideologically driven intolerance, a number of United Irishmen possessed a remarkable capacity for personal vindictiveness; there were sometimes dark passions lurking beneath the veneer of reason. Before 1800, such feelings had been focused on the forces of authority in Ireland, Britain and America; after Jefferson's victory, they were increasingly aimed at anyone who differed with the personal opinions of particular radicals. Duane was certainly not a man to be crossed. He once told an adversary in Philadelphia that "any man who would bring me a challenge, I would kick as long as my boots lasted, and I meant to keep my word." Driscol responded even to mild criticisms with outbursts of verbal violence; Carey had a ferocious temper; and Binns frequently came to blows with his political opponents, although he was not a man to hold grudges. Burk oscillated wildly between idealism and rage, and had a history of altercations that culminated in his death in a duel in 1808.[44]

One of the main issues that brought these powerful personalities into conflict, as it did within the Republican movement in general, was that of patronage. The same radicals who condemned the patronage system that excluded them in aristocratic Ireland fought fiercely over the plums in republican America. In this respect, few could exceed the expectations of Burk, who requested a government office from Jefferson on the immodest grounds that the president of a republic was obliged to give "patronage to the exertions of Genius." (Jefferson turned him down). Meanwhile, in Pennsylvania, Carey and Duane fought like two bears in a cage for a share of the spoils. Carey wrote hundreds of letters, pioneered lobbying techniques, and probably resorted to bribery for patronage purposes; in 1804, he won a lucrative contract to print the federal laws. Duane was equally aggressive, but less successful. Having alienated the moderate Republicans who controlled patronage, he was cut out of the picture, and became increasingly angry as a result.[45]

Along with these divisions over patronage, there was also a major struggle among the United Irishmen for control of the Irish vote, particularly in Pennsylvania where Republicanism was notoriously factious. In 1805, as has been seen, the Quid-Federalist alliance had beaten back the combined attempt of the city and country radicals to replace McKean as state governor. But both the Quid-Federalist and the city-country alliances were inherently unstable. By 1807, the Quids and Federalists had split over the broader issue of Anglo-American relations. At the same time, the urban Leib-Duane radicals were competing with their rural Snyder-Binns rivals for control of the state's democratic movement. The intra-radical divisions deepened and widened during the summer, shortly after Binns established the *Democratic Press* in Philadelphia. The paper gave the Snyderites a voice in the city, and operated as an alternative to Duane's *Aurora;* it may well have been funded in part by Carey and other moderate Republicans who welcomed any opportunity to damage Duane's position.[46]

After an initial period of apparent harmony, the conflicting aims and interests of Binns and Duane came out into the open. During the state elections of that year, Binns accused the Leib-Duane radicals of secretly plotting against Snyder and putting private ambitions above democratic unity. Duane replied in kind, blaming Binns's disruptive influence for democratic defeats in the state (including his own) and dismissing his rival as a man "without any thing but arrogance, vanity, egotism and impudence to sustain him." This had little to do with ideology—in most matters, Binns's and Duane's views were virtually identical—and much to do with power. The support of the Irish community was crucial in the outcome of this struggle.[47]

With his entrenched power base in the Irish strongholds of Southwark and the Northern Liberties, Duane was initially able to stave off Binns's challenge. The Duaneites expelled Binns from the St. Patrick's Benevolent Society, and conducted a smear campaign that accused him of betraying James Coigly in the trial of 1798. "This wicked lie was by many believed," Binns recalled, "and I was consequently looked upon with loathing." The accusation dogged Binns for the rest of his life; he attempted to exonerate himself in print, sued for perjury, and even appealed to Arthur O'Connor for support—not without irony, since the charge actually had some validity in O'Connor's case. Still, O'Connor came to Binns's aid, and added a blast of his own bitterness into the bargain:

> I am not astonished you should have been basely calumniated by some of our unworthy, intriguing countrymen. I do assure you, I have experienced more treachery, calumny, and vindictive envy and malice from some of these vile,

intriguing detractors, than from the most vindictive of our enemies on the side of the Irish and British Government, but I have ever treated them with the contempt they merit.[48]

Despite Duane's damaging counter-attack, the political tide in Pennsylvania began to turn in Binns's favor. Binns benefited from Snyder's victory in the 1808 gubernatorial election, and worked closely with the new governor's German supporters in Philadelphia to prize apart the formidable Irish-German alliance that Duane and Leib had forged. Describing themselves as the Old School Democrats, Duane and Leib rallied their forces for a showdown with the Snyderites, or New School Democrats, in the state elections of 1810. It was clear that major differences were emerging within the city's artisan community; Duane and the Old School attracted the support of poorer artisans and journeymen, while Binns and the New School appealed to the more prosperous master mechanics.[49]

During the campaign of 1810, incipient class conflict interlocked with the struggle for power and patronage and was intensified by bitter personal rivalries. Binns proved himself as adept at smear tactics as his rival, arguing among other things that Duane's accountant was an Orangeman. The idea, as the accountant himself pointed out, was "to pull down the colonel," Duane, and thus "make converts of the Irish." When the two men confronted each other at a ward meeting that July, things quickly got out of control. With Duane telling Binns that "*murder and perjury* were written on his countenance" and Binns calling Duane a "poltroon," they moved swiftly from verbal to physical violence, and would have inflicted serious injuries on each other had they not been physically separated.[50]

In the event, it was Binns who won the political fight. Backed by local bank promoters and building on Binns's personal following among more recent Irish immigrants, the New School Democrats finally broke the Leib-Duane grip on the Northern Liberties. The Old School Democrats were reduced to a rump in Southwark, where Duane still commanded considerable Irish support. Further isolating his opponents, Binns formed an alliance between the New School Democrats and the Madison administration, securing significant federal patronage for his newspaper in the process. There was no doubt, by this time, that the United Irishmen had become as fragmented as the Republicans in general.[51]

"You do not regret more than I do the unhappy divisions that have torn, and still divide the Irish Republicans here," wrote George Cuming in New York, where similar conflicts had splintered the United Irishmen between the Clintonian and Madisonian factions. Indeed, the infighting was so bitter that Cuming began to make dark predictions about "the degradation of the Irish character" in the New World. "Many are the difficulties a people labour under to preserve their liberties after they have been acquired," he concluded. As

"Brazen Projectiles, or, an enforcement of the solid arguments of the OLD SCHOOL" (1810). After their arrival in the United States, the self-proclaimed United Irishmen William Duane and John Binns fought bitterly for control of the Irish vote in Philadelphia. This cartoon depicts a fight that broke out between them at a ward meeting during the state elections of 1810. Duane, the editor of the radical *Aurora* newspaper and leader of the Old School Party, is about to hurl a candlestick at Binns, whose supporters are caricatured as wild Irishmen. Meanwhile, in the middle, the moderates look singularly unimpressed. Courtesy of the Boston Public Library.

Cuming's remarks suggest, such "unhappy divisions" and "difficulties" increased in direct proportion to the degree of political security experienced by the Republicans. During the first years of the nineteenth century, the decisive defeat of Federalism created the conditions in which internal conflict among Republicans could flourish.[52]

The United Irishmen participated in that conflict, with each faction blaming the others for the evil of factionalism. Thus Duane, of all people, complained to David Bailie Warden in 1811 about the "horrid spirit of intrigue which has destroyed the public virtue of the country." The only thing that would save the "principles of government," he wrote, would be "some foreign aggression such as will unite all men." And there was indeed much truth in this. The centrifugal tendencies within the Republican Party in general and the United Irishmen in particular would be countered by the centripetal force produced by the external conflict with Britain during the War of 1812.[53]

In the period between Jefferson's inauguration and the outbreak of war with Britain, the United Irishmen attempted to implement in America the political program that had been denied them in Ireland. Viewing the Federalists as an American version of the aristocrats and Orangemen who had defeated democracy in the Old Country, the United Irishmen were determined to give them no quarter in the United States. In the process, they frequently displayed the same kind of intolerance that they denounced in their enemies. On the radical edge of the American Republican movement, they pushed for liberalized naturalization laws, a more democratic and rational judicial system, constitutional revision in Pennsylvania, and the extension of full religious freedom to Catholics throughout the country; a militant minority also worked for a religious revolution that would turn the United States into a deist democracy. At the same time, their attempts to democratize the republic necessarily drew them into intra-radical conflicts; as this happened, the United Irishmen became less and less united. Nevertheless, the divisions over patronage and power were occurring within a specifically American frame of reference, and were focused on specifically American issues; in this sense, they actually contributed to the integration of the United Irishmen into American life.

There was one area, however, in which the United Irishmen would be consistently more radical than the rest of the population: their attitude to Britain. Their experiences in Ireland had produced an intense Anglophobia that few American-born citizens could match. And with the growing tensions in Anglo-American relations that culminated in the War of 1812, which compelled the Republicans to sink their differences in the face of a common threat, the United Irishmen were presented with the opportunity of simultaneously demonstrating their American patriotism and avenging the defeat of 1798. It was an opportunity that they were determined not to squander.

CHAPTER FOUR

Humbling the British Tyrant

During his imprisonment at Gloucester jail between 1799 and 1801, John Binns was visited by the former Home Secretary Henry Dundas, along with his wife and two daughters. During their conversation, Binns asked Dundas when he would be liberated, and received no clear answer. Mrs. Dundas, though, seemed more sympathetic, and said she could see no reason why Binns should remain in jail. "Why, my dear," explained Dundas, "if he were at liberty, he would only be doing mischief." "I am determined to go to the United States as soon as I am liberated," Binns told them. "Well, you should be doing mischief there," Dundas countered. "Well, sir, if I were," replied Binns, "I should not be doing mischief to you or your friends." Dundas paused, and said slowly and deliberately: "I am not so sure of that."[1]

Dundas's skepticism was well placed. Not just Binns, but all the leading United Irishmen in the United States emerged as American nationalists who advocated strong measures against Britain's attempt to control transatlantic trade during the Napoleonic War. The crisis in the Atlantic began in 1806, when France declared the British and Irish Isles in a state of blockade and threatened to seize neutral ships that carried British goods. In retaliation, Britain ordered that all neutral ships trading with the enemy must first be cleared in British ports, receive licenses, and pay duties. The French, for their part, made it clear that any ships submitting to British orders would be treated as enemy vessels. As the great neutral transatlantic trading power, the United States was being squeezed by both sides.

In theory, the British and French measures were equally unacceptable to the Americans. As the dominant Atlantic naval power, however, the British constituted the greater threat, and the Royal Navy's impressment of actual or alleged British subjects serving on American ships further aggravated Anglo-American relations. To break the British grip, the United States in December 1807 adopted the twin policies of an embargo and a Non-Importation Act; economic coercion, it was hoped, would force the belligerents to back down. When the trade sanctions proved impossible to enforce, they were replaced in the spring of 1809 by a Non-Intercourse Act, which opened up American trade to all countries except Britain and France. But the new legislation was a smuggler's paradise, and was widely interpreted in both Britain and the United States as a sign that America was losing the economic war.

After the breakdown of further negotiations with Britain, the United States in 1810 declared that it would resume trade with both countries, but added that if either one repealed its restrictions, a policy of non-intercourse would be renewed against the other. In response, the French foreign minister, the Duc de Cadore, issued a letter that promised to repeal the French decrees against American shipping. David Bailie Warden, who had by this time become the American consul in Paris, immediately smelled a rat. Despite the letter, he told a friend, France would not change its policy at all; his prediction turned out to be accurate. But Madison, possibly to increase the pressure on Britain, decided to take Cadore's letter at face value, and gave the British government three months to follow suit. When Britain refused, the policy of non-intercourse was resumed; within eighteen months, Anglo-American relations slid from commercial conflict into the War of 1812.[2]

Under these circumstances, the United Irishmen in the United States, like the Republicans as a whole, began to close ranks against the common enemy. The Anglo-American conflict effectively checked the internal fragmentation of America's first party system, and reinforced the Republican-Federalist alignments that had been established during the 1790s. In Pennsylvania, for example, the emerging Quid-Federalist party fell apart over foreign policy issues; there was no way that a moderate Republican such as Mathew Carey would stay in a coalition with Federalists who opposed commercial discrimination against Britain. At the same time, radical democrats such as Duane and Binns both agreed with the embargo, although the two men remained bitter personal and political rivals in all other respects. Britain's Atlantic policy appeared to confirm what the United Irishmen already felt in their bones: the same country that had perpetrated murders, tortures and house-burnings in Ireland was now beginning to turn against the last bastion of liberty in the world, the United States.[3]

Such feelings fused with a growing American anger about British aggression and arrogance. In their correspondence, United Irishmen such as George Cuming and John Chambers registered the general sense of resentment about "the Conduct of Gt. Britain in Blockading our harbours" and the "unwise, impolitic & brutal conduct" of British naval officers whose actions threatened to produce a pro-French backlash. "If they were paid by Bonaparte," commented Chambers, "they could not act with more propriety." A species of war fever broke out in the summer of 1807, after a Royal Navy ship fired on the USS *Chesapeake,* killed several members of its crew, and impressed four sailors who were deemed to be British subjects. In the chorus of outrage, the United Irishmen supplied some of the strongest voices. "Four of our citizens are borne off," exclaimed Burk, "wretched victims to satiate the rage of the British Moloch." Binns wrote of the "unanimous desire for revenge," Sampson and Emmet predicted war, and Driscol insisted that Americans must be "prepared to meet the British, in arms, by sea and land."[4]

Anger was soon transformed into action, as Irish radicals joined American militia units and raised companies of their own. "SONS OF ERIN, ASSEMBLE!" ran the cry in Washington, as Irishmen were exhorted to organize themselves into "a company of Invincibles" that would take inspiration from the memory of Montgomery, defend the American asylum of liberty against the British predators, and avenge the "murders . . . committed on the blood-stained fields of poor Erin." In Petersburg, Burk became captain of the Rifle Company, and instructed his men in the art of guerrilla war; the training he had received in the revolutionary underground of Dublin was now brought into service for America. One of the companies that formed in Baltimore was the Union Greens, whose banner of green depicted an eagle protecting a harp beneath its spreading wing. "*Fostered under thy wing,*" went the motto, "*we die in thy defence.*" Two years later, the *Shamrock* newspaper, the voice of United Irish nationalism in America, would adopt the same emblem for its masthead. In Philadelphia, Duane's Republican Greens toasted their namesake in New York, condemned foreign enemies and "domestic traitors," and anticipated "the hour approaching—when the hearts of 50,000 bold Irish boys, will beat in unison with Yankee Doodle." Here, it seemed, was the perfect antidote to American nativism. "The Hibernians in particular, who have been heretofore shamefully traduced by certain prints in the Union," commented one sympathetic editor, "display a spirit descriptive of freemen."[5]

It is significant that much of this spirit was animated by the issue of impressment. There were, of course, general objections to the practice; it was denounced as an insult to the national flag, an attack on individual liberty, and a means of forcing American sailors to participate in the plunder of their own country's commerce. But the Irish also had an immediate interest in the matter, since their own countrymen were much more vulnerable to impressment than were native-born Americans. From the British perspective, a strong navy was of vital importance in the struggle against Napoleon, and the country needed all the sailors it could get. Operating under the assumption that allegiance was inalienable, the British government had no compunction about compelling its subjects in the American merchant marine, including its Irish subjects, to serve in the Royal Navy. If this policy made sense for the British, it made equal sense for the Irish in America to resist it as strongly as possible. So important did the practice of impressment appear to Warden that he would later rank it as the principal cause of the War of 1812.[6]

The situation was exacerbated by the fact that the Royal Navy was intercepting passenger ships and impressing people at a time when Irish immigration to America was increasing. "Emigrants from every part of Ireland," wrote Chambers from New York in 1811, "are pouring in here, in unexampled number." Not all of them reached their destination. Among the many incidents that provoked outrage in the Irish-American community, none had a greater impact than the impressment of sixty-two passengers from the *Belisarius*, bound from Dublin to New York in the summer of 1811. It was boarded by the *Atalanta*, a British sloop from Halifax, and the passengers were removed on the grounds that they had not cleared the custom house in Dublin. "You shan't go into that damn'd Republican country," they were told; "we are going to have a slap at them one of these days, and you shan't be there to fight against us." Most of them were taken to St. John's Island (present-day Prince Edward Island) and told that they would become tenants on the estate of Lord Townshend; seventeen were forced into service with the Royal Navy.[7]

This incident was Irish America's *Chesapeake*. It was denounced throughout the country, amid outbursts of anger and demands for revenge, and was rapidly incorporated into standard United Irish interpretations of British oppression. The "late kidnapping," commented Edward Gillespy of the *Shamrock*, furnished "an additional proof, if additional proofs were wanted, of the perfidy of the British nation." Britain's policy of impressment, he argued the following year, was best understood as "a prosecution of a war waged against Ireland for nearly seven centuries, and which will never be terminated by concession, submission or treaty."[8]

Another writer went further still, and located the action of the *Atalanta* within genocidal interpretations of British imperialism—interpretations that clearly predated the Great Famine of 1846–51 with which they are usually associated. Such behavior, he believed, was only to be expected from "the bloody & ruthless nation that on one occasion reduced the whole population of Ireland to *eight hundred souls!*" And to destroy the oppressor, along with its remaining outposts in North America, was nothing less than to walk in the path of righteousness: "Irishmen in America!" he exclaimed, "*swear eternal vengence* [*sic*],—*vow holy hatred to British tyranny*, on the altar of patriotism; and Heaven will smile on the deed & accept the sacrifice. 'It is holy to the Lord,' . . . . Combatting too on the side of your *adopted* country, you will strike at once for vengence, for liberty, and holy retribution." This form of Irish-American nationalism combined modern notions of liberty and patriotism with the spirit of the Wars of Religion.[9]

Within the radical Irish community, there was widespread support for the embargo of 1807 as the most effective means of securing freedom of the seas, free trade, and an end to impressment. Through the embargo, it was argued,

America had the ability to bring Britain to its knees without firing a shot. This tactic would be effective because the United States imported manufactured goods and "luxuries" which it could easily do without; Britain, on the other hand, imported American food, which was a necessity of life. "By locking up her granaries," wrote Burk, "she [America] locks up the fountain of life from the colonies of her enemies, and haunts even the mother country with the giant spectre of famine." It is ironic, given subsequent nationalist arguments that the British deliberately created the Great Famine in Ireland, that the notion of using an artificially created famine for political ends had circulated within the United Irish community in America.[10]

The case for economic sanctions reached back to American precedents during the revolutionary era, when the Continental Congress had adopted similar measures on similar grounds. But there was an Irish dimension, nonetheless. In 1799, during the debate over the impending Act of Union, MacNeven had maintained that an independent Ireland could protect itself from British commercial retaliation by fighting and winning an economic war. Central to his position was the argument that the Irish imported "numberless luxuries" but exported the "necessaries" of life to Britain. Ireland's economic "backwardness," in this sense, could actually become a political advantage. When they argued for the embargo and non-importation from 1806, the United Irishmen could and did draw equally on American and Irish radical traditions.[11]

Economic sanctions, argued the Irish radicals, offered a route to victory that avoided the pitfalls of a standing army, a large navy, and a massive debt. In Duane's view, a powerful military establishment in the United States would produce massive tax increases, corruption, patronage and the abuse of power. A professional army, he told his readers, was comprised of people "whose trade is plunder, cruelty, and blood." An armed navy was nothing less than a "destructive den of *disease, crimes, immorality,* and *human debasement.*" And the debt needed to finance such a military force, he argued, would transfer money from the productive classes into the hands of the very people who would be most likely to oppress them. Anyone who doubted that need only look across the Atlantic to Britain, where the army and navy buttressed the power of an aristocratic minority that had unleashed a "REIGN OF TERROR" against republicans and democrats during the 1790s.[12]

But the embargo and non-importation acts were more than a substitute for war; they were also supported as a means of breaking America's neo-colonial relationship with Britain. By cutting off British competition, it was argued, economic sanctions would stimulate demand for domestic manufactures; this would create new opportunities for American agricultural goods and compensate farmers for the loss of their international markets. At the same time, a program of internal improvements could facilitate continental trade networks that would integrate the agricultural, manufacturing and commercial components of the American economy. In this way, the work of 1776 would be complete; the United States would enjoy the benefits of both political independence and economic emancipation.

In taking this position, the United Irishmen were applying their own country's anti-colonial tradition to American circumstances. During the late 1770s and early 1780s, the Irish Volunteers had supported domestic manufactures and launched a buy-Irish campaign. As the editor of the *Volunteers Journal* in 1783–84, Mathew Carey had pushed hard for protective tariffs to safeguard Irish industries and won considerable support from artisans and manufacturers who were suffering from English competition. After he arrived in the United States, he repeated the same arguments in a new context; in effect, his Irish economic nationalism became Americanized.[13]

In Philadelphia, Carey worked closely with Tench Coxe, one of the leading Republican advocates for American manufactures; together, they advocated the development of an internal market system characterized by transportation improvements, a sound banking system, and protective tariffs. Joining them was John Binns, whose grand-uncle had urged "the absolute necessity of a non-importation agreement, or protecting duties" to help his "starving brethren" in Ireland during the 1780s. Binns regularly opened the columns of the *Democratic Press* to Coxe, supplied him with information, and invited him to write editorials; when Binns was away from Philadelphia, he asked Coxe to run the paper for him. Unequivocally in favor of manufacturing in general and labor-saving machinery in particular, Binns believed that the industrial and the democratic revolutions would together eliminate economic and political oppression and create a new world order based on unparalleled prosperity and liberty.[14]

Other United Irishmen were equally enthusiastic about domestic manufactures. Duane warned American mechanics about the need to overcome "*foreign competition*," and Driscol rejoiced that "arts and Manufactures are every day coming to light." Burk saw great opportunities in the crisis of Anglo-American relations. "The mechanic arts will rise like a phoenix from the ashes of foreign monopolies," he wrote in 1808, "and we shall become by the blessings of Providence, in every sense of the word, a world within ourselves." As the joint owner of a paper mill near Petersburg, Burk himself had a stake in the growth of manufacturing, but it is clear that his politics transcended any narrow sense of self-interest; he was too much the romantic for that.[15]

For economic sanctions to fulfill their political and economic purposes, it was essential that they be applied rigorously. When the government began in 1809 to relax its commercial restrictions against Britain, the United Irishmen protested vociferously. Both Duane and Warden argued that any signs of American weakness would only encourage British aggression and actually bring about the conflict that the government was trying to avert; later in life, they were convinced that the repeal of the embargo led directly to the War of 1812. As tensions continued to build in the Atlantic, and as it became increasingly apparent that watered-down economic measures would not change Britain's position on the issues of impressment and neutrality, a growing number of Americans came to the conclusion that their country faced a choice between war and submission, and that submission was out of the question.[16]

Against this background, the United Irishmen established themselves in the vanguard of the pro-war movement. By 1811, Duane and Binns, despite their continuing personal and political rivalry, had come out strongly for war. In New York, the Hibernian Provident Society drank a St. Patrick's Day toast in 1812 to "War, vigorous War!—till the Nation's Wrongs are avenged, the Country's rights secured." Although their militancy was triggered by immediate events, it stemmed from earlier experiences. Bitter memories of British repression bubbled to the surface, and there was a strong desire to settle old scores. Federalists began to complain that Irish radicals were dragging the United States into an unnecessary war to satisfy their lust for revenge against Britain.[17]

Combining Hibernocentrism with American hyper-patriotism, the United Irishmen were convinced that Britain was attempting in America to complete the unfinished business, begun in Ireland, of eradicating republicanism throughout the world. Some of them even argued that Britain's real purpose was to hunt down and enslave the "Thousands of Irishmen" who had taken refuge in the United States. Others maintained that the fate of liberty in Ireland hinged on the outcome of events in America. A British victory, according to this view, would destroy democracy in America, and consolidate imperialism in Ireland; conversely, a British defeat would undermine aristocracy and empire, and pave the way for Irish independence.[18]

Operating from these assumptions, the United Irishmen in the United States threw themselves wholeheartedly into the war effort. Some of them, such as MacNeven, had already acquired significant military experience in their efforts to liberate Ireland; now, such knowledge would be applied directly to America. As a captain in Napoleon's Irish Legion, MacNeven had learned the importance of a "capable well organized general staff." Just as Napoleon had begun his mobilization of "raw recruits" by establishing a well-trained officer corps, he wrote, the United States must recognize that "good officers will soon form a good army." MacNeven also drew on his French training to develop plans for an American spy system; among other things, he discussed the kind of people who should be employed as informers and how much they should be paid. For all the moral outrage that the United Irishmen had directed against paid informers in Ireland, they found nothing remotely reprehensible about the practice when it served their own cause.[19]

Meanwhile, Duane produced a series of military manuals that were designed to emancipate Americans from their dependence on British military theory and applied Napoleonic models to the organization of the American militia. Nor did Duane and MacNeven confine themselves to military theory; they became militia officers, and exhorted their fellow countrymen to join them. In 1813, Duane was appointed the adjutant general of the Delaware river region, and ensured that his Old School allies were rewarded with contracts and positions. Binns, who became one of Governor Snyder's aides-de-camp during the war, with major responsibilities for ordnance, watched the progress of his rival with a mounting sense of frustration and fury. He tried to control his "personal indignation" in the interests of wartime unity, but became increasingly critical of both Duane and his patron, the Secretary of War John Armstrong, as the American army failed to make any headway in Canada.[20]

Among the United Irishmen who headed for the Canadian front in 1812 was Richard Caldwell, the young "general" in north Antrim during the 1798 rising. In Ireland, he had organized a makeshift force that joined the insurgents in Ballymena; in America, he raised "a very large company of men" from his new home in Orange County, New York, became a captain in the army, and participated in the march to Canada along the Lake Champlain route. At a personal level, this was an opportunity to avenge 1798: the execution of his friends, the torching of his family's home, his court-martial and sentence of death, the desperate pleading and prevarication to save his life, and the subsequent exile of the entire family to the United States. But failure in Ireland was followed by disaster in America. Suffering from dysentery, and exposed to severe storms while crossing the lake, Caldwell died before reaching the Canadian border. He was thirty-five years old, and left a wife and two children.[21]

The attempt to strike back at Britain through invading Canada was widely supported by the United Irishmen. In Baltimore, where the radical Irish organized Volunteer Companies of "*Irishmen and the descendants of Irishmen,*" a Catholic lieutenant urged that his countrymen and co-religionists "ferociously rush to destroy the perfidious *Britons.*" "This is the hour," he exhorted, "to humble the *British* tyrant in the *dust,* to *complete* the independence of America, and shatter into pieces the chains of poor unfortunate *Ireland*. Ireland will be rescued from British bondage on the plains of Canada, if *Irishmen* will, at this *decisive* moment, but religiously and gratefully discharge their *duty,* to both their *adopted* and *native* countries." From Albany, "A REPUBLICAN EMIGRANT" warned Canadians that thousands of émigrés, "particularly *from Ireland,*" were preparing to avenge British tyranny with the "thunder of American cannon." In New York, the Republican Greens were absorbed into the First New York Regiment of Riflemen; during the fall of 1812, they advanced with the state militia (whose officers included Robert Emmet, son of Thomas) toward Canada, only to stop at the border without engaging the enemy.[22]

Irish republicans also played a significant role in the defense of the country from British attacks. They rallied to the cause, for example, when De Witt Clinton in 1814 declared the city of New York in imminent danger of a British invasion, and called for volunteers to construct fortifications. On an August morning at five o'clock, some 1,500 Irishmen assembled to complete the ramparts at Fort Greene; they were joined by a number of Irishwomen who were "busily employed in laying sods and driving pickets." The city's Committee of Defense singled out the "PATRIOTIC SONS OF ERIN," without any mention of the equally patriotic daughters, for special commendation. "Their numbers, their zeal, their industry, the excellent organization, the great quantity of work accomplished by them and their universally correct deportment while on the field of labour, and throughout the whole day," noted the Committee, "were highly gratifying to the engineers who directed their labours." After working all day, the Irish volunteers, who included Emmet, Sampson and MacNeven, spent the night in celebration and music. "We blessed the land that gave us a home, and liberty, and equal rights," recalled Sampson; "and before we parted we resolved that either the enemy or we should be buried in those trenches, if he came so far."[23]

In defending the country against external aggression, the United Irishmen were able to present themselves as American patriots in a way that had been impossible during the late 1790s. In a striking reversal of roles, the United Irishmen now played the part that the High Federalists had assumed in during the Quasi-War of 1798. They argued that American liberty was threatened by the conjunction of external force and internal subversion, pressed for stronger measures against "domestic traitors" (including, in some cases, calls that internal enemies should be "*exterminated*"), and blamed many of the country's difficulties on the activities of foreign agitators. But now, of course, the external enemy was Britain, not France; the domestic traitors were Federalists, not Republicans; and the foreign agitators were loyalists, not democrats.[24]

Mathew Carey is a good case in point. Just as the Federalists during the 1790s had accused the Republicans of abusing the freedom of the press, Carey argued during the War of 1812 that the New England Federalist newspapers were deliberately and systematically spreading lies about the government. Most Federalists, Carey argued, were "as good citizens as ever existed" but were being manipulated by wicked and ambitious demagogues who put their own self-interest above the public good; the parallel with the Federalist attack on democratic republicanism during the 1790s is striking. And just as Cobbett had argued that America was in the grip of an international republican conspiracy, Carey in 1812 maintained that the government was facing a Federalist plot to pull New England out of the union and establish a pro-British state. "As early as 1793," he wrote, "the necessity of a separation was advocated by an assemblage of the highest talents & greatest influence Connecticut could produce. . . . To this project every thing has been rendered subservient." Such a scheme, he continued, could not be defeated by reason alone; this was to fall victim to "the pernicious[,] the fatal idea, that the good sense of mankind is a fair match for the machinations of the wicked. Every page of history proves the destructive fallacy of this opinion." Exactly the same argument had been made by the Federalists in support of the Alien and Sedition Acts in 1798.[25]

Unless the Federalist conspiracy were exposed and eliminated, insisted Carey, the country would tear itself apart in civil war. He urged Madison to support legislation that would make any attempt to dissolve the union a "high crime & misdemeanour, subject to a severe penalty," and argued that a series of Union Societies should be established throughout the United States to mobilize popular support for national unity. When it became clear that Madison was not going to follow his advice, Carey responded with a mounting sense of frustration and anger. In a remarkable series of letters to the president in 1814, Carey blamed him in advance for the "rapine, desolation and slaughter" that would inevitably befall the country without firm and decisive action. "None of the human race, without positive guilt," Carey continued, "ever made so awful, so deplorable, so irrecoverable a sacrifice of human happiness as you have done." Madison took this in his stride, commenting in his reply on Carey's "valuable & seasonable service" and "laudible views" on national unity while ignoring the denunciations; the reaction must have driven Carey to distraction.[26]

But while the High Federalists after 1800 remained on the far right of American politics, Carey attempted to establish a coalition of militant moderates that would isolate the extremists on both sides. In 1814, he published the *Olive Branch,* which argued that prominent and pro-union Federalists should be brought into the government. On the one hand, he attempted to undermine the ultra-Federalists in New England by arguing that they did not represent the true economic and political interests of the people; as Edward Carter has argued, Carey was trying to foment social conflict in the region for the greater good of the country. On the other hand, he was equally critical of radical republicanism; his old enemy Duane, in particular, was singled out as a doctrinaire democrat who had refused to support the financial and military measures necessary to win the war. Among the United Irishmen who agreed with him was William Sampson, who praised the "pure and manly patriotism" of the *Olive Branch* and adopted it as a political reference book.[27]

The ideal of "pure and manly patriotism" may have been interpreted in different ways, but it was central to the United Irishmen's sense of identity in both Ireland and America. Nevertheless, their general situation as Irish-born people living in America during a time of war with Britain contained potentially dangerous ambiguities. The British government regarded all the Irish in the United States as British subjects, and thus as traitors to the crown, no matter what their claims to American citizenship may have been. But the American government regarded Irish immigrants who had not yet become citizens as alien enemies, no matter what their politics may have been. In both cases, the United Irishmen fought hard to ensure that their radical compatriots were treated on equal terms with the native-born American population.

The British position was expressed in the Prince Regent's proclamation of October 1812 that all his subjects who were captured while fighting for the

United States would be executed as rebels-in-arms. This position was the logical outgrowth of earlier British justifications for impressment: allegiance was inalienable; claims to American citizenship were irrelevant. The proclamation sent shockwaves of terror throughout the radical transatlantic community. Naturalized citizens in the militia expressed considerable alarm, and immigrant-based volunteer companies talked about disbanding; fear spread quickly. In response, a meeting of naturalized citizens was held in Philadelphia at the beginning of 1813, with Binns in the chair. They drafted an address to Secretary of State Richard Rush emphasizing their loyalty to the United States and urging strong counter-measures. Binns also served on a committee that wrote Madison and petitioned Congress; almost 2,000 people demanded that the government hold British prisoners as hostages and carry out reprisal executions. Similarly, the Hibernian Provident Society in New York pressed for a "RETALIATION LAW," and sent its own communication to Congress.[28]

The pressure worked. Replying to the Philadelphia committee, Madison agreed with Binns that Britain's policy was "repugnant to reason & humanity," and promised to protect citizens from Britain and Ireland who fought for "the rights & safety, of their adopted Country." In March 1813, Congress passed a law giving the president the power of retaliation, and twenty-three captured British officers were selected as hostages for the equivalent number of British- and Irish-born captives held in Quebec. As a result of this action, the British backed down; the prisoners were exchanged, rather than executed, and the Prince Regent's proclamation was neutralized.[29]

For the naturalized citizens, this was a clear victory. The position of Irish non-citizens in the United States, however, remained highly ambivalent. Many of them were staunch republicans, and a significant number served in the militia. Technically, however, they were subjects of the crown, and as such were classified as alien enemies. The crunch came in February 1813, when the Department of State instructed all alien enemies who lived within forty miles of tidewater and who were engaged in commerce to move inland; those who were not engaged in commerce had to apply for permission to remain where they were.[30] The intention was to prevent British supporters from supplying information to the enemy, but the effect was to unleash a storm of protest from radical immigrants who complained about unjust treatment. By classifying Irish democrats as British subjects, by treating them as anti-republican, and by uprooting them from their new homes and businesses, the regulation struck at their sense of identity, their political self-definition, and their economic and social well-being.

Over the next year, the administration was deluged with petitions from immigrants who either professed their loyalty to the American constitution or sought permission to leave the country. Among the self-declared patriots, the Irish were by far the largest group, although there were also many English and Scottish radicals who shared their sentiments. The petitions allow us a rare glimpse into the lives and attitudes of otherwise unknown figures who reacted with horror to the regulation. For example, Thomas Burke of Philadelphia wrote:

> There are hundreds of persons in this district who are it is true alien enemies in the legal sense of the words. But, Sir, there are very few of them who would not if necessary risk their lives for this country against the Government which drove them by its tiranny [*sic*] from their own native and oppressed land. That there may be many persons in the United States who ought to be watched I have not a doubt. But I believe that few if any of them are Irishmen. For myself I can truly say that I am as strongly attached to the Country and Government as if I were bound by all the solemn obligations prescribed by law. . . . I should be mortified if I were to be ranked as an enemy. I consider that I have been to blame in neglecting to become a Citizen having resided in the united states since the year 1802. But this neglect was not in the slightest degree the effect of doubt or indecision it was wholly unintentional.[31]

Other petitioners expressed similar views. James Frazer related how he had left "my oppressed country, Ireland" for the "Land of Liberty," settled in Savannah, Georgia, and joined the city's militia. "My sentiments accord with the principles of a Republican Government," he declared, "and willingly would I expose my life to maintain the rights of independence of this, the only Republic upon earth, which affords an Asylum for the persecuted and oppressed of all nations." Another immigrant, John McClintock, wrote that he had

> emigrated from Ireland to the United States in May 1806. Having for his object the enjoyment of Liberty and a better prospect to procure a sustenance than in his native Country. . . . He believes the war in which the United States are now engaged is just and necessary and his attachment to the Country of his adoption is such, that he would forfeit his existance [*sic*] rather than give aid or comfort to its enemy.[32]

Most of the petitioners from Ireland were not United Irishmen themselves, although their political opinions placed them firmly within the republican nationalist tradition. The United Irishmen had generally arrived earlier, and had already become American citizens. They agreed that firm measures were needed against alien enemies, but argued that "enemies" should be clearly distinguished from "aliens." Duane, Binns, Emmet, Sampson and Cuming all wrote letters on behalf of their fellow countrymen who were caught in the net cast for non-citizens.[33] Ireland, they insisted, was a special case; the fact that the Irish were lumped in with the British was yet another disastrous consequence of the failure of 1798.

Fearing that Irish non-citizens might turn against a government that regarded them as enemy aliens, the *Shamrock* urged its readers to "acquiesce cheerfully in the late order of the Executive" and predicted that the regulations would only be enforced against manifestly pro-British elements. At the same time, the paper formulated a classic statement of the "emigration-as-exile" theme that came to dominate Irish-American political discourse during the nineteenth and twentieth centuries. While recognizing that only a minority of the Irishmen in American were "directly exiles by the edicts of the British government," it argued that the vast majority of emigrants had been driven out by the "forfeitures and confiscation" of the seventeenth century, which had reduced the population to penury and forced them to seek refuge across the Atlantic. But if they were forced out of Ireland, they nevertheless chose to come to the United States, the only country in the world that enjoyed the "blessings of liberty." As a result, the article continued, Irish immigrants owed gratitude and allegiance to the country that offered them sanctuary, despite the Alien Enemies Proclamation. Above all, they should remember that there was a "sympathetic kindred of soul between the United States and the people of Ireland," and that the cause of America was also the cause of their native country.[34]

When the war was over, the United Irishmen saw the outcome as both the consummation of the republic and the confirmation of their new identity as patriotic Americans. "We have come out of the War without obtaining the object of it," wrote Chambers; "but we have given such earnest of a fighting capacity, by sea & land, as much undoubtedly raise the National Reputation high indeed!" Not only was the national reputation raised, the radicals argued; the Irish in America had provided much of the leverage. Thomas Macdonough, the American naval commander who "captured the whole Br. fleet, on Lake Champlain," was of Irish ethnicity; General Macomb, "before whom Sir George Prevost fled with a large regular army," was the son of a Belfast man; Andrew Jackson was not simply an American hero, but an American hero whose family came from Carrickfergus. The Irish contribution to the cause was recognized and respected in wider Republican circles; Richard Rush, for example, singled out John Binns for special praise, arguing that "no one can adequately estimate the benefits to the Nation of the resolute and patriotic labor of that Press [Binns's *Democratic Press*] during the years 1812, 1813, and 1814."[35]

If the war increased America's international standing and bolstered a sense of national pride, it also produced significant political realignments within the United States. The foreign policy issues that had divided Federalists and Republicans were now removed from the political agenda. At the same time, there were no longer any clear-cut party differences on such issues as states' rights, federal power and a central banking system. As the old party system disintegrated, American politics became characterized by a maze of shifting allegiances centered on questions of power and personality. Even those who participated in this species of jockeyship, as Paine might have called it, were disgusted by what they saw as the degeneration of American politics. Duane, who had already delivered several jeremiads before the war, became something of a political misanthrope. "Your knowledge of men and things formerly," he told Warden in 1821, "would not enable you to comprehend things now"; although Warden knew of the "knaves & hypocrites" in the political arena, wrote Duane, he "could have no conception of the extent to which meanness and treachery is daily carried."[36]

Binns, his old rival, came to much the same conclusion; personalities were replacing principles, and the lust for power was superseding the public good. Even Andrew Jackson, whom Binns had revered as the hero of New Orleans, turned out to be nothing more than an unscrupulous man-on-the-make. By 1834, Binns pronounced the old party system dead. The country was now divided into pro- and anti-Jackson factions, he wrote; the result was to turn "the people into a nation of office hunters and our elections into mere battle grounds to secure the spoils of office." "Cannot these dreaded & mighty evils be averted?" he asked. "If so, how can it be done? Is there virtue, honor and manly independence in our own Public Men to effect it?" For a while, he advocated the formation of a new party that would put principles above the sordid struggle for personal gain. But Binns answered his own question in the negative more than twenty years later, when he wrote in his memoirs that the spoils system, with all its corrupting consequences, had become an entrenched feature of American political life. "This is," he commented, "a state of things greatly to be regretted."[37]

There was, then, considerable disillusionment in the air, along with strong feelings of national pride, in the postwar period. But there were also broader issues that confronted the rising American empire and continued to grip and engage those United Irishmen who remained politically active. As American nationalists, they grappled with the questions of economic protectionism, the banking system, western expansion and national unity. And as Irish-born citizens, they fought manifestations of nativism that intensified with the new influx of predominantly Catholic Irish immigrants after 1815. The émigrés had already formed their political principles in the period before 1812; they would now attempt to implement them in a rapidly changing economic and political environment.

As has been seen, the United Irishmen had long supported domestic manufacturing to promote American economic independence. During the War of 1812, the country's industrial sector had expanded at a rapid rate; the task now was to protect American manufactures from the renewed influx of cheap British imports. In Philadelphia, Carey emerged as a prominent protectionist. Central to his analysis was a radical reinterpretation of Adam Smith's *Wealth of Nations,* the bible of nineteenth-century political economy. Smith had argued that a healthy manufacturing sector meant a healthy home market and that the home market was a major determinant of agricultural prosperity. But if that was the case, responded Carey, then Smith had actually undermined the whole basis of his free trade position. In the United States, Carey argued, free trade would result in the return of British economic hegemony and the destruction of American manufacturing. On Smith's own reckoning, he continued, this would weaken the home market and undermine the agricultural sector. With such arguments, Carey contributed to the theoretical foundations of the American System that was developed by Hezekiah Niles and Henry Clay. Indeed, Clay's famous speech on the tariff bill of 1824 drew heavily on information that Carey had supplied.[38]

True to form, Carey became an active and energetic lobbyist for protectionism. He played a leading role in the Philadelphia Society for the Promotion of National Industry, and worked closely with the United Irish triumvirate of Sampson, Emmet and MacNeven in New York, all of whom shared his views. Sampson was a leading member of the New York Society for the Promotion of Domestic Manufactures, and wrote to Carey in February 1817 about the possibility of forming a national organization that would press for protectionism. In the same month, Sampson traveled to Washington to lobby Congress for a protective tariff; his presentation to the House of Representatives' Committee on Commerce and Manufactures, he told his wife, was received "kindly and favorably."[39]

During his campaign, Sampson attempted to enlist the support of Jefferson, and elicited an encouraging response. Jefferson wrote that he had changed his mind about manufacturing, and had come to realize that "the inventions of latter times, by labor saving machines, do as much now for the manufacturer, as the earth for the cultivator." He agreed with Sampson that British competition was damaging American interests, but doubted whether protectionist duties would be sufficient to withstand the pressure. America's best hope, Jefferson continued, was for a political revolution in Britain that would liberate the country from monarchical and aristocratic rule. During the revolutionary crisis itself, he predicted, the British economy would be thrown into chaos, and American manufactures would have the breathing space to establish themselves on a secure foundation. Nor would America be the only beneficiary of such a revolution: "No country, more than your native one," Jefferson told Sampson, "ought to pray & be prepared for this."[40]

The protectionist cause was also supported in New York's *Shamrock*, which was edited after 1814 by the United Irish émigré Thomas O'Connor. In 1816 O'Connor, along with Emmet and MacNeven, helped found the Shamrock Friendly Association, which was closely aligned with De Witt Clinton's Republican faction in the city. "Agriculture, manufactures and commerce," ran one of its St. Patrick Day toasts in 1818: "the first is necessary to our existence, the second to our independence, the third to our rank as a nation. The entire must be maintained at whatever price we would pay for liberty." In its support for economic protectionism, transportation improvements in general, and De Witt Clinton's canal-building program in particular, the Shamrock Friendly Society neatly combined United Irish political economy with the immediate interests of recently arrived Irish immigrants. Protectionism would not only safeguard American independence but also boost the manufacturing sector in which immigrants were searching for work. Canal construction would integrate the home market, strengthen national unity, promote prosperity, and provide jobs for the growing Irish labor force. Not surprisingly, one of the first actions of the Shamrock Friendly Society was to request Clinton's support for the employment of Irish workers in the state's construction projects.[41]

Just as the war had brought the issue of protectionism and industrial expansion to the political forefront, it also raised new questions about the relationship among banks, economic growth and political democracy in the American republic. In 1810–11, there had been United Irish opposition to the recharter of the Bank of the United States, on the grounds that it was a monopoly dominated by British stockholders.[42] The most conspicuous exception to this position, in United Irish circles, was Mathew Carey, who had been convinced that the consequences of shutting down the bank would be catastrophic. But the opponents of the bank carried the day, and the government subsequently fought the war with a shortage of hard money and a widely fluctuating currency. After lurching through a series of financial crises, America found itself on the brink of bankruptcy in 1814. Given such experiences, there was significant support in the postwar period for the establishment of a new central bank. The pendulum had swung back to Carey's position, and fellow Irish radicals such as Binns, Chambers, MacNeven and Sampson joined him in welcoming the second Bank of the United States in 1816.[43]

Generally speaking, the United Irishmen believed that a sound banking system was a necessary condition for economic growth and equality of opportunity; in this respect, as in so many others, they were very much in the Paineite tradition. In Carey's view, the principal beneficiaries of such a system were the "most useful and industrious part of the community, the merchants, the traders, the manufacturers, the mechanics and the artists." Binns argued that the banks played a crucial role in providing capital to improving farmers, and was not particularly concerned about borrowers who overextended themselves and went bankrupt; the general good, he believed, exceeded the sum of individual losses. MacNeven broke with Jackson in 1834 over the president's attack on the Second Bank of the United States, with the result that, according to his daughter, "a storm of party rage was directed against him." In the crowd that attacked MacNeven's house in protest were many recent Irish immigrants who regarded the Bank as a bastion of privilege.[44]

Among the United Irishmen, it was Duane who had first given effective voice to such anti-bank sentiment. Before the War of 1812, he had supported banks in general while opposing the Bank of the United States as a British-controlled engine of oppression. During the postwar depression, however, he came to blame America's economic problems not simply on the renewed central bank but on the entire paper money system itself. The banks, he argued, had encouraged a frenzy of speculation that provided the illusion of prosperity without the solid foundation of real wealth. Now, in 1819, the results were coming in at the rate of fifty bankruptcies a week in Philadelphia alone. And beyond the immediate crisis lay a broader malaise; the prevalence of paper money and easy credit, Duane believed, created a parasitic moneyed aristocracy that fed off the productive classes and promoted the values of greed and corruption in place of hard work and honesty.[45]

Apart from Duane, most of the United Irishmen who were still involved in politics during the 1820s and 1830s believed that the fundamental prerequisites for the rising American Empire of Liberty consisted of a strong and stable central banking system, as well as economic protectionism and internal improvements. Despite their anxieties about Jacksonianism, they remained confident that the United States would fulfill its revolutionary destiny as the greatest force for economic and political emancipation in the world. The population, Warden noted, continued to double each generation, while the economy was expanding on all fronts; manufacturers were developing the new technology of the Industrial Revolution, merchants were opening up new markets in Asia and Latin America, and farmers were pushing farther and farther into the West.[46]

The continent would indeed be the conqueror, United Irishmen believed. With the Louisiana Purchase, observed Warden, "a wilderness, inhabited by a few savages," was being occupied by a "civilized population," steeped in the principles of civil and religious liberty. "The accession of the Floridas," commented Chambers in 1821, "rounds off our southern Quarter"; the event was seen as part of the natural order of things. "In the half century which I have resided in the United States," wrote Binns toward the end of his life, "she has obtained many millions of acres of land, and by conquest obtained many more millions of land." Far from being disturbed by the notion of "conquest," he welcomed it as expanding the boundaries of freedom, and supported an even more aggressive approach to the acquisition of new territory. So far, he argued, the South had been the principal beneficiary of American expansionism; this imbalance should be redressed. "Is it not time," he asked, "would it be anything but sheer justice, to turn our eyes to the North? Why not look to the Canadas, with their three millions of white inhabitants? to say nothing of Nova Scotia, etc." The possibility that those inhabitants might actually prefer to remain subjects of Britain rather than become United States citizens was never considered; they would be forced to be free, in the finest Rousseauist tradition.[47]

Binns's remarks not only revealed a great deal of hubris; they also indicated that territorial expansion could generate severe sectional tensions within the United States. Other radicals, such as Warden, were acutely aware of the "tendency of so great a country to separate into different empires, from the strength of factions, or the opposite interests of different sections of the country." As good nationalists, the United Irishmen wanted strong central institutions that would hold the country together. Emmet, for example, supported a broad construction of the Constitution, and argued that the doctrine of states' rights would "open the door to constant collisions and quarrels between the federal and State Governments and eventually subvert the Union itself." Binns expressed alarm at the "perversion" of "State Rights and State Sovereignty" in the South, although he was equally troubled by Jackson's apparent attempt to "engross the whole political power of the States & of the U. States." And Carey opposed secessionist sentiment in South Carolina with the same passion that he had directed toward New England separatism during the War of 1812.[48]

"The United States stand in a situation of the most solemn responsibility to the whole human race," wrote Carey in 1830. "It is with them to determine the all-important question, whether man is capable of self-government. A more important question never was at issue, [and] the past experience of mankind unhappily leads to the negative of the proposition."[49] If the United States was to answer the question in the affirmative, it was essential not only to counter the centrifugal forces of an expanding empire but also to preserve a liberal and tolerant polity within its borders. In this respect, one of the most disturbing developments was something that affected the United Irishmen directly and immediately: the persistence and prevalence of nativist attitudes in the American republic.

Before the War of 1812, nativism had been directed mainly against the political activities of the United Irishmen, although competition for work had also been a factor. In the postwar period, the economic and religious aspects of nativism became increasingly pronounced. Anxieties over employment fused with a deep-rooted anti-Catholicism to produce a ferocious backlash against the Irish immigrants who were coming into the country during the 1820s. Nativist sentiments seeped through every pore of the political system, and permeated both major political parties. Despite their highly visible and vocal patriotism during the war, Irish radicals remained targets of discrimination. In Philadelphia County during the 1830s, for example, the Democratic Party excluded naturalized citizens from holding offices in the district; Binns organized an effective counter-campaign against this "evil and proscriptive spirit."[50]

As one of the few United Irishmen to remain politically active in the 1840s and 1850s, Binns continued to defend his increasingly embattled community from nativist attacks. He was horrified by the Philadelphia riots of 1844, when Protestant crowds burned down a Catholic church and desecrated its cemetery in a conflict that ended in around twenty deaths and a hundred injuries; the old specter of religious intolerance was beginning to haunt the asylum of liberty. Binns lived long enough to witness the rise of the Know-Nothing Party, which he connected directly with the attitudes and actions of the 1844 rioters. With their fraternal rituals and their intense anti-Catholicism, the Know-Nothings appeared to him as an American strain of the Orangeism that the United Irishmen had fought in the 1790s. He denounced them as a "band of conspirators" and a "den of robbers" whose influence must be eradicated from the United States. Nativism, after all, hit all the most sensitive United Irish nerves; it ran counter to their ideology, threatened their community, and contradicted their image of America as an asylum of liberty. On balance, though, Binns was optimistic enough to believe that the storm could be weathered; in an ironic twist, he thought that nativism was "doomed to destruction" precisely because it was un-American.[51]

To be American, in this view, was to embrace the principles of democracy, the program of civil and religious liberty for which the United Irishmen had fought in their own country during the 1790s. It was a matter both of sentiment and of reason. Warden, whose Glasgow education had taught him the importance of benevolent feelings in strengthening the social compact, believed that "the State of National feeling is principally ascribable to the liberty of the press and to the efficient representation of the People."[52] Other factors that sustained this consciousness of Americanism, he argued, were peace, prosperity, religious freedom and a broad social egalitarianism. It was essential, however, to ensure that the people continued to recognize the benefits of staying together under democratic republican principles, of belonging to the world's only Empire of Liberty. And here, the "diffusion of knowledge" was of central importance. The "people"—meaning the white, propertied, male people—must be educated for democracy. Through the creation of a distinctly American literature, theater, music and sense of history, it was believed, the cultural basis for national unity and liberty would be established. In the process, the educational system, broadly conceived, would produce nothing less than a New Citizenry for this New World. No group of people threw themselves more wholeheartedly into this endeavor than the United Irishmen.

CHAPTER FIVE

Marching to Irish Music

"A fundamental mistake of the Americans has been, that they considered the revolution as completed, when it was just begun," wrote Noah Webster shortly after the War of Independence. "Having raised the pillars of the building, they ceased to exert themselves, and seemed to forget that the whole superstructure was then to be erected. This country is independent in government; but totally dependent in manners, which are the basis of government." Above all, Webster wanted to emancipate the United States from English cultural models. Hence his new dictionary, with its attempt to create a new spelling system for the United States; to spell "plough" as plow, or to omit the "u" from colour, was to make a cultural declaration of independence from Old World obscurantism and take a stand for the enlightened rationalism of New World republicanism. Among the other Americans who participated in this project was Benjamin Rush, the radical physician from Philadelphia, who saw political independence as the prerequisite for a fundamental transformation of American manners, morals and medicine. At the core of this cultural revolution would be an educational system that attempted "to convert men into republican machines."[1]

Although this cultural nationalism had indigenous American origins, it struck a responsive chord among immigrants from the so-called "Celtic fringe" countries of Scotland, Wales and Ireland, where radical intellectuals had been grappling with their own questions of national identity in the face of increasing Anglicization. In a prize-winning essay delivered at the American Philosophical Society in 1793, the Scottish-born William Thornton went far beyond Webster and argued that the American alphabet itself should be revolutionized, to shake off English linguistic imperialism and create a new language based on the phonetics of liberty. Morgan John Rhees searched the wilderness for Welsh-speaking Indians, supposedly descended from Prince Madoc; the carriers of original Cambrian freedom would, it was hoped, join with modern Welsh democrats to form a new community of liberty in the American West. And the United Irishmen, who had participated in their own country's first Celtic Revival, transferred their cultural nationalism from Ireland to the United States, where the prospect of success appeared much greater.[2]

Central to this common endeavor was a widely shared belief in Lockean notions of the malleability of human nature; if people were products of environment and education, then it would indeed be possible to reconstruct them as model republican citizens. Operating from the principle that, in Duane's words, "the character of man ever has been and ever must be formed *for* him," and believing that the first impressions were the strongest, the cultural nationalists emphasized the importance of childhood in the formation of personality and the development of ideas. "Children are, in general, what parents are pleased to make them," maintained Warden. "If they will not be influenced by the hope of reward, they can be awed by the fear of chastisement. . . . There is a modesty and ductility in the minds of youth which fit them for any impression." On these grounds, he strongly supported the establishment of elementary schools in the country, and believed that "the General influence of Common Schools, where the first lasting impressions are received, will serve more than Scientific institutions to support the Democratical principles of the American Constitution and Laws." Mathew Carey agreed.

> These Schools take the child in a state of innocence, when the mind is a mere *tabula rasa,* and imprint on it, in indelible characters, the rudiments of justice and knowledge, which can scarcely fail to have powerful and beneficent influence throughout life; and may probably convert into an exalted benefactor of mankind—a Washington or a Franklin—the being, who, under other circumstances, might prove a Luttrel, or an Arnold, or a Robespierre.[3]

Accordingly, the United Irishmen were deeply concerned with creating a sound educational system in the United States. To turn theory into practice, Carey helped to found the Sunday School Association in 1790, and counted it as among the "various efforts made of late years to diminish crime, to increase the comforts of the poor, and to meliorate and elevate the character of society." Warden welcomed such schemes, and was particularly impressed with the Washington city council's policy of taxing luxuries to finance "the education of the poor of the city"; the result, he believed, was the improvement of morals and the spread of "the inestimable blessings of knowledge." Another Irishman who involved himself in educational reform was Samuel Knox, a United Irish sympathizer and Presbyterian minister from Belfast who arrived in America in 1795. Drawing on his own experiences, he argued that the

United States should establish special colleges to facilitate the smooth adjustment of foreign teachers to their new environment; he also pioneered the idea of teachers' training colleges to improve the quality of education and promote the "National Blessings of civil and religious liberty."[4]

Within American schools, the United Irishmen attempted to develop appropriate curricula for the new generation of republicans. "The method of education is best adapted to inform the infant mind," wrote Duane, "which renders the knowledge of things most simple, clear, and distinct." He was particularly impressed with the Pestalozzi system that he encountered in Philadelphia; it combined a highly structured curriculum with a question-and-answer approach that involved the student in the learning process, and was based on the assumption that the pursuit of knowledge should be enlightening and enjoyable. "The Pestalozzi system proceeds with effect that will render it *indistructible* [*sic*]," he told Jefferson in 1810, "and get it but once into general use—there is an end to error."[5]

Duane himself attempted to get the Pestalozzi system into general use the following year, in the *Epitome of the Arts and Sciences* that he prepared for use in American schools. Believing that the customary educational emphasis on the liberal arts was the product of "borrowed prejudices" from abroad, Duane adopted a utilitarian approach geared toward the farmers and artisans who formed the economic backbone of the country. The *Epitome* also outlined the practical benefits of democratic republicanism, and argued that political knowledge would enable ordinary people to recognize and resist threats to their liberty. With its emphasis on useful information and democratic politics, the book functioned as a Jeffersonian Republican primer for the productive classes.[6]

Where Duane drew on the Pestalozzi system, Warden brought progressive Irish and Scottish approaches to education into the United States. Among other things, he attempted to adjust teaching to the students' level of understanding, and emphasized plain speech over the grand style of rhetoric. Such methods proved to be highly controversial. As the principal tutor at Kinderhook Academy (where his students included the future president Martin Van Buren) and Kingston Academy in New York, Warden was praised in some quarters for bringing in more students, and denounced in others for diluting educational standards. His workbooks indicate that the attacks were misplaced; the classes were comprehensive, rigorous and demanding. Although he shared Duane's functionalist view of education, Warden rejected narrow notions of utilitarianism. Rather than merely attempting to slot students into existing occupations, he argued, teachers and parents should impart as much scientific information as possible and foster an innovative spirit that would promote individual learning. Nor did he dismiss the importance of classical knowledge; he taught Greek and Latin, and translated Antoine L. Thomas's eulogy on Marcus Aurelius into English, to "inspire youth with virtue & sound patriotism." Appropriately, given his politics, he dedicated the book to Jefferson.[7]

Warden was one of many United Irish émigrés who became teachers in America. "These miscreants," snarled Cobbett in 1798, "not by their superior knowledge, but by their superior impudence, get admission into almost every country School that they fix their eyes upon." When they were not indoctrinating their students with democratic ideology, he continued, they spent their days drinking and debauching their "female scholars." "Thus," Cobbett concluded, "one way or the other, almost every part of Pennsylvania is more or less stocked with their lousy-looking breed and their infamous principles." Among his targets were John Black and Samuel Wylie ("singular names" for democrats, he added) of the University of Pennsylvania; Wylie in particular was denounced for his "violent and daring" expressions. They were joined at the University by their fellow United Irishman and old friend Robert Patterson; he taught mathematics, rose to vice-president of the institution, and in 1805 became the director of the federal mint.[8]

Another mathematician and United Irishman who wound up at the University of Pennsylvania was the brilliant and eccentric Robert Adrain. According to one story, he had been shot in the back by his own men after getting into an argument with them the day before the battle of Saintfield; after the defeat, his friends circulated a rumor that he was dead, and smuggled him onto a ship bound for the United States. He spent most of his American career at Columbia College in New York, where he established his reputation as one of "the most distinguished mathematicians of this continent." He was less effective as a teacher, however, and had as much difficulty controlling his classes as he had with his troops in 1798. Fortunately for him, his students were not armed.[9]

Along with their contributions to the theory and practice of education in America, the United Irishmen were on the leading edge of attempts to fashion a new literature for the New World. From his bookstore in Philadelphia, Mathew Carey developed a national distribution network through which democratic and republican publications could be transmitted. Although many of these works were imported from Europe, Carey encouraged the emergence of a distinctly American literary canon that would set new international standards. During the 1780s, he launched *The American Museum* to provide a platform for American poets and writers. Shortly after the Republican victory in 1800, he began working for an American Book Fair, modeled on that of Frankfurt and Leipzig, which would promote the country's publishing and bookselling trade. His case for literary nationalism was grounded on utilitarian principles; it would, he argued, increase the independence of the United States, strengthen the "patriotic spirit of fostering domestic arts and manufactures," improve the "arts and sciences," and stimulate economic growth. For Carey, literary emancipation was the cultural counterpart of political and economic independence, and remained a central goal throughout his career.

"Carey's labors on behalf of cultural nationalism," Edward Carter has argued, "may well have constituted his most lasting contribution to his nation's development."[10]

If Carey's principal cultural role was to create conditions in which American literature could flourish, John Daly Burk aspired to become (and thought he actually was) the greatest poet, historian and playwright of the American Republic. Convinced that the "expansive feelings and spirit" of literature constituted powerful weapons for liberty against "the insolent assumption and exercise of power," Burk set out in 1797 to write "The Columbiad," an epic poem on the American Revolution. He worked on it for two years, and regularly printed extracts in his own newspaper, the *Time-Piece*. In twelve books of blank verse, the poem attempted to "ennoble and immortalize" the Revolution, which was presented as the culmination of all earlier libertarian writings and the harbinger of universal regeneration. "The Columbiad," he believed, would instill a sense of pride and glory among the new generation in America's revolutionary heritage.[11]

The only trouble was that the poem was dreadful. Attempts to raise subscriptions got nowhere, and Burk's prosecution for seditious libel in 1798 further disrupted his plans for publication. Three years later, he sent a copy to Jefferson. "Should you estimate highly as I do the value of my Poem," he wrote, "I ask for it your public patronage & exertions." The appeal did not work; the poem remained unpublished. But Burk retained an unshakable belief in his own poetic genius; if his work would not be read, he ensured that it would at least be heard. While visiting the home of Judge John Tyler in Petersburg, Burk recited his poetry in installments over the breakfast table. Trapped in the corner was John Tyler junior, the future president. What Tyler remembered most about those mornings was the reaction of "the worthy and practical old housekeeper, Mrs. Bagby," to the recitals. She would wait until Burk got to the "most affecting part of his effusion," and then give "a prolonged sneeze, whose effect was to completely demolish the sentiment of the poet and provoke a more than audible smile on each face." It is, on balance, reassuring that so many attempts by extreme cultural nationalists to mold the minds of a new citizenry are so often met with prolonged sneezes.[12]

In Burk's view, poetry was only one aspect of a general cultural campaign to sustain the revolutionary democratic tradition in America. Equally important, in his view, was the role of historical writing in fostering a sense of pride in the country's progress. History, like art, was approached in functionalist terms. There was no clear distinction in Burk's mind between "the pen of the historian and of the poet," and both history and literature were conceived as the continuation of politics by other means. It is true that Burk the historian was concerned with documentation in a way that Burk the poet was not. In preparing his monumental *History of Virginia*, the major United Irish contribution to American historiography, he borrowed a file of newspapers from Jefferson (which he never returned), plagiarized whole sections of Robert Beverley's earlier history (which he nonetheless condemned as pro-royalist, unsystematic and tedious), and claimed to have access to new and valuable sources (which never actually appeared in his work). It is also true that Burk the historian paid lip service to the concept of impartiality, and maintained that he was taking a scientific approach to his subject. Yet the purpose of the work contradicted this professed position; its aim was to glorify Virginia's leading role in the struggle for America's freedom, rather than make any attempt at analytical detachment.[13]

Such an approach was typical of its time, and characterized historical writing on both sides of the Atlantic. It is instructive, in this respect, to compare Burk's treatment of Irish history with his work on Virginia. Immediately after the Rising of 1798, Burk wrote and published his *History of the Late War in Ireland,* which defended the United Irishmen against their detractors. It was an angry book, which registered the shock of repression and expressed Burk's views in their most concentrated form. His argument was characterized by a black-and-white position that cast people as heroes or villains and judged all their actions accordingly. He wrote as if the unity that the United Irishmen sought had actually been achieved, and praised the "private integrity," "public spirit," and "daring courage" of the revolutionaries; "there was not one," he asserted, "who did not die proudly and intrepidly." But the heroes were crushed by vicious and vindictive tyrants who burned and tortured their way through the country. When describing counter-revolutionary atrocities, Burk's language shook with rage; words like "butchered" sprang readily to his mind. Revolutionary violence, in contrast, was sanitized and rationalized; the People would "pick off" rather than butcher their enemies, and were goaded into insurrection by the "*brutality and insolence*" of their oppressors. In any case, he added, "there was not a single instance of perfidy among the United Irishmen." For Burk, this was truly a struggle between Vice and Virtue, and the forces of Evil had temporarily triumphed.[14]

Exactly the same kind of categorization and moralization appeared in Burk's history of Virginia; the form remained the same, but the content became Americanized. In his treatment of Bacon's Rebellion of 1676, Burk simply projected his interpretation of the Irish revolutionary movement onto the American past. Nathaniel Bacon, who led a rising of frontiersmen against Governor William Berkeley, was reinvented as a republican democrat before his time; Burk identified so closely with Bacon that the narrative verges on autobiography masquerading as history. Glossing over Bacon's desire for self-aggrandizement and his attempt to exterminate the Native Americans, Burk praised the rebel leader as "a youth amiable and popular," who possessed "a bold and dauntless courage." Bacon did not always consider the relationship between ends and means, Burk conceded, and sometimes became carried away by his own passions. But such minor drawbacks did not diminish his "real fame." "When the liberties of a people are in danger, or have been violated," Burk wrote, "it is perhaps right to trust less to the doubtful value of calculations, and the cold suggestions of prudence, than to the ardor and enthusiasm of liberty, and all the heroism and glory they will inspire." Such an argument reveals far more about Burk's political outlook than it does about Bacon's Rebellion.[15]

The parallels can be pushed still further. In his history of Ireland, Burk argued that the United Irishmen enjoyed the support of the whole people, save for a handful of dupes and knaves. His history of Virginia made the equally specious assumption that the colonists were united behind Bacon, save for a handful of loyalists in Gloster County. Once these categories had been established, the same double standards that characterized his writings on the Irish revolution were applied to Bacon's Rebellion. "Actions on the way," as Wilcomb Washburn remarked about Burk's *History of Virginia,* "are judged good or bad not according to what they are but by whom they are done." When Bacon lied about his dealings with the governor, Burk was relatively unconcerned; if there was duplicity, at least it was duplicity in a good cause. When Bacon confiscated loyalist estates, it was a necessary part of the revolution; but when Berkeley confiscated rebel estates, it was an outrageous act of oppression. Just as Burk denied that the United Irishmen had been implicated in revolutionary atrocities, he maintained that Bacon was "never reproached with shedding innocent blood, save what was unavoidably spilt in the heat and hurry of battle." Berkeley, in contrast, was charged with unleashing a counter-revolutionary terror that matched the horrors of 1798.[16]

Burk's moralistic and romantic approach to history extended far beyond Bacon's Rebellion and the Rising of 1798, to embrace an idealized version of life in Ireland and Virginia before English imperialism tightened its grip. In theory, Burk rejected "illustrious origins" arguments as myths perpetuated by the privileged to justify their hereditary power. But in practice, he was more than willing to adopt such myths himself, when they suited the purposes of national liberation and democratic republicanism. Pre-conquest Ireland, Burk believed, was an idyllic land of chivalry, simplicity and learning. His nostalgia even got the better of his republicanism, as he convinced himself that the kings were just and the people happy, in "the only innocent appearance that monarchy ever assumed."[17]

The same concept of a Golden Age, with suitable adjustments for time and place, was applied to the founding of Virginia. The colony was established, argued Burk, at one of those rare historical moments when the English were "tolerably free of moral taint and contagion"; the London Company behind the colonization was described as a "democratical" organization that carried the seeds of liberty across the Atlantic. In the case of Ireland, the Golden Age myth was both a reaction against English cultural denigration and a source of inspiration for the revolutionary movement. For Virginia, it connected the present with the past, viewed Jeffersonianism as the fulfillment of democratic destiny, and placed the state at the moral center of the world. By reading the history of Virginia, or at least his *History of Virginia,* Burk believed, "afflicted humanity will find consolation in the prospect of a better order of things." And the Irish, it was clear, were the most afflicted of all.[18]

To make the teleology work, Burk had to slide over many unpleasant and awkward facts, explain away others, and indulge his propensity for wishful thinking to the full. The existence of black slavery in this land of white liberty was largely ignored; a people who were highly visible in Burk's Virginia became virtually invisible in Burk's history of Virginia. White attacks on Native Americans were either extenuated as necessary defensive measures or condemned as aberrant instances of aggression. Burk's treatment of the settler community was riddled with contradictions. In fact, the putatively "democratical" London Company initially ruled the colony with a rod of iron; far from being the home of religious freedom, seventeenth-century Virginia was consistently and vigorously intolerant; during the English Civil War, the supposedly liberty-loving colonists were actually on the royalist side. Burk slid round all this by insisting that the [illegible] of the London Company was the temporary product of specific circumstances, the colony's religious laws were not actually enforced, and the royalism was more illusory than real. The point, after all, was to reinvent the past for the purposes of the present.[19]

It was this usable past that made the book so successful; Burk told his audience what they wanted to hear, and reaped the rewards. "The judge, the lawyer, and the man of literature," ran one review, "have not hesitated to pronounce it as possessing peculiar charms to distinction, and as holding the most elevated rank among historical productions." "The work before us," ran another, "is superior to other histories of a distinct state." Burk's *History of Virginia* was still regarded as a standard work at the end of the nineteenth century, and was described as recently as 1973 as "essential for any student of Virginia"—although by that time, this was very much a minority verdict.[20] Neither its admirers nor its detractors, though, connected the book with the author's Irish experiences. Whether as a subliminal history of the Rising of 1798 or as a compensatory myth for the failed democratic revolution in his own country, Burk's history had as much to do with Ireland as Virginia.

This was also true of Burk's plays, which brought him even greater recognition than his historical writings. His *Bunker-Hill,* in particular, was hailed as the "Dawn of the Columbian Drama," played to packed houses in Boston and New York, and remained one of the most popular patriotic plays in the country right up to the middle of the nineteenth century. In using the theater to imprint democratic, republican and nationalist ideas on the collective mind, Burk was participating in a wider revolutionary cultural movement that stretched across the Atlantic from Paris to Philadelphia. The French Jacobins had emphasized the power of the theater in their attempt to form a new collective personality for the state; because of its ability to appeal to the eye and the ear, the theater, it was argued, could reach out and touch common people who lived within and beyond the literate world. In America, there was an equally strong sense that the theater was a powerful force for good or for ill. Benjamin Rush believed that republican drama would help to shape the American character, and radical democrats condemned traditional plays that elevated noblemen while belittling the common people. What was needed, according to the cultural nationalists, was a revolution in theater that would match the revolution in politics.[21]

Irish radicals in the United States fully supported this objective. In Dublin, Mathew Carey had organized a protest campaign at the Crow-Street Theatre against a play entitled "The Poor Soldier," in which an Irishman was portrayed as a coward. "The offence was, in my estimation," added Carey, "infinitely enhanced by the writer being an Irishman." Dublin audiences, he argued, would show that they were "not to be insulted with impunity." In the event, the demonstration fizzled out, and Carey found that he enjoyed the play despite himself. The struggle, however, would be continued across the Atlantic. The Irish editors of the *American Patriot* in 1803 wanted state-run theaters that would "promote charity, reform morals, foment patriotism, and refine the taste and manners of the people." Burk agreed that the theater should become "a moral, delightful and republican *entertainment*," and believed that drama was "a potent engine in lashing the follies and absurdities of mankind." But while most cultural commentators restricted themselves to the realm of theory, he would attempt to put his beliefs into practice.[22]

Bunker-Hill was first performed in Boston in February 1797, less than a year after Burk arrived in America. Based on one of the first battles of the revolutionary war, when British troops met fierce resistance and suffered heavy losses in taking the ground overlooking Boston, it was a work of high melodrama that pitted the villainous British General Gage against the virtuous American General Warren. There was also a subplot, in which a British officer, Colonel Abercrombie, was torn between a false sense of honor to fight for a cause he knew was wrong and the natural ties of love and affection he felt toward a patriotic American woman, Elvira. The dialogue was stilted, forced, and long-winded; the American characters were given interminable speeches in which they compared themselves to Roman heroes, while the British commanders conspired to crush the rebellious colonists. In the end, Abercrombie put his military reputation as a soldier over his love for Elvira; he was killed in the battle, and Elvira was driven insane with grief. Meanwhile, General Warren insisted on staying with his troops until they had all left Bunker Hill, and was shot during their retreat. But he died happy in the knowledge that his men fought like the Spartans and Romans of old, and looked forward to joining Brutus and the "virtuous souls immortal" in the next world. "Live the Republic," he gasped with his last breath. "Live; O live, forever."[23]

As a work of drama, *Bunker-Hill* is unspeakably bad; it is easy to sympathize with the nineteenth-century critic who remarked that the play "had not a particle of merit, except its brevity." But as a work of politics, and particularly as a guide to the map of Burk's mind, it is highly revealing. Burk wrote the play when he was crossing the Atlantic in 1796, before he ever set foot in America; it reflected his idealized image of the New World, and was detached from any first-hand knowledge of American political life. But he did, of course, have first-hand knowledge of Irish political life from his attempt to organize an underground revolutionary movement in the country.

At various points in the play, Burk's Irish attitudes and experiences were projected onto ostensibly American scenes. His depiction of Warren as a man of action, who would sacrifice everything for the "sacred voice of country," fit perfectly with Burk's revolutionary self-image. Similarly, his view of the American people-in-arms was closely connected to his aspirations for Ireland. The American patriots were presented as an elemental, unstoppable force of nature, united in both their patriotism and their hatred of British power, who rushed at the occupying American army "with fury next to madness." This was more than a heroic version of the Battle of Bunker Hill; it was also a declaration of hope for a coming Irish revolution. And if his dream of Irish democratic unity remained chimerical, his sense of Irish revolutionary anger proved to be remarkably accurate. When the Rising occurred in 1798, the British officers repeatedly commented on the "enthusiasm" and "fury" of the "rebels" in language that proved strikingly similar to the words that Burk put into the mouths of the British officers in his play.[24]

At another level, *Bunker-Hill* can also be seen as an attempt to bring United Irish revolutionary ideology into the American mainstream. Acutely sensitive to charges that he and his fellow radicals were "rebels," Burk pointed out that the British had viewed American patriots in exactly the same way during the Revolution. "When nation's [*sic*] lose their rights," he had General Warren say, "words of best sense / Are tortur'd to mean what the rulers please." In the hands of the British, Warren continued, the word "obedience" had been twisted to mean "a base, unmanly fawning" to arbitrary power, while the word "rebellion" had been misused to represent what was in fact "the glorious act / Of a *whole people,* bursting from their chains." Once words had been restored to their correct meaning, Burk believed, the identity of the American and Irish struggles would be impossible to deny.

There could be no doubt, from the play's perspective, that radical republicanism was the true legacy of the American Revolution. As he lay dying, General Warren imagined an egalitarian and democratic future for his country; at his funeral, the standards that were furled around the bier implicitly connected Boston's anti-British past and the "spirit of 1776" to the ideology of revolutionary France. It is no wonder that President Adams (to whom Burk had originally considered dedicating the play) disliked it so much. Nor is it surprising that the Federalist *New-York Gazette* warned that anyone who saw *Bunker-Hill* must "have in his mind the situation of America, and that period when the British was [*sic*] to be considered as endeavouring to deprive this country, if possible, of its right and darling idol, Liberty, and not the present period, when it is hoped, perfect amity will, in future, be the prominent feature of the two countries."[25]

For the most part, though, the play was a phenomenal success; it attracted audiences of up to three thousand a night, who responded with "one incessant roar of applause, from beginning to end" of the fourth and fifth acts. Such reactions had as much to do with the play's style as its content. *Bunker-Hill* was not only the first play to bring battle scenes from the Revolution onto the stage but also the first to use the constructed set rather than the painted background. Burk devoted considerable attention to the revolutionary special effects in the play. There was a hill with enough room for twenty men, there were guns and cannons firing ("windows on the stage should be open to let out the smoke"), and a backdrop was painted with the appearance of a town on fire. "When the curtain rises in the fifth," Burk wrote, "the appearance of the whole is good—Charlestown on fire, the breastwork of wood, the Americans appearing over the works and the muzzles of their guns, the English and American music, the attack of the hill, the falling of the English troops, Warren's half descending the hill and animating the Americans, the smoke and confusion, all together produce an effect scarce credible."[26]

Americans had never seen anything quite like it before. Traditionalists such as William Dunlap dismissed it as so much "smoke, noise, and nonsense," and lamented that bad theater was driving out the good. A rival company in Boston attempted to recover lost audiences by featuring an erupting volcano in its next production. But Burk knew his Lockean psychology, and had absorbed the French Jacobins' approach to theater earlier in the decade. This was sheer spectacle, bringing in people who had "never before seen the inside of a Theatre," whom Dunlap described as a "mere rabble," and filling them with patriotic fervor. And this, Burk was convinced, was the beginning of a truly national American theater, the kind which he and his fellow radicals had hoped to create in Ireland. "If it succeed," wrote one critic shortly before the play's first performance, "of which there scarce remains a doubt, we may hope to see the long list of London Comedies, which teem with low and vulgar obscenity, and are calculated only to please the corrupted manners of a licentious metropolis, banished from our stage." Six years later, Burk's old friend Denis Driscol suggested to the Thespian Corps of Baltimore that they leave aside "the dramatical representation of chimerical scenes and love intrigues," and put on instead *Bunker-Hill,* a play which "corresponds with our notion of patriotism and humanity."[27]

As it turned out, however, Burk never repeated the stunning success of his first play. He followed it up in 1798 with *Female Patriotism, or the Death of*

Joan D'Arc, which plummeted to new literary depths. Burk had clearly exhausted his limited stock of creativity; phrases, images and dramatic techniques from *Bunker-Hill* were recycled, a whole section from Shakespeare's *Henry VI* was brought in to supply the imaginative deficit, and the plot was crude and inconsistent. Recreating the past in the image of the present, Burk transformed the medieval French into modern revolutionaries. The leaders of the French camp spoke the language of liberty, equality and fraternity, believed that government should rest on Rousseauist notions of the "general will," and would willingly have established a republic had the people only been enlightened enough to accept one.[28]

The theme that the people were not yet ready for republicanism—a problem with which the United Irishmen had grappled earlier in the decade—was brought out most clearly in the actions and attitudes of Joan herself. As the "British" (another of Burk's anachronisms) were closing in on the French, Joan rallied the troops by announcing that the future had been revealed to her:

> God's mother deigned to appear to me,
> And in a vision, full of majesty:
> Wish'd me to leave my base vocation;
> And free my country from calamity.
> Her aid she promis'd and assur'd success.

Once victory had been secured, however, she revealed the truth; her story about the vision was actually a "pious fraud" to "raise the fainting courage of the land." Joan's inspiration, it transpired, came from the secular source of patriotism and the "innate exertions" of the human mind; she had been educated in the principles of classical republicanism, and had long denounced the "crimes of tyranny and kings."[29]

Joan had, in effect, become a revolutionary heroine, whose mission had a much deeper purpose than first appeared. Amid shouts of "*Liberty and equality,*" she explained her purpose to the people:

> 'Tis not to crown the Dauphin prince alone
> That hath impell'd my spirit to the wars,
> For that were petty circumstance indeed;
> But on the head of every man in France
> To place a crown, and thus at once create
> A new and mighty order of nobility,
> To make all free and equal, *all men kings,*
> Subject to justice and the laws alone:
> For *this great purpose* have I come amongst you.

Because the people were only just emerging from "the darkness of the middle age," she explained, the day of liberty had not yet dawned. But dawn it inevitably would; seeing far into the future, Joan revealed that "a virtuous band of English colonists" in an unknown land far across the sea would "first throw down the gauntlet to Kings," and that "France would follow her example: shall overturn all thrones, and exterminate all tyrants." "Your country," she prophesied, "will one day become a mighty Republic, in the glory and immensity of which all former governments will be lost."[30]

Now, much of this was simply bad writing. Burk wanted to end the play with a ringing declaration of republicanism, and Joan was the obvious person to make it. In giving Joan supernatural powers of prophecy, however, Burk contradicted his earlier depiction of her as a secular patriotic heroine. But there was more to it than bad writing. In effect, Burk was attempting to give the audience his own "pious fraud" that would raise the fainting republican spirits in Federalist America. And in moving so easily and effortlessly between Joan's initial deception of the people and her higher goal of human emancipation, Burk revealed and reflected the United Irish willingness to employ dubious means (including pseudo-religious prophecies) in the service of democratic ends.

Flushed with the success of *Bunker-Hill,* Burk expected great things from his new play. "Such a drama," he wrote, "ought to elevate the minds of the audience to enthusiasm, and literally drown the stage with tears." In fact, it was hissed off the stage, and Joan's prophecy in particular was greeted with derisory laughter; the play was pulled after only one night, never to be performed again. This was not so much a reaction to the writing—*Bunker-Hill,* after all, had been a success—as a question of technique, theme and timing. *Female Patriotism* lacked the spectacular special effects of *Bunker-Hill,* and was weakened by poor performances from the male actors, whose talents were not quite up to the material. While *Bunker-Hill* had tapped into indigenous American patriot traditions, *Female Patriotism* identified liberty with the French Revolution, at a time when Franco-American relations were deteriorating rapidly. The play came out on April 13, 1798, only a few days after the publication of the XYZ dispatches meant that American patriotism now defined itself against revolutionary France. Not even a good pro-French play could have withstood the wave of American anger; *Female Patriotism* did not stand a chance.[31]

This was not, however, the end of Burk's career as a playwright. After he moved in 1801 to Petersburg, a town with a long theatrical tradition, Burk became a leading figure in the local dramatic society. The only extant play from that period is his *Bethlem Gabor,* which drew on William Godwin's 1799 novel *St. Leon* for its setting and characters, not to mention its dialogue. But where Godwin's novel was a complex and imaginative study of the interaction between socio-historical forces and human consciousness, Burk's play was just silly. The plot was full of inconsistencies, there were loose threads hanging all over the place, and the story was so predictable that Burk's earlier membership in the Telegraphic Society begins to take on an entirely different meaning.[32]

Bethlem Gabor was the early nineteenth-century equivalent of a Hammer Horror movie. It featured a physically disfigured and emotionally lacerated Transylvanian lord (played by Burk himself), who was consumed by hatred and revenge after the murder of his family. It moved through a world of ventriloquism and seemingly magical mirrors, as it took the audience into underground vaults, secret passages and dungeons. And it concluded with the obligatory battle scene, complete with cannons, music and smoke, and Turkish invaders flying off in all directions at once, swiftly followed by the amazing resurrection of Bethlem's wife and children, who had been "miraculously preserved" to provide the equally obligatory happy ending.[33]

The most fascinating thing about this High Gothic production is the way in which Burk, following Godwin, occasionally stumbled across important insights about the human condition, only to ignore their deeper significance. One theme of the play concerned the destructive and cyclical nature of vengeance; the thirst for revenge was tearing Bethlem Gabor apart and threatening the lives of innocent and [illegible] people around him. There was also a fleeting sense that the oppressed can behave as badly as the oppressor. "Will Bethlem Gabor," asks one character, "who has suffered so much from the tyranny of the world, will he imitate its tyranny, its injustice, by which his happiness has been overthrown?" But the question was left hanging, and quickly disappeared in the smoke and mirrors of the melodrama. And it was certainly not something that Burk ever asked about himself or his fellow United Irishmen, despite—or possibly because of—its obvious relevance to the Irish revolution. As far as Burk was concerned, the United Irishmen were Good and their enemies were Evil, and that was the end of it. In that sense, the dominant tone was struck not by a passing question in *Bethlem Gabor,* but by the ringing words at the end of *Female Patriotism:*

> Frenchmen to arms,
> Gird on your swords, and put your armour on.
> The spirit of the lovely Joan of Arc,
> Doth hover o'er the field, and shrieks for vengeance.[34]

Similarly, Burk's treatment of Bethlem's madness raised important but unexplored questions about the relationship between private feelings and public behavior. Devastated by the murder of his family and living in a hell of the mind, Bethlem learned that the Austrians and Turks were attacking his castle. He wanted to die, and decided to die fighting the foe. And so, he charged out: "Speak of the former glory of Hungary, and its present debasement," he declared, "—repeat the bloody tyranny of the Austrians and Turks—breathe into their souls, the flame of liberty! Liberty! Liberty or death!" The intensity of Bethlem's patriotism stemmed from his inner torment, and his courage in battle sprang from a death wish. This opens up the larger issue of the extent to which people who shout "Liberty or death!" are actually projecting their personal crises onto the public stage. But the opportunity for a discussion of motivation, of the relationship between the private and public spheres, was totally ignored. Burk was more interested in setting the scene for Bethlem's role in the battle than in exploring the psychology of militant patriotism.[35]

Despite Burk's consistent avoidance of anything that smacked of self-examination, his whole approach to art rested on the general assumption that emotions were the best route to Reason. He was not, of course, alone in this view; Noah Webster, for example, maintained that "the *heart* should be cultivated with more assiduity than the *head*." On both sides of the Atlantic, radical democrats believed that music, along with theater, was one of the most effective ways of reaching the heart and instilling a sense of patriotism. Benjamin Rush argued that "vocal music" played an important role in "civilizing the mind, and thereby preparing it for the influence of religion and government." In Ireland, the United Irishmen had pressed music into the cause of nationalism and republicanism. Robert Simms, later described by Lord Castlereagh as a traitor of the "deepest cast," had been among the organizers of the Belfast Harpers' Festival of 1792, which had been timed to coincide with the city's Bastille Day celebrations; the idea was to stimulate a sense of patriotism by reviving the "Ancient Music and Poetry of Ireland." Later in the decade, revolutionary songs became an integral part of the United Irish movement, and were an essential ingredient in political meetings from Dublin to London; to this day, one still hears references to the "musical wing of the national struggle."[36]

It is not surprising, then, that United Irish émigrés carried this tradition over to the United States, and turned it into an expression of American nationalism. Almost inevitably, the center of this enterprise was Burk's Petersburg, Virginia. When the Scottish traveler John Melish passed through the town for an overnight coach stop in 1806, he was immediately taken to a music session, where a "liberal circle" of "agreeable young men" (almost certainly including Burk himself) mixed jigs and strathspeys with American tunes like "Yankee Doodle." By the time he got back on the coach, he was in a euphoric mood about the "spirit of unity" and the "bond of peace" that drew people together in the United States. He was also left with the mistaken but understandable impression that the town was composed almost entirely of Irish people. Although this was something of an exaggeration, the town was indeed a magnet for United Irishmen; "they are distinguished for frank liberal manners and high-spirited patriotism," commented Melish.[37]

One of Burk's closest friends in Petersburg was another United Irish exile, John McCreery. Inspired by the example of Scotland's Robert Burns and

Ireland's Thomas Moore, Burk and McCreery set out to publish a songbook that would combine traditional Irish melodies with modern American words; they intended to transform the airs of Ireland into the national music of the new republic. Although Burk was killed before the project could be completed, McCreery carried on by himself. Other United Irishmen in the town offered their encouragement; one of them, Thomas Robinson, wrote the introduction to the collection when it was finally published in 1824.[38]

By far the most successful product of this venture was McCreery's "The American Star," composed in 1810 and set to the tune of "Captain O'Kane." During the War of 1812, it became one of the most popular songs in the country, rivaling "The Star Spangled Banner" in the patriotic repertoire. At the same time, Irish marches were being incorporated into the music of the American militia. In New York, traditional Irish tunes were given modern American titles, such as "Governor Tompkins's Quick Step." The same process was occurring elsewhere in the United States: "If an Irishman was there," remarked Driscol after observing a general muster in Augusta, "to be sure the cockles of his heart would not be raised to see Americans march to Irish music!"[39]

And here we have the perfect metaphor for United Irish cultural and political activities in the United States. In their approach to education, literature, history, theater and music, as in their approach to politics, the United Irishmen were putting American words to Irish music. Precisely because it was the words that were most audible and visible, the origin and nature of the underlying melodies can easily be overlooked. It was not immediately apparent, for example, that Burk's historical and dramatic writings, or Carey's economic and cultural nationalism, or Sampson's opposition to the common law, followed melodic patterns that had been marked out in Ireland; the American content obscured the Irish form. But the Irish music was there nonetheless, beneath the surface of the words, resonating deeply within the consciousness of the new republic, and transforming itself into something that was no longer Irish. This was the case not only with culture and politics, but also with religion—and especially with the matter of millenarianism, as it was carried across the Atlantic by radical Presbyterian ministers such as Thomas Ledlie Birch.

CHAPTER SIX

Signs of the Times

In 1775, shortly after the outbreak of Anglo-American hostilities at Lexington and Concord, the Reverend Ebenezer Baldwin delivered a sermon in Danbury, Connecticut, which attempted to guide his congregation through the troubled times that had befallen the country. The American colonies, he explained, were "the Foundation of a great and mighty Empire; the largest the World ever saw, to be founded on such Principles of Liberty and Freedom, both civil and religious, as never before took place in the World; which shall be the principal Seat of that glorious Kingdom, which Christ shall erect upon Earth in the latter Days." Baldwin estimated that the American population was around three million, and that it was doubling every twenty-five years. Projecting these figures into the future, he predicted that by the year 1975 the North American continent would contain 192 million people, who would be brought up in accordance with the fundamental principles of civil and religious liberty. By this time, the Old World would be up to its neck in tyranny, luxury and corruption; there could be no doubt that "Liberty, as well as Learning and Religion, has from the Beginning been travelling Westward." From his reading of the Bible and the calculations of his contemporaries, Baldwin was convinced that the millennium was scheduled to begin on or about the year 2000. "And since it is in the last Ages of the World that America is to enjoy this prosperous State, and as this is the Time, in which Christ's Kingdom is to be thus gloriously set up in the World," he concluded, "I cannot think it chimerical to suppose, America will largely share in the Happiness of this glorious Day, and that the present Scenes are remotely preparing the Way for it."[1]

Such views were by no means confined to Ebenezer Baldwin; many of his fellow ministers believed that the American Revolution represented the fulfillment of prophecies in the Book of Revelation, and convinced themselves that the Americans were the new Chosen People. With the outbreak of the French Revolution in 1789, similar apocalyptic visions appeared in Europe; the secular millenarianism of Paine's *Rights of Man* fused with the religious prophecies of James Bicheno's *The Signs of the Times* to create a highly charged sense of impending and cataclysmic change. In London, Richard Brothers began to distribute enormously influential millenarian tracts that predicted the success of the French revolutionary armies, and prophesied that London would be destroyed for its wickedness by an earthquake on the king's birthday in 1795. On the appointed day, the city was hit by the one of the worst thunderstorms in its history; when John Binns took shelter in a public house, he found fifty terrified people praying for deliverance. He later met Brothers, who explained that "the earthquake had, at his earnest and oft-repeated intercession, been by the Almighty, postponed, and the destruction of London averted." Even such rationalist philosophers as Joseph Priestley and Richard Price were highly receptive to the millenarian mood in the air, and believed that the American and French Revolutions were part of the divine plan to destroy the forces of Antichrist.[2]

Similar sentiments surfaced in Ireland, where United Irish ideology was permeated by intimations of the apocalypse. Radical Presbyterian ministers rejoiced that the French Revolution would sweep away all church-and-state establishments and pave the way for a new political and religious era. Samuel Neilson's *Northern Star* advertised Bicheno's *Signs of the Times,* praised its contents, and recommended it to the "friends of liberty." "Christ in Triumph, Coming to Judgment!" ran a religious prophecy that was circulating in County Tyrone in 1797. "As Recorded in the Most Holy Sacred Scriptures, by the Holy Prophets and Evangelists, Predicting, that there will be great wars and commotions in several parts of the world. . . . Likewise, Foretelling the utter destruction of the Heathens and Turks." In the tense and volatile atmosphere of the time, the political implications were clear to the authorities and revolutionaries alike. "The ignorant country people," commented the magistrate who discovered the handbill, "will take many meanings out of it, that suit their present way of thinking."[3]

As the millenarian spirit spread, it caught not only the rural population but also the United Irishmen and their supporters in the United States. "Hail auspicious day," proclaimed one such figure in Boston, when he learned of the 1798 Rising; "welcome, thrice welcome this political millenium!!!" Not even deists were immune: Denis Driscol, needling his religious opponents in America, argued that Daniel and John were Jacobins before their time and would have been prosecuted for sedition by the British government had they been alive during the 1790s. But no one exemplified the Irish-American character of the millenarian impulse more clearly than the revolutionary United Irishman and Presbyterian minister from Ulster, Thomas Ledlie Birch.[4]

For the most part, Birch is a forgotten figure today; historians of the period rarely mention him at all, and often get him wrong when they do. The only person to compile a selection of Birch's writings, Brendan Clifford, took as the centerpiece of his work a pamphlet entitled "The Causes of the Rebellion in Ireland"; this would have come as a surprise to Birch, since he did not actually write it. Similarly, one of the few historians to comment on Birch's reaction to the Second Great Awakening in America mistakenly placed him in the Revivalist camp by attributing to him another pamphlet he did not write. Birch would also have been somewhat depressed to discover in the *Dictionary of National Biography* that he died in 1808, since he actually lived for another twenty years. Birch's Irish historians have ignored his American career, just as the small number of American historians who know about him have ignored his Irish background. Yet he was the minister of one of the largest Presbyterian congregations in Ireland, the founder of the United Irishmen in County Down, and a stormy figure in western Pennsylvania whose activities generated intense controversy within the American church. His career reveals a great deal about transatlantic Presbyterianism in general and its millenarian component in particular.[5]

Brought up in the Presbyterian heartland of County Down, Birch followed a well-trodden path to Glasgow University in 1770, where around one-third of the students came from Ireland. Among his professors was Thomas Reid, the self-styled "True Whig" and founder of the Common Sense school of thought, whose theoretical emphasis on benevolent feelings did not stop him from complaining about the "stupid Irish teagues" who attended his classes. Another was John Millar, the radical social philosopher whose son would dream of establishing a New Caledonia in the New World. Closely associated with the New Light, liberal-rationalist wing of Presbyterianism, Glasgow University sent a steady stream of students back into Ulster's Presbyterian church. Known as the "young fry," these Glasgow-educated ministers gradually effected a kind of quiet revolution in the Synod, which became increasingly New Light in character toward the end of the century.[6]

Along with several other Irish students, Birch belonged to a "little debating club" in Glasgow that was continued in Ireland after they graduated. More impressed by the political than the religious liberalism of Glasgow, he remained theologically orthodox; he referred to himself as an "old side Presbyterian," and was described by a friend as being "truly Calvinistick." Birch was equally opposed to the "heresies" of Arianism and Unitarianism on the one hand, and the emotionalism of evangelicalism on the other. At the same time, he believed that true religion could only flourish under conditions of civil liberty, and strongly opposed aristocratic power in church and state. Such a combination of religious conservatism and political radicalism was not at all uncommon; David Miller has shown that about half of the Presbyterian clergymen who were accused of rebellion in 1798 belonged to the Old Light camp.[7]

Birch already had a reputation for radicalism when he was ordained as the minister of Saintfield, County Down, in May 1776. He and his congregation held fasts "for the humiliation of Britain in desolating America" during the War of Independence. When, in 1784, the Yankee Club of Stewartstown congratulated Washington on his victory, Birch ensured that the correspondence was published in the *Belfast Mercury*. As the chaplain of the Saintfield Light Infantry, he was on the radical wing of the Volunteer movement, and welcomed its principal achievements: freedom of trade, the easing of civil disabilities facing Presbyterians and Catholics, and the assertion of legislative independence. Such reforms were steps in the right direction, Birch believed, but needed to be taken further; the task ahead was to democratize the legislature and to abolish all remaining religious discrimination in the country. And yet, during the late 1780s, he came to feel that even the limited gains of the Volunteers were being rolled back. Instead of carrying on the fight, he complained, the leaders had deserted the people, and had put their pocketbooks above the patriot cause.[8]

All this was changed, in Birch's view, by the French Revolution, with its message that everything was possible, that for a people to be free it was sufficient that they will it, that the days of hereditary rule and episcopal privilege were numbered. Twenty-two million Catholics in France, he argued, had demonstrated that they were capable of winning and enjoying their own freedom; at the same time, "the worthy generous Roman Catholic of Ireland, long ignorant and treated like a stranger in his own country, is now become as enlighten[e]d as others." Preaching the gospel of liberty to the United Irishmen in Saintfield, arguing for Catholic emancipation at public meetings in Belfast, delivering anti-war sermons to the Freemason Lodges of County Down, Birch was convinced that the time was right for political revolution in Ireland and that the work of the Volunteers could finally be completed.[9]

Under these circumstances, Birch's radicalism rapidly assumed millenarian dimensions. The first glimpse of this outlook appeared in November 1792, amid celebrations in Antrim and Down for the French victory over the Prussian invaders at Valmy, the battle that saved the Revolution. "Having such mighty and [a]stonishing events presented to our view," he wrote, "certainly without being chargeable with a spirit of enthusiasm, we might be led to assert, that the fall of the beasts as described in the revelation, or of unreasonable civil, and religious tyranny, and the peaceful reign of a thousand years, or something like them, are fast approaching." These views found their fullest expression in a remarkable sermon that Birch delivered to the General Synod of Ulster in June, 1793, at the invitation of the Moderator, his fellow United Irishman William Steel Dickson. Here, he argued that gospel ministers must lead exemplary lives in "this *Important Period,* when the Prophecies are Seemingly about To Be Fulfilled in the Fall of Antichrist." Above all, he believed, this involved a serious and sustained effort to bring the system of government into line with the principles of Christianity.[10]

"It is the duty of Ministers of Religion, who would let their light shine before others," he declared, "to bear public testimony against, and to endeavour to Reform the corruptions of the State." The "salvation of souls," Birch argued, was impossible without the eradication of "public corruption." Ministers must therefore "adopt the precepts of Religion as a standard, by which to judge the conduct of their Governors." And they must apply equally rigorous criteria to themselves: "A Christian, and especially a Teacher," he reminded his fellow ministers, "must be eminent for his spotless life, no lewd debauchee, attentive to his sacred calling, of becoming humility, accommodating in his behaviour, charitable to those in distress, no drunkard, no quarreler, or contentious person, scorning little petty chichanery [*sic*] and double dealing. . . ." As they walked in the way of the Lord, and worked for civil and religious liberty, they must display an inflexible integrity: "We must brave all opposition, and take up our cross and follow our Redeemer through good and evil report, to the loss of our substance, good name, or even life."[11]

This determination was all the more important, in Birch's view, given the political changes that portended the millennium. "We live," he said, "in a very advanced and enlightened period of the world, when ignorance and superstition are falling like lightning from Heaven, and knowledge is making very rapid strides." The power of the Antichrist, symbolized by the Beasts in the Book of Revelation and surviving in the "spiritual tyranny" of church-and-state establishments, was already on the wane, he argued. Working through the scriptures to decode their hidden messages, he concluded that the Beasts had been destined to experience "some remarkable *Fall*" between 1760 and 1790.[12]

There was overwhelming evidence, Birch was convinced, that recent events matched ancient prophecies. The American Revolution had struck a blow for civil and religious liberty in the New World, and papal authority was waning in the Old. In Birch's view, the war between revolutionary France and the counter-revolutionary European powers was nothing less than the ultimate cosmic struggle between God and Satan. "We may observe in a *certain Contest,*" Birch informed his audience, "that seemingly literal accomplishment of the Prophecy of the Battle of Armageddon, in which the Beast and his Adherents are to be cut off, as a prelude to the peaceful Reign of a Thousand Years." Not only that, but Birch believed that he had actually discovered the very year when the millennium would begin; through a close analysis of the Books of Revelation and Daniel, he pinned it down to "the Year Eighteen Hundred and Forty-eight, or nearly Fifty-five Years hence."[13]

It is not recorded how his sermon was received. But we do know that the

General Synod was deeply divided between radicals and conservatives; if some ministers nodded their heads in agreement, others must have squirmed in their seats. Significantly, all six of Birch's attempts to become Moderator were rejected; his politics were too extreme, and his personality rubbed too many people the wrong way. Within his own congregation at Saintfield, where he lived on "Liberty Hill," he generated extreme reactions. Although the majority strongly supported him, a significant minority found his views so offensive that they left the church and joined the Seceders, a rival Presbyterian denomination. While Birch combined democratic politics with doctrinal orthodoxy, the Seceders were on the conservative evangelical wing of Ulster Presbyterianism; they were generally (but not exclusively) loyalist in politics, and appealed more to the emotions than the intellect in their religion. The Seceders had been expanding rapidly in late eighteenth-century Ulster, and were now making inroads into Birch's Saintfield congregation. And this was something that he was determined to stop.[14]

Birch attacked the Seceders with concentrated fury in a pamphlet that quickly went into nine editions, *Physicians Languishing Under Disease.* He saw himself as one of "the Soldiers to be employed by the *Great Captain of our Salvation in that Glorious conflict,* in which he is finally to defeat *the Devil and all his Agents,*" and would give no quarter on the battleground of Saintfield. The Seceders, he argued, exploited and fomented divisions within congregations to advance their own creed; they were "like the archapostate, who seduced our first parents." Instead of practicing the Christian virtues of love and reconciliation, wrote Birch, they were a destructive force that disgraced true religion. "The name Seceder! cheat! hypocrite! defamer! reviler! disturber of the church's peace! destroyer of the happiness of families!" he exclaimed, "are now reckoned . . . to be words of the like import!"[15]

While orthodox Presbyterians emphasized the importance of an educated ministry, Birch continued, the Seceders rushed their students through university, and then had the nerve to present themselves as the "*the destined propagators of the only true religion.*" In place of the sober and serious worship of God, they attracted crowds by creating religious fairs, in which meeting tents were surrounded by "*stalls of merchandize,*" some of which even sold liquor. This, Birch believed, was a species of profanation, which mocked the religious principles it pretended to propagate. To make matters worse, the Seceders had accused him of being soft on Catholicism, and had petitioned the government in 1783 and 1784 against parliamentary reform. There was only one way to deal with such people; if they did not change their ways, the Seceders must be treated as "the outcasts of society!" "If you have received any wounds in our conflict," he told his antagonists, "blame not me; I was only upon my own defence: You threw the first and second stones."[16]

As well as fighting the Seceders, Birch became increasingly embroiled in conflicts with the loyalists in his district. In 1797, eleven members of his congregation were arrested for attacking the house of Hugh McKee, a local farmer who opposed the United Irishmen and kept the authorities informed about their activities. When he attended the trial, Birch himself was arrested for comments he had supposedly made the previous fall, promising to join a French invasion of Ireland and warning a conservative neighbor that the price of resisting liberty would be death. Meanwhile, a loyalist member of his congregation, Joseph Harper, claimed that Birch had offered him a fifty-pound bribe to stop informing on the United Irishmen, and claimed that the minister had incited a mob to attack his home. Birch was acquitted on the charge of supporting the French. Harper's case was deferred until the spring of 1798, but it never came to court, for Harper was assassinated on the Belfast-Saintfield road a few days before the trial. In his own account of these events, Birch omitted this minor detail, remarking only that he was "acquitted for want *of prosecution,* and discharged after being exposed to enormous *expence and trouble.*" As far as his enemies were concerned, the "cloven-footed Preacher" had cheated justice; the incident was still fresh in their minds when the Rising broke out a few weeks later.[17]

On Saturday, June 9, Birch and many of his "hearers" joined the insurgents who were gathering at Saintfield; six weeks earlier, he had been elected chaplain of the United army. One of the first acts of the revolutionaries was to settle old scores with Hugh McKee. In what has been described as the only United Irish atrocity in County Down, the McKees' house was burned down with the entire family inside. Birch's own reactions were ambivalent; he condemned the attack as "a piece of inconsiderate rash folly," implied that McKee brought it on himself by shooting at peaceful passers-by, and then added that the man who led the atrocity turned out to be a zealous loyalist. A few hours later, Birch witnessed the battle of Saintfield, when the United army defeated the Yorkshire Fencibles and captured their weapons; the victory, he later wrote, "shews what the determined spirit of freemen can effect." The following day, Pike Sunday, as it became known, he preached to his troops at Creevy Rocks. According to local tradition, his text was Ezekiel IX, 1: "Cause them that have charge over the city to draw near, even every man with his destroying weapon in his hand." As a student of American guerrilla warfare and an admirer of Washington's military tactics, he urged the revolutionary leader Henry Munro to consolidate his forces near Saintfield, on terrain that would favor the insurgents. His advice went unheeded; on Monday, June 11, the United army marched to Ballynahinch, and Birch marched with them.[18]

His movements over the next two days are unclear; he claimed to be back in Saintfield, burying the soldiers. There is no evidence that he was in Ballynahinch on Wednesday, June 13, when General Nugent's soldiers took the town after the fiercest battle in the north, and the cavalry swept through the countryside in a rage of repression. Three days later, in the early hours of the morning, Birch was seized by the dragoons and bundled off to Lisburn, where a military court tried him for treason and rebellion. Among other things, he was charged with seditious preaching, "setting forth from Scripture prophecy," as he put it, "the extension of the redeemer's Kingdom over the whole Earth; and the establishment of a peaceful happy State, when every power in opposition to Christ's Kingdom would be put down and wars would cease."[19]

More immediately, the court-martial accused him of encouraging the rebels as they assembled at Saintfield. In his defense, Birch argued that he was nowhere near the United army, and brought in a host of witnesses to corroborate his story. It was not, in truth, a convincing performance. Some of the witnesses were themselves United Irish supporters, who had hidden weapons and ammunition in their houses; others gave contradictory evidence in their rush to provide alibis. As the trial progressed, his enemies confidently expected him to hang.[20]

And then, after three days of denying that he had anything to do with the United Irishmen, Birch made a remarkable statement in his closing address to the court. "Gentlemen," he said, "I may have done wrong but it was an Error. I love my King & Country & shall ever pray for their Happiness. I have the most perfect Confidence in the Justice & Humanity of this Court & most chearfully resign my Honor & Life to its Disposal." This was pure hypocrisy; having attempted to cover his actions with a smokescreen of deception, he now pretended to admit the "Error" of his ways, while professing what was in fact a thoroughly spurious loyalty. Yet it saved his life. The key to this unexpected turn of events lay with Birch's brother George, a loyalist magistrate and commander of the Newtownards yeomanry. After Thomas's arrest, George used his influence with Lords Downshire and Londonderry to reach a compromise. In return for a confession of error and a statement of loyalty, Thomas would be spared from the gallows and exiled to America.[21]

When the verdict was announced, the Orangemen in the Lisburn yeomanry were outraged. Some of them had lost friends and relatives in the Rising, reckoned that one of the principal instigators of insurrection had been spared by aristocrats who put private connections above public justice, and decided to take matters into their own hands. Immediately after the trial, while Birch was still in custody, a leading Orangeman in the yeomanry held a loaded pistol to his head and threatened to shoot him on the spot. A few days later, when Birch was being conveyed from Lisburn to Belfast, his coach was surrounded by a party of yeomen who were out for his blood. On both occasions, he was saved by the regular soldiers, who considered it a point of honor to keep their prisoners alive.[22]

He was sent to the *Postlethwaite* prison ship in Belfast Lough, where there were enough Presbyterian ministers to have formed a revolutionary denomination of their own. William Steel Dickson, who had been arrested just before the Rising, was there, along with Robert Steele from Dungiven, William Sinclair and James Simpson from Newtownards, and the licentiate David Bailie

Warden. Except for Dickson, all these men went to America, along with other radical Presbyterian ministers such as John Glendy, who became chaplain of the House of Representatives and a close friend of Jefferson and Madison. Altogether, nearly fifty Presbyterian ministers and licentiates were implicated in United Irish politics during the 1790s; three of them, James Porter, Robert Gowdy and Archibald Warwick, were executed, and a dozen wound up in the United States.[23]

It would be a mistake, however, to assume that such figures were representative of Irish Presbyterianism as a whole. On the contrary, they appear as a militant minority whose revolutionary activities were rejected by most of their fellow ministers. Within the General Synod, there were many conservatives who drew the line at reform, and many reformers who drew the line at revolution; in the aftermath of 1798, they closed ranks and condemned the Rising in the strongest possible terms. In August, the Synod issued an "Address to the People," pointing out that the Rising had resulted in death and disaster, arguing that conditions in Ireland did not justify revolution, and urging everyone to behave in a peaceful, orderly and respectful manner.[24]

At the same time, they sent a loyal address to George III, disassociating themselves from "those few unworthy members of our Body, whose conduct we can only view with grief & Indignation." They promised to do their utmost "to recall the deluded from their Errors & Crimes, to make a strict Inquiry into the Conduct of our delinquent members; and to withstand to the best of our Abilities those pernicious foreign Principles which threaten alike the Temporal and Eternal Interests of Mankind." There were purges in the presbyteries. When Warden asked the Bangor Presbytery to provide him with credentials of his licentiate status so that he could preach in America, they turned him down flat. "FAREWELL!" he exclaimed at the end of a bitter pamphlet against the "junto" who had rejected him; "that your conduct towards me, may be the last instance of your MEANNESS, *injustice,* and CRUELTY, is the sincere wish of D.B. Warden."[25]

When they crossed the Atlantic, Birch and his colleagues encountered an equally divided Presbyterian church in the United States. And in 1798, the high-point of Federalism, the conservatives were firmly in control. Shortly before their arrival, the General Assembly, which was the American equivalent of the General Synod, had issued a pastoral letter warning of the dangers of revolutionary democracy. It ran:

> When formidable innovations and convulsions in Europe threatened destruction to morals and religion, when scenes of devastation and bloodshed, unexampled in the history of modern nations, have convulsed the world, and when our own country is threatened with similar calamities, insensibility in us would be stupidity; silence would be criminal. The watchmen on Zion's walls are bound by their commission, to sound a general alarm at the approach of danger.[26]

The causes of this danger, asserted the Assembly, were rooted in a moral crisis that was spreading from Europe; "a vain and pernicious philosophy" was infecting an American society that was already steeped in corruption. "Profaneness, pride, luxury, injustice, intemperance, lewdness, and every species of debauchery and loose indulgence greatly abound," it was reported. The "solemn crisis" of the Quasi-War was interpreted as God's punishment for American irreligion. Even the Presbyterian ministers themselves were not immune; the Assembly castigated them for being apathetic and hypocritical, and for displaying "a contempt for vital godliness, and the spirit of fervent piety." What made the situation still more alarming, from this perspective, was that some of the ministers coming in from Europe were actually carrying the disease with them.[27]

Accordingly, against the background of the Alien and Sedition Acts, a majority in the General Assembly pushed through a set of "Rules and Regulations" that were designed to filter out undesirable foreign ministers from the American church. In future, a newly arrived minister would be examined on his educational background and religious faith before being allowed to join a Presbytery for a one-year probation period. The Presbytery would then conduct further tests to determine his suitability, and refer the decision back to the General Assembly for ratification. "No such minister or licentiate, after being rejected by one Presbytery," it was stipulated, "shall be received by any other"; aggrieved ministers could, however, appeal their cases to the General Assembly. The Rules were strongly attacked by the radical minority within the church; the general Federalist-Republican polarization in America was reflected in the politics of Presbyterianism. One of the centers of opposition was the Baltimore Presbytery, where such leading figures as James Muir argued the case for a more open policy. Even more outspoken in its criticism was the Presbytery of New York, which condemned the Rules as "unnecessary, unconstitutional, uncharitable, and inconsistent."[28]

Traveling through a transatlantic network of radical Presbyterians, Birch was put up in New York by Samuel Miller, a fellow minister and kindred spirit. Miller supported the French Revolution, blamed the Federalists for the Quasi-War, and shared Birch's belief that the millennium was at hand. In the same year that Birch had presented his apocalyptic sermon to the General Synod in Lurgan, Miller was delivering a similar message to the Tammany Society in New York. To establish his credentials as a Presbyterian minister, Birch brought with him testimonials from the Belfast Presbytery. One of the signatories was the radical minister and former Volunteer Sinclair Kelburn, who had just been released from Kilmainham jail after a year's imprisonment for his United Irish activities; he had toured America earlier in the decade, and was well known in Presbyterian circles on both sides of the Atlantic. Another was Alexander Henry, the minister at Castlereagh, who had been charged and acquitted of sedition in 1794.[29]

Mixing with radical Presbyterians in New York and Philadelphia, Birch denounced the General Assembly's Rules and Regulations as the religious equivalent of the Alien Law. The church's legislation, he wrote, was "a shutting out of strangers, and a declaration of war against the sister churches in the old countries." Birch was equally critical of the Assembly's comments about the pernicious influence of democratic and deistical principles in America. The real threat to religion, he argued, came from church-and-state establishments rather than deism, and Americans should direct their hostility to the source of corruption. At the same time, he attempted to break the negative political stereotype that conservative Americans held of radical immigrants. One of the main reasons that he wrote and published his *Letter from an Irish Emigrant* in 1798 was to counter the influence of those "designing men" who portrayed British and Irish democrats as bloodthirsty Jacobins. It was precisely this desire to rescue the reputation of the United Irish exiles that prompted Birch to describe them as "forming the most respectable emigration which has taken place to your United States since the settlement of the New-England Colonies."[30]

With the triumph of the Republicans in 1800, and the growing realization that the democratic movement in Ireland had been decisively defeated, Birch increasingly viewed America as his new home rather than a place of temporary exile. The United States came to represent a release from the traumas of 1798, a refuge from persecution. Although the forces of darkness had triumphed in Ireland, the people of America could walk along the broad road of civil and religious liberty. "They have no fear of loosing [*sic*] heads upon blocks, and planted upon market-houses," he wrote; "of expiring at stakes, on gibbets, or racks; or lingering in prison ships or dungeons, like their friends in the old countries; or banishment over an immense ocean, into a dreary wilderness, like their forefathers, or encountering the innumerable horrors of a late revolution. No!"[31]

Just as the country was given a new start in 1800, Birch himself was offered the opportunity of a new beginning. A number of other revolutionaries from his Saintfield congregation had resettled at Washington, in western Pennsylvania. They invited Birch to become their minister, and he duly accepted. Here, in the trans-Allegheny West, Birch and his congregation attempted to build a Christian republican community that would prepare itself for the Second Coming. And here the millenarianism that he had preached in Ireland became Americanized.[32]

Everything had been foretold in the Book of Revelation, with its mysterious visions of a woman giving birth to a man-child and of the menacing red dragon with seven heads, seven crowns and ten horns, ready to devour her offspring. God had carried the man-child to heaven, and had enabled the woman to seek sanctuary in the wilderness. To Birch, the full meaning of all this had finally become clear; the woman symbolized the church, the man-child signified a powerful and vigorous church, and the dragon represented the union of wicked spiritual power with the crowns of monarchy, the tyranny of church and state. Nor could there be any doubt about the identity of the dragon and the current whereabouts of the woman. The dragon had the mouth of a lion, and everyone knew that the lion was "the ensign of Britain." Moreover, God had given the woman the wings of an eagle to fly to the wilderness: "America, as would seem evident from the name, wilderness; America being emphatically long so styled in the old countries, and *her emblem the eagle*."[33]

Viewing the Age of Revolution through the prism of the Book of Revelation, Birch interpreted American history as the unfolding of Divine Destiny. The New World had been designed as "the place of refuge for the persecuted gospel church"; the War of Independence had been fought to protect the woman from the dragon. America, Birch exulted, was like "him who sat upon the white horse, followed by the army clothed in white, the gospel soldiers upon earth, led forth by their generals, under the supreme command of the blessed Jesus." Having withstood the onslaught of Britain, the United States could now spread the "spirit of light and reformation" across the world, and deliver a fatal blow to "civil and religious tyranny throughout the old countries."[34]

But the Beast still stalked the world, and the times remained turbulent. The forces of Antichrist had combined to defeat the French Revolution and "finally blot out liberty from the face of the earth." The dragon "hurled destruction" on all the "friends of reformation" who were within his reach, inflicting "pains.., imprisonments, banishments and tortures" upon the reformers. According to the scriptures, the dragon would become even more haughty and insolent after its wings had been plucked, just as Britain had become more aggressive after the loss of its colonies: "let it be witnessed by her conduct in different parts of the world, and particularly the influence of her wealth and merchandize in the cities of America, the insolence and tyranny of her navy to American citizens, with the impressments and piracies committed upon distressed foreign emigrants, under their protection, even in their harbours." And, "most humbling to observe," Birch continued, the dragon had insinuated himself into America itself; the activities of the Federalists and their hated Alien and Sedition Acts were proof enough of that.[35]

But the Federalists had fallen in 1800, and the days of the dragon were numbered. The "signs of the times," Birch believed, pointed to the approaching consummation of history. In Ireland, there had been reports of ghost armies marching silently across the countryside. The night sky had appeared "clothed with a mantle of blood," and on the western horizon, toward the Land of Liberty, there was "sometimes the resemblance of an immense pile of fuel, the flame just breaking out." Across the Atlantic, the first appearance of the Aurora Borealis occurred at the very time of the American Revolution: who would dare to say that this was merely a coincidence? At the beginning of the new century, when the Republicans came to power, the United States had been lit up by a ball of light ("of such notoriety as not to require any authorities to be adduced") that sped across a thousand miles in two minutes; this could only have been another sign from God. In Birch's new home, in Washington County, there had been strange pillars of light on each side of the sun. "Judicious people," he commented, "notice an uncommon change in the seasons." God was speaking through Nature; the first rumblings of the millennium were becoming audible, rolling in like the sound of distant thunder.[36]

Birch already knew that the millennium would begin in 1848; now, in America, he pinpointed the place as well. Since the gospel had traveled progressively from the east to the west, and since the eastern seaboard of America was already succumbing to "worldly refinement and pride," it seemed clear that Christ's return would take place west of the Alleghenies. Since Pennsylvania had been "most exemplary for its brotherhood," it appeared probable that God would begin the millennium in that state. And since one of the towns in western Pennsylvania had been named after George Washington, the "*illustrious founder* (under God) of American liberty," there could be little doubt that the Second Coming would occur in Washington, Pennsylvania, the very place where Birch and his fellow countrymen just happened to live. Everything was beginning to come together, to make much-needed sense. Far from being exiles on the edge of the western world, the Saintfield revolutionaries had been placed by God at the very center of the universe. Far from losing control over their lives, they were a new Chosen People.[37]

In taking this position, Birch was contributing to powerful millenarian currents in American life, which reached back to the colonial era and looked forward to the Millerites and a myriad of communitarian groups later in the century.[38] Birch's chiliasm, born in the traumas of revolutionary turmoil, had been transmitted across the Atlantic and transmuted into an American tradition. Yet it also retained its individual, idiosyncratic character. Birch combined an intense millenarian outlook with radical democratic politics and rigid Presbyterian theological orthodoxy. It was a highly volatile worldview, in which apparently insignificant events could easily assume eschatological dimensions. This grandiosity fitted in with Birch's tendency toward self-dramatization; he was very much at the center of his own universe. His own life served as a microcosm of the apocalypse; his personal vicissitudes were projected onto a cosmic canvass. The battle between Christ and Antichrist had driven him out of Ireland; God had given him, like the woman in the Book of Revelation, a sanctuary in the wilderness.

And yet the utopia that he sought proved maddeningly elusive. When he moved to western Pennsylvania, Birch ran straight into the Second Great Awakening, which was pioneered by evangelists who made the Irish Seceders pale in comparison. Birch and his congregation became embroiled in a protracted and bitter conflict with the revivalists over the religious and political identity of the American Republic. The struggle pitted recently arrived Irish immigrants against earlier settlers, Republicans against Federalists, and orthodox Presbyterians against their evangelical rivals. Its sheer intensity reflects the moral totalitarianism of the antagonists; while the evangelists saw the Great Awakening as the outpouring of the Holy Spirit in the trans-Allegheny West, Birch and his supporters viewed it as a species of religious showmanship that imperilled the millennium. This conflict was not just a local squabble among obscure people in a remote frontier region; to the participants, nothing less than the consummation of human history was at stake. Birch threw himself into the battle with such urgency that by the time it was over he had traveled four thousand miles by horseback in the American West. He argued his case so tenaciously that it dominated the proceedings of the Ohio Presbytery for several years and became a matter of central concern to the General Assembly.

The first sign of trouble came in October 1800, when Birch applied to the Ohio Presbytery (which had jurisdiction over Washington in western Pennsylvania) to be "taken under their care." He was examined according to the Rules and Regulations governing foreign ministers, rejected on the grounds that he had not demonstrated sufficient "soundness in the faith," and replaced by a revivalist minister from Virginia. Twice more Birch applied for admission to the Ohio Presbytery; twice more he was rejected. He and his congregation continued to meet anyway, pending an appeal to the General Assembly in May 1801. After hearing both sides, the General Assembly attempted to reach a compromise. The Ohio Presbytery was within its rights to decide who could preach in its jurisdiction, went the judgment, but Birch should not be prevented from being taken up by "any Presbytery, to which he may apply." Although it seemed like a reasonable decision, it pleased neither side; far from settling down, the situation became even worse.[39]

Believing that the General Assembly had fully vindicated its position and convinced that Birch was unfit for the church, the Ohio Presbytery launched an all-out attack on his character. John McMillan, a leading revivalist and prominent figure in the Presbytery, began to spread stories that Birch had been "staggering drunk upon the road" after the General Assembly meeting, and denounced his antagonist as a "Minister of the Devil." Not only was Birch a heavy drinker, his enemies in Washington reported; he "was found lying in bed with a woman" who was not his wife, and apparently had his leg over her. Rallying to his defense, Birch's congregation condemned McMillan and his supporters, and demanded that their minister be allowed to preach in Washington. Birch himself petitioned for admission into the Ohio Presbytery, on the grounds that the General Assembly had established his theological credentials, that the General Assembly was a superior body to that of its presbyteries, and that he had been allowed to apply to any Presbytery he chose. Predictably, he was rebuffed yet again.[40]

Never one to give up easily, Birch charged McMillan with "slander and unchristian threats," and insisted that the Ohio Presbytery deal with the matter. If he won the case, Birch believed, he would restore his reputation and destroy McMillan's influence in the church. McMillan was suitably unrepentant; he brought in a small army of witnesses who swore that Birch drank whiskey at breakfast, noon and night, rolled through the streets in an alcoholic stupor, and repeated the same garrulous stories over and over again. He had described Birch as a Minister of the Devil, said McMillan, because that was precisely what Birch was. McMillan carried the day; he was admonished for using "harsh and unguarded" language against Birch, but otherwise exonerated. Birch had lost the power play, and he was furious. He appealed the decision at the next General Assembly meeting in 1802, where he received the same verdict as before and was warned not to preach within the bounds of the Ohio Presbytery without permission. Undeterred, he requested such permission at the earliest possible opportunity, and was denied yet again. Birch stormed out of the meeting, declared that he would have no further dealings with the Presbytery, and initiated civil proceedings against McMillan for defamation of character. He eventually won $300 in damages, although the decision was later overturned by Pennsylvania's Supreme Court on the grounds that civil courts had no jurisdiction over ecclesiastical affairs.[41]

Meanwhile, Birch's future prospects in the Presbyterian church were becoming bleaker. When he applied for permission to preach in the nearby Huntingdon Presbytery, he was turned down because of rumors emanating from Ohio about his "moral character." At the same time, his intransigence began to alienate some of his most influential allies: the fact that he had openly defied the General Assembly by continuing to preach in the Ohio Presbytery only strengthened the arguments of his enemies. The crunch came in 1803, when the Assembly debated his case for two full days. As it became clear that his position was hopeless, Birch "withdrew in a contemptuous manner, signifying his intention to decline the jurisdiction of the General Assembly." In response, the Assembly expelled him from the church, and left him to fend for himself. Five years after arriving in the Land of Liberty, Birch had apparently lost everything: his career, his reputation, and his dreams of making Washington a fit site for the Second Coming.[42]

At one level, the conflict between Birch and McMillan can be explained as a clash of powerful personalities, a fight between two men who were more similar than they cared to admit. Both men knew that they were right, believed that compromise contradicted integrity, and were outspoken in the denunciation of their enemies. As far as McMillan was concerned, Birch was outspoken in every sense of the word; on one occasion, McMillan told an acquaintance that Birch was "an everlasting talker, and [he] hated to be in his [Birch's] company." The same charge had been leveled in Ireland, where he was known as "Blubbering Birch." If he talked in the same way that he wrote, the accusation was not without foundation. But the clash of personalities only exacerbated deeper divisions between the two men and their respective followers over larger questions of religion and politics. And these divisions mirrored and magnified the earlier struggle between Birch and the Seceders in Saintfield.[43]

The central, inescapable issue facing the Presbyterian church at the turn of the century was the religious revival that was sweeping through the West. It began in Kentucky and Virginia, where fire-and-brimstone Presbyterian preachers like James McGready combined verbal terrorism about the horrors of hell with the promise of eternal joy for those who experienced the new birth. In sharp contrast to the intellectual and frequently dull style of traditional Presbyterian preaching, the revivalists offered an orgy of emotion. Among other things, they pioneered camp meetings, which attempted to create a total religious environment conducive to mass conversions. From Cane Ridge, Kentucky, to western Pennsylvania, the results were astounding; thousands of people experienced the new birth amid an ecstasy of fits, fallings, groans, barking, dancing and leaping. Young children, apparently possessed by the Holy Spirit, exhorted the adults to repent and open their hearts to God. Amazed audiences heard children spontaneously reciting whole chapters of the Bible and women speaking in tongues. No one seemed immune; even some of the orthodox ministers who intellectually rejected the "excesses" of the revival succumbed to it themselves, and fell crying and groaning to the ground. The evidence appeared overwhelming; the word of God was spreading like wildfire throughout the West.[44]

In the Ohio Presbytery, McMillan and his supporters were at the heart of the revival. From their "College of Grace" at Cannonsburg, they issued certificates of "real conversion" to people who would continue the work of proselytization. Most of the church elders in the region were ordained by McMillan, and shared his belief that the Holy Spirit could directly and immediately operate on the minds of sinners. The Ohio Presbytery, Birch observed, was full of revivalists who took Paul's conversion as their model, and who portrayed the terrors of hell in lurid colors to the "shrieks and groans of the seemingly terrified audience." There was also a sense in which the revivalists connected the Awakening with the development of a distinctive western identity. One church elder informed Birch about the "common sentiment that the Ministers raised upon the west of the mountain, were not only equal in oratory to those upon the east side, but had the inward part the other wanted." The revival, from this perspective, was a declaration of western cultural independence.[45]

Not surprisingly, such "extraordinary" and "unusual" events generated considerable controversy within the Presbyterian church. After initial misgivings, a majority of the General Assembly welcomed the "outpouring of the Divine Spirit" as an antidote to the "infidelity" that had threatened to take over the country. But deep divisions remained. Rationalist preachers denounced what they saw as the dangerous emotional extravagances of the Awakening; the revivalists accused their opponents of being closet deists. Major disputes blazed up over the ordination of new ministers. To meet the new demand and to care for the converted, the revivalists began to license preachers from their congregations. Their opponents complained that the traditional Presbyterian emphasis on an educated ministry was being undermined, and that well-established rules were now being broken. Each side strongly and sincerely believed that the other was full of hypocrites. Throughout the West, congregations split over the revival; rival factions jockeyed for control of churches, and excluded their enemies if they could. The center could not hold; in a crisis of unprecedented growth, the church was hit by a series of schisms.[46]

In this context, Birch's experiences in western Pennsylvania appear much more intelligible. In Ireland, he had attacked the Seceders for their emotionalism, their religious fairs, and their supposedly lax approach to an educated ministry. In America, he encountered the same tendencies writ large. Even though he had been the minister of one of the largest Presbyterian congregations in Ireland for over twenty years, he was rejected by the Ohio Presbytery because he could not demonstrate that he had directly experienced the new birth. Meanwhile, people whom he considered ignorant laymen were being elevated to the ministry in his place. The revival, he believed, was theologically unsound and logically absurd; it confused emotional spasms with true faith, ignored the role of study and reflection in serving God, and forgot that the Divine Spirit manifested itself through people's actions over a long period of time. The revival, from this perspective, was actually the very antithesis of true religion. The subtitle of his book on the subject summed it up: "Instructors Unexperienced—Converters Unconverted—Revivals Killing Religion—Missionaries in Need of Teaching—or, *War Against the Gospel by its Friends.*" In Ireland, he had tried to turn the Seceders into the outcasts of society; in America, the revivalists succeeded in doing precisely that to Birch.[47]

But there was also an important political dimension to the conflict between Birch and McMillan, as both sides acknowledged. "Parties . . . [were] running high, (for purposes not of a religious nature)," commented Birch's supporters in their petition to the General Assembly in 1801. The following year, McMillan argued that his own examination before the Ohio Presbytery was the product of "political and ecclesiastical divisions existing in this place." And here was the problem: If the revival in the West was socially and religiously radical, it was led by political conservatives; Birch, in contrast, combined religious conservatism with political radicalism. McMillan was firmly aligned with the Federalists; during the gubernatorial election of 1808, he was a strong supporter of James Ross, whose role in the Naturalization Law of 1798 and whose efforts to prevent Jefferson's victory in 1800 had made him anathema to immigrants and Republicans alike. It was not surprising, then, that he condemned Birch's hearers as "followers of Tom Paine" and complained about Birch himself for rambling on about "the political sentiments of the Revd. Mr.

Porter," the minister who was hanged at Portaferry in 1798. Nor was it surprising that McMillan and his supporters attempted to use Birch's United Irish past against him, portraying him as a fugitive from justice and an enemy of order.[48]

Birch responded with the familiar United Irish argument that the American War of Independence and the Rising of 1798 were part of a common struggle for civil and religious liberty against the imperial power of Britain. The "justice" from which he had fled, wrote Birch, was the same "justice" that had slaughtered 50,000 American citizens, turned their churches into stables and play-houses, raped American women and murdered American prisoners. And he made no apologies for his continuing radicalism in the United States; the people must never cease to be vigilant, he declared, since "errors are never likely to be rectified by those who have an interest in preserving them." Birch had no time for those who argued that, because America had more freedom than Old World countries, the process of reform had gone far enough. The momentum must be maintained, he believed, so that Americans would be fit to meet the Messiah when he arrived, as arrive he surely must, in 1848.[49]

In the meantime, Birch remained deeply troubled by his relationship with the Presbyterian church. Despite his [illegible], he never gave up hope that he might be readmitted, and worked to counter the influence of the Federalists and evangelists in its midst. It took six years before he could bring himself to apply for reinstatement to the church, and it took two sessions of the General Assembly to squeeze a full and unreserved apology out of him. In 1810, Birch acknowledged that he had "done wrong in his conduct before the Assembly," expressed "hearty regret for his conduct," and retracted his publications against the church. Allowed to return to the fold, he was received the following year by the Baltimore Presbytery, which had long opposed both the revival and the Rules and Regulations against foreign ministers. The ministers included his fellow Irishman and radical Samuel Knox, who had heard Birch's millenarian sermon in Lurgan back in 1793. In a highly unusual and controversial move, the Baltimore Presbytery allowed Birch to stay in western Pennsylvania, so that he could preach to his flock in Washington without interference from his old enemies in the district.[50]

As he made his act of contrition before the General Assembly in 1810, Birch must have had strong memories of the similar "confession" that he made before the court-martial at Lisburn twelve years earlier. There is little doubt that his religious apology was as hollow as his political one had been. Just as he had continued to express democratic republican views after his public declaration of loyalty to the king in 1798, Birch continued to condemn in print the McMillan wing of western Presbyterianism after his declaration of penitence in 1810. The man who prided himself on his inflexible integrity in both politics and religion wound up dissembling in both areas: in Ireland to save his life, and in America to save his career.

In many respects, Birch's American career reads like a replay of Irish themes in an altered context. The same struggle for political democracy that pitted him against the loyalists in Ireland was conducted against the Federalists in America, where at least he was working with the grain of history. The same struggle to protect orthodox Presbyterianism from the Seceders in Ireland was fought against the revivalists in America, where Birch suffered a series of crushing defeats that paralleled his political experiences back home. And the millenarianism that had been central to his political and religious outlook in Ireland was carried over to the New World and charged with a new American content.[51]

The last glimpse of Birch's millenarianism appears in November 1810, shortly after his readmission to the church. Typically, it stemmed from a small event that was quickly magnified into cosmic proportions. That fall, the students at Washington College put on an exhibition in which there was fencing, boxing, fiddle music and stageplaying; there was also a comedy routine that was full of Irish jokes. In response, "Bonus Homo" complained about the sinful nature of the proceedings and the negative depiction of the Irish, adding some sarcastic remarks about the impact of the revival on western morals. His comments triggered a debate that raged through the columns of the *Washington Reporter* for two months.[52]

One of the participants was an anonymous writer from Mingo Creek, who poked fun at Birch's predictions for Washington. Tongue firmly in cheek, the writer confessed to an initial skepticism when he encountered Birch's millenarian writings; now, however, the sudden appearance of "*extraordinary reformers*" in the town had made him think again. These reformers, he continued, wanted nothing less than to revolutionize morals, religion, literature, education and government; Birch himself had been given the "political department," and was single-handedly working to force the British to change their policies so that "peace will pervade the whole world, & the long expected millenium usher forth in all its glory." Birch was "raised up for no common purposes," the writer added; he had been "urged on by the force of genius to ascend to the pulpit without waiting for the tedious process of regular authority." "Taking all these circumstances, together with others that might be mentioned, the conclusion is inevitable," he wrote. "The millenium!! Hail, happy period! Hail highly favoured Washington! Hail, 'O ye people'!!"[53]

Birch was not amused. Do not be deceived by this "facetious squib," he wrote; do not believe "that all things civil and religious are just as they ought to be." The millennium was not to be mocked by arguments that "provoke you to hold in contempt the idea of reformation" and "lull you asleep to what are really the *signs of the times*." And the signs of the time, he insisted, were clearly visible in Washington: the majority of the clergy were "avowed aristocrats," the exhibition at Washington College showed that there were "sinful pursuits in the seminary," and his own persecution revealed the vindictiveness and viciousness of the "junto" of ministers in the region.

Birch had been singled out for such treatment, he believed, because he was "an Irishman and a democrat." Without the efforts of people like himself to fight Britain's belligerence in the Atlantic, and without the thoroughgoing reformation that was ridiculed by his enemies, he continued, there was no hope for the United States in general and Washington in particular. He wrote:

> And happy will you be O ye people, should your Birches prove successful in scourging those tyrants of the world, who infest your shores, impress and murder your citizens, and menace your tranquility [*sic*]. But if on the contrary all attempts should fail, and all things among you civil and religious continue as they are; then woe to thee O Washington! woe woe woe to you O ye clergy!!! and woe to you ye people![54]

On this reading of reality, the fate of humanity, the United States, and western Pennsylvania hung in the balance, as the clock ran down to 1848 Birch continued to fight the good fight. in 1809, we find him at the Hibernian Provident Society in New York, proposing a toast to the "friends of liberty" and a "general reformation"; six years later, he praised Jackson's victory at the battle of New Orleans as a manifestation of divine providence. Birch continued to be at the center of controversy; in 1813, a widow in Washington accused him of swindling her out of a "large sum" of money, and the mud flew in all directions. After that, he begins to fade from view; he attended the General Assembly several times for the Baltimore Presbytery without attracting any attention to himself, and he carried on with his religious duties in Washington. It is most unlikely, though, that his low public profile reflected any weakening of his convictions or transition toward tranquillity; he was simply not the kind of person who would go gentle into that good night.[55]

In retrospect, Birch might seem an absurd, crankish figure, and in some respects he was. But it is dangerous to dismiss him in this way; he had been, after all, one of the most prominent Presbyterian ministers in Ireland, and an equally forceful figure in America. It is more instructive to see Birch's career as being symptomatic of deeper stresses and strains in the Age of Revolution. Both his political radicalism and his theological conservatism were deeply rooted in the northern Irish Presbyterian culture; similarly, his millenarianism combined his religious background with the secular hopes generated by revolutionary change. The traumatic events of 1798 intensified his vision of the apocalypse, and accentuated his persecution complex. It is not surprising that he projected his hopes and fears onto the American scene, where they combined and clashed with similar manifestations of political and social change, the millennial impulse and the religious revival. Nor are the issues raised by

Birch's career quite as anachronistic or bizarre as they might at first appear. Questions of political democracy, religious toleration, theological conservatism, apocalyptic visions, and the paranoid style all continue to mutate in the American mind as we move into the next millennium. And who could deny that Birch's principal target, politically conservative religious revivalism, remains a powerful presence in American life?

CHAPTER SEVEN

No Excluded Class

Although the political radicalism of the United Irishmen is not in doubt, their attitude toward social issues has been a matter of debate among historians. On the one hand, Marianne Elliott maintains that their "demand for universal suffrage did not signify any egalitarian thinking," and finds that there was "no trace of any social programme" in the movement. On the other, Jim Smyth argues that the radicals had a strong sense of conflict between the "productive" and "parasitic" classes, and contends that there was a wide spectrum of opinion about the desirability, nature and extent of social change. "It makes more sense," he writes, "to view radical ideology, as it relates to the social question, as unformed and contradictory."[1] One way to approach this debate is through the attitudes of the United Irish émigrés in the United States. As prominent radicals in Jeffersonian America, they were forced to articulate their social prescriptions for a democratic republic. Issues that had been remote and abstract in Ireland assumed an immediate and practical importance. The United States, in this sense, becomes a laboratory in which to observe the social values of the United Irishmen.

On the question of "egalitarian thinking," the American evidence is clear: one of the things that the United Irishmen most admired about the United States was its relative social equality and wide diffusion of prosperity. "It is the duty of governments," commented Burk, "instead of making inequalities greater, to lessen and correct them." There was a general consensus among the émigrés that the American government had succeeded in this task. This was, they believed, a society without beggars or aristocrats, in which the productive potential of each individual could be realized, and where people were judged by merit rather than birth. America, from this perspective, appeared as a classless society, whose central social and political principle was inclusiveness. "The elective franchise," wrote Warden, "is nearly universal, and there is no excluded class, whose irritated feelings threaten destruction to a system that subjects them to degradation."[2]

Such egalitarianism would sometimes be pushed to its extreme anti-authoritarian conclusion. "'Political leaders,'" ran one of the Hibernian Provident Society's toasts, "—May that Anti-Republican phrase be forever expunged from the vocabulary of freemen." This position grew directly out of the radicals' earlier experiences of "betrayal" in Ireland. After the defection of "a few men of the class generally called the 'great'" during the Volunteer agitation of 1783, argued an article in the *Shamrock,* Irish democrats had come to realize that the "people" must take control of their own affairs; Birch had made the same point in his survey of Irish politics.[3]

And yet, for all their commitment to inclusiveness and classlessness, the United Irish émigrés' definition of the "people" was actually quite limited. Black slaves, Native Americans, and women remained beyond the political pale, and white males who organized themselves into trade unions were regarded as a threat to the ideal of individualism. In their approach to race and gender, the United Irishmen generally proved to be cautious and conservative; a few of them also turned out to be racist and chauvinistic, even by the standards of the day. Not only did their egalitarianism stop at the boundaries of white male society, but it refused to countenance class conflict within those boundaries. The same vision of society that pitted them against any lingering "aristocratic" tendencies in America also explains their hostility to anything resembling a working-class movement within the country.

As good democrats who were steeped in the language of liberty, the United Irishmen emerged from a political culture in which slavery of all kinds was regarded as oppressive and unjust. This was particularly the case in the Presbyterian north-east, where Scottish enlightenment thought reinforced local anti-slavery traditions. Many years later, Warden still remembered John Millar's lectures on civil law at Glasgow: "the mind revolts at the idea of a serious discussion on the subject of slavery. Every individual, whatever be his country or complexion, is entitled to freedom. . . . Negro slavery is contrary to the sentiments of humanity and the principles of justice." In Belfast, Thomas McCabe, one of the founders of the United Irishmen, had organized a successful campaign against the attempt by Waddell Cunningham and other Belfast merchants to form a company that would ship slaves from Africa to the West Indies. Similarly, William Drennan in 1792 planned a boycott of sugar and rum to force West Indian planters to end the slave trade and ultimately abolish slavery itself.[4]

To a significant degree, the United Irishmen who crossed the Atlantic carried these attitudes with them. In 1810, when the *Shamrock* began carrying advertisements for slaves, one angry correspondent invoked the memory of McCabe in his protest against the practice. "Ireland justly boasts of never having participated in the slave trade," he wrote, "and I hope none of her sons in this land of freedom will countenance the dishonorable traffic." The storm of protest was so strong that the editor quickly backed down and agreed not to carry such advertisements in future. Among the New York Irish, both the Hibernian Provident Society and the Juvenile Sons of Erin delivered toasts condemning slavery and demanding its immediate abolition.[5]

Thomas Emmet's anti-slavery position was a major reason why he chose to live in New York rather than Virginia. "You know the insuperable objection I have always had to settling, where I could not dispense with the use of slaves," he told a fellow radical (who had no such scruples himself), "and that the more they abound, the stronger are my objections." Emmet's first court appearance in New York was to plead the case of a fugitive slave; he subsequently became counsel to the city's Manumission Society, although his role in the organization has sometimes been exaggerated. Among the other United Irishmen who were drawn to New York, Warden continued to argue against slavery, which he attacked as "the grand evil in the United States."[6]

From Virginia, Burk took a superficially similar view; the introduction of slaves into the colony, he wrote, had been "an evil, than which none can be conceived more portentous and afflicting." He outlined, and dismissed with disgust, the principal arguments that were used to justify this "infamous traffic": the belief that blacks were suited to work in a torrid climate; the notion that they were the descendants of Cain and thus "consigned to bondage" by God; and the view that they were intellectually inferior to whites. Acutely embarrassed by the presence of slavery in the land of liberty, he tried to convince himself that most white Virginians condemned the practice and were generally "humane and liberal masters." At the same time, he covered his discomfort by saying as little as possible on the subject; the silence is deafening.[7]

While Burk retreated into extenuation and evasion, his friend Denis Driscol moved rightward on the question of slavery at the same speed with which he had moved leftward on political matters in Ireland. When he arrived in the United States, Driscol was one of the most militant anti-slavery figures in the country; he denounced the practice as a "disgraceful *stigma*," and reminded Americans that "their *practice* is *at war* with their *theory!*" "The law of the U. States," he pointed out, "says that Liberty is established forever; and the laws of Maryland, Virginia, &c. say 'have slaves; they are your property, buy and sell them.' This appears to be a mere mockery, and an attempt to impose on the good sense of mankind."[8]

And yet, as Driscol became increasingly acculturated to white American society, such a position proved harder to sustain. "SLAVERY IS ODIOUS WHEREVER IT IS PRACTISED," he shouted in November 1802. But he added in a whisper that in the United States, "slavery is freedom, comparatively speaking." Before long, and particularly after he moved to Georgia in 1803, the whisper became louder and louder, and Driscol himself began to exhibit the same discrepancy between theory and practice that he had earlier attacked. In the introduction to his *Augusta Chronicle,* he promised to promote "republican principles" through the force of "Reason and Truth"; immediately underneath was an advertisement offering a $30 reward for a runaway slave. Then, to compound the irony, he printed an article arguing that "those who prefer liberty to slavery" in Ireland could only welcome a French invasion of the country.[9]

While Warden was translating Henri Grégoire's work on the intelligence of Negroes, Driscol's paper ran a regular column entitled "Negro Intelligence" that had a very different meaning; it presented news about the capture of runaway slaves. Despite the froth about slavery in America being comparative freedom, a typical captive was described in the column as being "very much marked on the back with the whip." Driscol's new attitude was reflected not only in such notices but also in the double standard he displayed on the issue of capital punishment. Although he did not believe in the death penalty for criminals, he proved remarkably flexible in his views when the race line was crossed. "This example," he commented after the execution of a black burglar, "it is to be hoped will be a lesson to others, and deter them from courting the rope and an untimely end."[10]

Nor was Driscol the only United Irishman who thought this way; those who settled in the South generally became slaveowners themselves. Harman Blennerhassett, for example, bought ten slaves to work for him at Belpre Island on the Ohio River; his wife, Margaret, complained bitterly that two of them had "taken advantage" of the family's distress after the Burr expedition and run away. Even while he was languishing in Richmond jail in 1807, Blennerhassett carefully noted the low price of slaves and planned to move into the market while conditions were favorable. After his release, he bought a cotton plantation with eighteen slaves in the Mississippi Territory, and remained there until the enterprise collapsed during the War of 1812. Some of the leading United Irishmen outside the South also owned slaves. Despite his radical libertarianism and his fulminations against "the foul pollution of slavery," John Binns fell into this category. But Binns's attitudes toward blacks were mild in comparison to those of his chief competitor for the Irish vote in Philadelphia, William Duane.[11]

Writing to Jefferson during the War of 1812, Duane discussed the way in which the British "have arrayed the white Protestant against the white Catholic in Ireland," and anticipated that "the enemy will endeavor to use the black population against us" in the same manner. To prevent this from happening, he argued, American whites must incorporate black slaves into the army as quickly as possible. This would not be difficult to accomplish, since "American born blacks, even in the Southern states where slavery is yet suffered, feel a sentiment of patriotism and attachment to the U.S." The slaves were attached to the country that enslaved them for three reasons, Duane wrote. First, slavery was actually "congenial to the habits of thinking and to the condition of the actual Africans and their immediate descendants"; it was, so to speak, part of their cultural heritage. Second, slaves in America were much better off than their ancestors had been back in Africa; there were echoes here of Driscol's "comparative freedom" argument. And third, the blacks liked to imitate the "manners and habits of white men," and thus imbibed the values of white patriotism.[12]

The blacks in question may have been less patriotic, however, had they known what Duane had in store for them during the war. One of the chief advantages of forming black battalions, he told Jefferson, would be "to save so many of the whites"; the blacks, who were clearly expendable, would fight and die for the liberty of whites, whose lives were much more valuable in Duane's scheme of things. Not only that, he argued, but the incorporation of black slaves into the army would be "the best force by which the refractory of their own color could be kept in subjection." Besides, it was dangerous to have the whites away in the army while the blacks were still on the plantations; under these circumstances, the blacks might feel their strength and become highly receptive to British plots for a slave rebellion. Precisely why they would want to rebel given their putative patriotism and the supposed congeniality of their condition was a question that Duane left unasked.[13]

The attitudes of the United Irishmen in the United States toward slavery, then, ran the spectrum from opposition through reluctant acquiescence to straightforward support, from the moral outrage of Emmet to the cynical manipulation of Duane. Although some of the New York Irish called for immediate emancipation, the United Irishmen in general did not align themselves with militant abolitionism. Despite anti-slavery sentiment within Ireland, and despite early signs of solidarity between Irish radicals and African Americans, it proved increasingly difficult for immigrants who sought acceptance and respectability to identify with people whom white Americans regarded as an inferior race.[14]

There was also a strand of exceptionalism within radical Irish nationalism that militated against identification with African Americans: what Liam Kennedy has called the MOPE factor in Irish politics, the view that the Irish were the Most Oppressed People Ever. Some Irish republicans argued that their sufferings at the hands of the British far exceeded anything that had been experienced by black slaves. Life for an Irishman who had been impressed into the British navy, claimed one writer in the *Shamrock,* was much worse than that of a slave on a plantation. "The negro raised in ignorance, is contented, nay often pleased with his lot," ran the argument. But the Irishman, who "possesses at least those feelings and sentiments for liberty and enjoyment which God and nature have implanted in his breast," had a much greater consciousness of his oppressed condition. Nobody, from this perspective, suffered quite like the Irish.[15]

Together with the desire for respectability and the persistence of Irish exceptionalism, the overriding United Irish commitment to national unity fostered conservative attitudes toward slavery. Believing that abolitionism would tear the country apart on sectional lines and leave the democratic republican experiment in ruins, the United Irishmen generally viewed militant anti-slavery sentiment as a dangerous and destructive force. Mathew Carey may have shared the dominant United Irish view that slavery was an "evil," but he nevertheless responded with rage to a New England newspaper article that attacked the brutal treatment of blacks in the South. Such arguments, he wrote, stemmed from an "unholy and demonaic spirit" that had been "incessantly employed to excite hostility between the different sections of the union."[16]

Rather than pressing for abolition, Carey sought to integrate slavery into his program for economic nationalism. Slave labor, he argued, could profitably be employed in Virginia cotton factories; this would not only prepare slaves for eventual emancipation, but also stimulate southern manufacturing and reduce the "jealousies and heart-burnings that prevail upon the subject of the protecting system." In this way, Carey believed, his proposal would "knit more closely the bonds of union between the different sections of the country." Nation-building came first; the slaves would have to wait until they were deemed to be ready for freedom.[17]

It had been relatively easy for the United Irishmen to condemn slavery from the safe distance of three thousand miles across the Atlantic. Once in the United States, however, they were confronted with the practical difficulty of remedying the situation. Burk had argued that abolition would occur once it was "safe and practicable" to proceed. But Warden's environmental analysis of slavery concluded that the institution had created a "vicious and degraded population" that lacked the political, educational and economic skills to cope with immediate emancipation. "Universal immediate emancipation," concurred Carey, "would be the greatest curse not merely to the masters, but to the slaves, utterly unfit as they are for such a novel situation."[18]

How, then, could slavery be abolished? The owners would not voluntarily relinquish their slaves, Carey answered; at the same time, the costs of compensation were astronomical, and the notion that the North might coerce the South was "too absurd to be discussed." That left the possibility of an armed slave uprising, which he believed the abolitionists, with all their inflammatory talk of human bondage and the right of resistance, were unwittingly encouraging. But such a rising, Carey continued, would produce a "horrible convulsion" that would destroy masters and slaves alike; visions of Saint Domingue haunted his imagination. "We may, therefore, fairly conclude the object of immediate universal emancipation wholly unattainable," he wrote, "or, if attainable, at too high a price."[19]

The irony of this position completely escaped Carey and most of his United

Irish colleagues in America. As they of all people should have known, similar arguments had been made in Ireland by Protestant loyalists against immediate universal emancipation for Catholics. Irish Catholics, it had been said, were too ignorant, impoverished and superstitious to cope with the political, economic and religious responsibilities of freedom; many loyalists viewed them as a vicious and degraded people who must be kept in check. Emmet, during his imprisonment at Fort George, had recognized the parallel: "Some supposed—what has also been asserted of the negro race—that the Irish were an inferior, semibrutal people, incapable of managing the affairs of their country." And the irony was increased by the fact that the loyalists had cast the United Irishmen in exactly the same role that the United Irishmen were now casting the abolitionists, as impractical visionaries who were oblivious to the consequences of their actions and whose policies would culminate in civil war.[20]

Given their view that slavery was evil but that its immediate abolition was impractical, some United Irishmen believed that a long-range solution could be found by encouraging the immigration of free whites into the United States. But such a policy of dilution would take many years, and still left the question of what to do with the "discharged slaves." One possibl[illegible] the "colonization" of slaves to Africa. As early as 1786, only eighteen months after his arrival in the United States, Carey had published a futuristic fantasy about the resettlement of freed slaves in Africa and the establishment of an all-white America. "Very few blacks remain in this country now," ran his imaginary report from a Charleston newspaper in 1850, "and we sincerely hope that in a few years every vestige of the infamous traffic carried on by our ancestors in the human species, will be done away." Later in life, he continued to argue that colonization schemes would bring "incalculable" benefits to both the United States and its slaves.[21]

Binns took a similar view, and insisted that all surplus government revenues be applied to the purchase and transportation of slaves to Africa. By such an act of "national justice," he wrote, Americans would remove the stain of slavery from their "free institutions," atone for the "countless evils" that had been inflicted on the blacks, and supply "Africa's benighted regions" with a stream of former slaves who had become sufficiently Americanized to enlighten and civilize the continent. There were material advantages as well; the returned slaves, Binns believed, would provide a ready market worth millions of dollars for American manufactures and produce. But all these arguments, with their twin appeals to morality and self-interest, failed to impress the southern slaveowners. On the contrary, several grand juries in South Carolina and Georgia recommended that Binns be strung up for his efforts. As for the slaves themselves, Binns never bothered to enquire whether they actually wanted to be shipped across the Atlantic to Africa; they were to be given no voice in the matter.[22]

Unable to find any viable alternatives to slavery, but unwilling to countenance immediate emancipation, the United Irishmen equivocated and temporized. If slavery could not be abolished, they argued, then it could at least be humanized. "Let not the whip and the cowskin be so constantly uplifted," advised Driscol in 1802. Rather than aggravating the situation by confronting the masters, argued Carey, opponents of slavery should appeal to their humanity and to their personal interests; through humane treatment, he wrote, the condition of the slaves would be ameliorated and the risk of a rebellion would be correspondingly reduced. But apart from demanding more enlightened attitudes from the slaveowners and hoping that slavery would eventually wither away, they felt that nothing could be done. The United Irishmen who took this position were assimilating ideas that were commonplace in white society and had previously found expression in Jefferson's *Notes on the State of Virginia;* in this, as in so much else, Irish radicals were becoming true Jeffersonians.[23]

The United Irishmen had traveled far from the abolitionist sentiment that had characterized the radical movement back home. The distance was clearly revealed during the early 1840s, when Daniel O'Connell berated Irish Americans for acquiescing in slavery. In response, Binns argued that Irish Americans had deliberately avoided the divisive issue of abolitionism so they could focus all their energies on repealing the Act of Union. It was both ignorant and insulting, he continued, for O'Connell to attack Irish Americans for adopting a strategy that was designed to strengthen the repeal movement in Ireland. There could be no doubt about Binns's priorities. Nationalism, in both its Irish and American forms, took precedence over abolitionism; if slavery was an evil, it was one that could be tolerated without too much difficulty.[24]

A similar ambivalence characterized United Irish attitudes toward Native Americans in the United States. Although the subject had attracted little attention in Ireland, it had not been entirely ignored. At Trinity College during the early 1790s, the Historical Society debated the question "Whether the conquest of barbarous nations for the purpose of civilization was justifiable?" The result of the debate is unknown, but there is little doubt that the participants, including the radicals in the Society, regarded Native Americans as "barbarous." Most of the United Irishmen in the United States, had they been asked that question, would have fully accepted the notion of "civilization" while expressing serious qualifications about the question of "conquest."[25]

Convinced that they represented the most advanced views on political and economic liberty in the world, the leading United Irishmen in America believed that they were bringing enlightenment to the savages. Warden and Burk, for example, supported state-sponsored schemes to introduce "spinning, weaving, and agriculture" into Native American communities, and noted with satisfaction the apparent acculturation by the Creeks to white norms. Duane, as a journalist in Calcutta during the 1780s, had already praised the supposedly benevolent consequences of British civilization in India; "we plant science and give peace and prospering security to her long oppressed natives," he had written. In the United States, such notions became Americanized and were applied to the indigenous population. Among other things, Duane suggested that Native Americans be represented in Congress to accelerate their integration into the Empire of Liberty.[26]

But if the attempt to civilize the "barbarous" nations of North America appeared fully justifiable, conquest that stemmed from aggressive war was unequivocally condemned. In contrast to the "cruelties of the Spaniards in Mexico and Peru," wrote Burk, "where millions of Indians were sacrificed at the shrine of bigotry and avarice," the North Americans had a much more benign approach to colonization. "Their attachment to liberty," he asserted, "forbade them to encroach on the rights of others: the lands, which they might have seized by the sword, were procured by purchase, while treaties, on their part, religiously observed, secured to them the confidence and respect of the Indians." This idealized version of the past doubtless boosted an American sense of superiority and self-righteousness, but bore little relation to reality. Hamilton Rowan, who was equally opposed to [illegible] and conquest, took a much more clear-eyed view of the situation. "I will go to the woods," he told his wife in 1796; "but I will not kill Indians, nor keep slaves. Good God! if you heard some of the Georgians, or the Kentucky people, talk of killing the natives! Cortes, and all that followed him, were not more sanguinary in the South, than they would be in North America."[27]

There were, however, certain circumstances in which conquest was deemed to be permissible. If the Native Americans were actually attacking the United States, and particularly if they were acting with the encouragement of the British government, then they should indeed be treated as a conquered people, it was argued. None of the United Irishmen, however, pushed the argument as far as Jefferson did during the War of 1812. "This unfortunate race," he wrote Warden, "whom we have been taking so much pains to save and to civilize, have by their unexpected desertion and ferocious barbarities justified extermination, and now await our decision on their fate."[28] Some United Irishmen were drawn in the same direction, but pulled back from justifications of genocide; their attitude toward Native Americans was a complex combination of attraction and repulsion. No one exemplified this more clearly than Burk, whose *History of Virginia* was by far the most extensive United Irish treatment of Native American culture.

On the one hand, Burk wrote of the "unadulterated purity and innocence" of pre-colonial Native American life, praised "the sagacity and natural eloquence of this people," and regarded their leaders as repositories of ancient chivalric values. In the process, he intermittently moved toward cultural relativism, and insisted that Native Americans should be judged on their own terms. "We must not argue from cities to the wilderness," he wrote; if the

Native Americans appeared lazy to European eyes, it was only because they had lived in relative abundance and had no need to develop "arts and civilization." The Native Americans, he believed, were uncorrupted by "luxury and wealth," and close to the spirit of classical republicanism. Not surprisingly, he viewed their values as being virtually identical to those of the Spartans.[29]

On the other hand, Burk could not fail to recognize that Native American resistance to white settlement threatened the colony of Virginia. As his attitude to the indigenous people shifted from respect to fear, Burk developed a negative stereotype of Native Americans that ran counter to his romantic image of their life. The Natives became devious, untrustworthy and unpredictable; the "subtle and vigilant savage" professed friendship with the settlers by day while secretly plotting their destruction by night. And although he was frequently critical of the settlers for provoking, corrupting and exploiting the Natives, Burk believed that ruthless measures were sometimes required to safeguard the colony. In the face of Powhatan's hostility after 1609, Burk noted, "the corn and habitations of the natives were every where burnt without pity." "It was thought necessary to strike terror," he continued, "by some signal examples, and the humanity of [John] Smith was obliged to give place to policy." In the next breath, however, Burk could argue that Powhatan, with his "sagacious mind," had correctly anticipated "the mischiefs of a foreign establishment" on his land.[30]

By the time he had finished, there were enough contradictions to dizzy the mind. The incoherence was clearly related to the tension in his thought between the "noble" and "savage" aspects of the imagined Native character, but there was more to it than that. As an Irish radical who was one of the most anti-colonial figures of his generation, Burk identified at some level with the Native Americans who fought against the encroachments of foreign settlers. Despite his horror at their actions, Burk admired such Native leaders as Powhatan and Opechancanough for taking a stand against the external forces that threatened their community. On one occasion, and contrary to much evidence that he himself had presented, Burk exonerated the "Indians of Virginia" from the "general charge of barbarism and treachery" in language that echoed his defense of the United Irishmen after the Rising of 1798.[31]

At the same time, though, Burk also identified strongly with the colonizers of America. He praised Columbus as exemplifying the scientific spirit of Newton (once again reading history backwards), and believed that the story of Virginia was the march of progress and liberty. The Native Americans, in Burk's view, were on the wrong side of history: hence his comments about the unfortunate necessity of striking terror into them, which stand in striking contrast to his passionate denunciation of similar acts of terror against the natives of Ireland in the 1790s. Burk's anti-colonialism prompted him to side with the Native Americans; his democratic republicanism meant that his primary allegiance was to white American society. The stresses and strains tore his argument apart.[32]

If United Irish attitudes to race in America were deeply ambivalent, the question of gender was hardly raised at all. As far as most United Irishmen were concerned, the Rights of Man really were the rights of man. This viewpoint was, of course, dominant in the early republic, although more radical ideas were beginning to circulate. As early as 1790, a remarkable article in the *Aurora* complained that women had been written out of history and called upon them to claim full civil, political and social equality with men. Mary Wollstonecraft's *Vindication of the Rights of Women* was reprinted and serialized in America during the 1790s, and customary notions of male superiority were being challenged by the playwright Susanna Rowson.[33] Such radicalism, however, failed to make much impression on the United Irishmen in the country. On the few occasions that they did consider issues of gender, the United Irishmen combined traditional attitudes about the role of women in society with more modern language about female patriotism. It was, however, the traditionalism that preponderated. For example, the toasts given by United Irishmen during their St. Patrick's Day celebrations heaped praise upon Irish and American women for their patriotic virtues, viewed them as a source of inspiration for the men who fought the battles, and objectified them as symbols of their country.

Predictably, this idealization found its fullest expression in the writings of Burk, who romanticized women with the same passionate intensity that he brought to Irish history, Virginia history, the United Irishmen, American Republicans, and (in their Rousseauist mode) Native Americans. In Burk's *Female Patriotism,* Joan D'Arc embodied the spirit of her country, and inspired the demoralized menfolk of France to defeat the English invader. She was at once a warrior and a woman; the Duc de Chastel was impressed by both her "warlike ardor" and "virgin modesty." And although she could lead the men into battle and defeat her enemies in single combat, Burk was careful to ensure that the "woman" did not become lost in the "warrior":

> Sometimes the weakness of my sex prevails
> And I do shudder at the noise of arms;
> And oft when I have slain some warlike chief
> And seen life's current issue from his wound,
> My heart seems broken so intense my grief,
> And pity issues gushing from my heart
> As if the fund of sorrow was a spring.

Chastel was impressed by this woman who wept for those she had slain; for him, Joan united all the virtues, "the soft, the mild, the warlike, and the grand."[34]

But it was also clear that Joan's warrior side was the product of exceptional circumstances. Once those circumstances changed, she intended to return to her former life and become fully feminine again:

> For tho'
> The love of liberty sublimes my soul
> And make me do such things to compass it,
> As my soft sex would shrink at; Yet I feel
> Those timid, soft, and virgin sentiments
> Play on the silken fibres of my heart,
> Which speaks me all the woman; let me heaven
> Sooner resign my laurels in an hour
> Than loose [*sic*] one single thought that's feminine:
> This is the females [*sic*] jewel and of worth
> More than a world. . . .

With peace, both men and women could be faithful to their true and separate characters, and live simple and virtuous lives in a state of rural bliss. Female patriotism, in Burk's view, was conditional and limited; in his writings, traditional sexual stereotypes were reinforced rather than reexamined.[35]

According to Burk, women in modern society were on an "equal rank" with men; he did not allow the fact that women could not vote, or that husbands controlled the property of their wives, to get in the way of his argument. His notion of equality turned out to be highly one-sided; Burk's central preoccupation was the way in which women could influence the behavior of men. Women, from this perspective, were kinder and gentler creatures, whose virtue and benevolence could improve male society. As the "connexion between the sexes became more lasting, more rational, and endearing," he wrote, "the men were daily improving in humanity and virtue, under the soft and bewitching influence of beauty, rendered more interesting by the graces of culture and education."[36]

At one level, such an approach continued to place women in an ancillary role, and confined them within their "separate sphere" as nurturing mothers and loving wives. But it also opened up new cultural and educational possibilities within that role for women in the American republic. Precisely because they were virtuous care-givers, it was argued, women were uniquely placed to transmit republican values to their husbands and children. From the idea of the "republican wife" and the "republican mother," it was a short and logical step to argue that women should be educated in the principles of republicanism for the greater good of the community. In effect, this represented an attempt to politicize the domestic sphere of women. Among the United Irishmen who supported this notion were Warden and Duane.[37]

"It is the want of education," insisted Warden, "which has stamped the female sex with mental inferiority and formed a severe distinction destructive to society and impious in the eye of that Being, who has blessed them with minds equally rational." As the principal tutor at Kingston Academy in New York, he became an early advocate for women's education; later in life, he praised women who asserted their independence and dignity against "the tyrant man." Duane's views on women's education fitted the "republican mother" model so well that the entire ideology could be distilled from his writings. "The infant mind receives its first impressions from the mother," he argued; "upon mothers, principally depend the future happiness and virtue of children, and of society at large; it is, therefore, of the first importance, that females should possess correct ideas of that knowledge which is requisite for children of both sexes." His *Epitome of the Arts and Sciences* attempted to provide a practical, political and moral education for women as well as men, and was designed to be part of the core curriculum in the rapidly increasing number of schools that were being opened for girls and young women in the United States.[38]

This view of female education was applied mainly to women of the middle class. Lower down in the social scale, especially in the seaboard cities, the growing number of women who worked as seamstresses or in domestic service were more concerned with basic matters of survival than with becoming "republican wives and mothers." Only Carey, among the radical Irish émigrés, directly addressed their situation and argued against their exploitation. In 1831, in a pamphlet on "the sufferings of the seamstresses," he publicized their condition and attacked the employers who paid them below subsistence wages.[39]

Carey began by taking on four "erroneous opinions" associated with the "school of political economists": that everyone willing to work could find employment; that the poor, "by industry, prudence, and economy," could support themselves without charity; that their sufferings were the product of their own idleness and dissipation"; and that taxes for the support of the poor only encouraged them in their laziness. These opinions, which have an eerie modern ring, completely ignored the realities of the situation, in Carey's view. The poor in general, he wrote, were subject to seasonal and cyclical unemployment, and seamstresses in particular were victims of both "the superabundance of female labour" and "the direful effects of over-driven competition." Through a detailed statistical analysis, he demonstrated that no matter how hard they worked, the seamstresses could not pull themselves out of poverty.[40]

What, then, was to be done about such "enormous and cruel oppression"? Essentially, Carey aimed to bring public and private pressure to bear against exploitative employers and to moralize the so-called laws of supply and demand. Just as he had attempted to humanize slavery, Carey now tried to mitigate the "evil" treatment of seamstresses; in both cases, he was more concerned with reforming people's attitudes than revolutionizing the social system. Among other things, he called on "ladies" to work on behalf of their oppressed sisters, through expressing sexual solidarity and influencing their male friends to lobby employers. The idea was to ostracize those employers who were "*grinding the faces of the poor*" in the name of political economy. Carey also urged middle-class women to establish schools for seamstresses, to open up alternative avenues of employment. One alternative that he ruled out, however, was domestic service; that, in his view, would be to move from one overcrowded and oppressive situation to another. Many masters and mistresses, he wrote, treated their servants harshly, so that domestic service was little more than a species of domestic slavery.[41]

Although Carey's old friend and fellow radical William Sampson generally liked the pamphlet, he took issue with its arguments about domestic service and female education. "Poor female children," Sampson wrote, could benefit from domestic service; he and his wife, for example, employed two Irish girls who had "no wants, no painful anxieties," and who sent money to their parents across the Atlantic. "They are useful," he continued, "and not so exposed to temptation or seduction." Educating women above their station was a dangerous thing. A "lady of good understanding," he noted, remarked that "these infant schools, by refining too much[,] inspire them with pretensions very unfavorable to their peace and contentment and that instruction in domestic occupations and qualifications would be more for their advantage and that of their community." "It is better to know less and know it well," Sampson added, "than for a whole community to be philosophers like those of the flying Island[,] better for a young maiden to learn plain cooking than the theory of extracting sunbeams out of Cucumbers." Rather than being educated to fulfill their potential, women were to be trained to know their places, on the grounds that they would be happier that way. This was not an argument that Sampson would ever have countenanced in relation to disfranchised men in Ireland.[42]

The concept of separate spheres, closely connected as it was with images of the "softer sex," continued to consign women to a subordinate status in society. Whether they were objectified as patriotic symbols or idealized as a humanizing influence on society, whether they were to be educated as republican wives and mothers or confined to such domestic chores as cooking and cleaning, women were expected above all to meet the needs of men. This view was widely held throughout American society, and was shared by both sexes. It is not surprising that it was reflected and reinforced in the writings of the United Irishmen in the United States, when they bothered to think about the issue at all. But there were glimpses of a changed attitude, remote possibilities for the future; Warden had argued strongly that women were the intellectual equals of men, and the introduction of politics into female education could have unforeseen consequences. It remained a long way, however, from Sampson's Laputa to Elizabeth Cady Stanton's Seneca Falls.

Carey's concern for the plight of seamstresses, together with his attempt to temper the doctrines of political economy with a sense of humanitarianism and justice, raises the more general question of United Irish attitudes toward poverty and property relations in the American republic. The two most radical figures, in this respect, were Driscol and Burk, both of whom rejected the notion of absolute property rights while accepting the general framework of the market economy. In Ireland, Driscol had been imprisoned for advocating an agrarian law: "The earth is the common inheritance of all men," he had argued. "Every man has a right to a proportionate share of the country he lives in. He, who possesses a greater share of the land he lives in, than another, is a monopolist and an usurper of the rights of his fellow citizens." This was revolutionary talk, indeed; the practical result of his position, as he fully realized, would be to break the Anglo-Irish monopoly of land ownership and reverse the expropriations of the seventeenth century. It would be mistaken, however, to infer that Driscol was a "social leveller," as his enemies insisted; his target was landed wealth, rather than private property in general, and he had no objection to healthy competition among free and independent individuals.[43]

But healthy competition, for Driscol and Burk, was not the same thing as untrammeled competition. Both men were influenced by deep-rooted notions of the "moral economy," in which customary conceptions of a "just price" and a "fair wage" challenged the emerging orthodoxies of the free market. The *Dublin Evening Post,* during the early 1790s, carried articles that called upon the Lord Mayor to "REGULATE the assize of BREAD," and attacked corn merchants for engrossing and forestalling. Burk expressed identical views in America, where he supported severe penalties against "forestallers and engrossers" and published attacks on them for attempting to deceive and cheat the poor. "Rouse, then, my Fellow-Townsmen," ran one such piece in the Boston *Polar Star,* "and, in open Townmeeting, let us unanimously agree to raze every stall, and leave not a trace behind to shelter the heads of such pests to society." In Baltimore, Driscol argued for a more effective regulation of the sale of bread, so that the poor paid a fair price and the bakers received a fair profit.[44]

The idea was to regulate the market rather than replace it with common property ownership. Burk regarded economic leveling as an "evil," and argued that when property lines became "too vague and uncertain," there were no incentives for "enterprize and industry." But he also rejected the view that the accumulation of property should be the central goal of the republican polity, and reminded his readers that the rights of man were life, liberty and property, in that order of importance. Much the same position was taken by Driscol. When he wrote that "the whole moral system, as far as it respects property, must be revised," Driscol was referring to social values and attitudes rather than the institution of private property itself. People should not put their own selfish interests above the needs of their fellow men, he maintained, and should never exploit their neighbors' necessity. Driscol was not a proto-socialist; nor was the question of property relations a central concern in his writing, which was preoccupied with political and religious rather than economic issues.[45]

Above all, the radicals appealed to men in the "middling spheres of life." Farmers and artisans, wrote Driscol, "feel a pride in preserving liberty and equality"; they would resist any attempts to oppress them, and had neither the means nor the desire to oppress others. Duane took a broadly similar position, arguing that farmers were by far the most important interest in the country, and including artisans among "the *useful members*" of society. The independence and well-being of both groups, in his view, depended on free and fair commerce. "No reasonable man," he asserted, "can expect that the spirit of commerce can be restrained in a free nation; commerce like water will always find its level; yet the attempt to make water run up-hill is not more absurd than the attempt to check the operations of our commercial spirit." In Britain and Ireland, the principal threat to free and fair commerce emanated from the aristocracy; in the United States, he believed, it came from financial monopolies and the "speculators in commerce" who made no contribution to the real wealth of the community. Emphasizing the dignity and self-respect of productive laborers, Duane attacked "the propensity of the *idle*, the *imbecile*, and the *profligate* speculator to treat with affected contempt those classes of *men—mechanics* and *farmers*, to whose virtue and toil those excrescences of society owe their very existence."[46]

The emerging picture seems reasonably clear; the United Irishmen supported useful citizens against the idle rich, free commerce against monopolies, the self-reliant individual against excessive government. The best way to achieve the greater good, they believed, was to create conditions in which the creative potential of each person could be realized. Even the most radical figures supported intervention in the marketplace only as a limited response to exceptional circumstances. The principal threat to their individualistic ideal came from above, in the form of aristocratic rule or monopolistic corporations. But there were also new challenges emanating from below, as journeymen on both sides of the Atlantic increasingly attempted to defend their living standards by organizing themselves into trade unions that stood primarily for collective rights. Like the Jeffersonian Republicans in general, the Irish émigrés opposed the emerging trade union movement; they did so with the same energy and from the same principles that they had directed against aristocracy.

The United Irishmen had first confronted the issue of workers' combinations in Ireland during the 1790s. Against the background of increasing capitalization and concentration of ownership, Dublin's journeymen organized themselves into trade unions, and attempted to raise wages, reduce hours, and restrict access to their crafts. Among other things, they sought to limit the number of apprentices, keep out country workers, and stop women from taking over their work. A bill in 1792 to curb such combinations generated massive demonstrations in the city, in which journeymen were pitted against their masters. Almost without exception, the United Irishmen backed the masters and supported the anti-trade-union legislation. Only William Paulet Carey, brother of Mathew, took up the journeymen's cause, and even he did not approve of combinations; his point was that the rich had been combining against the poor, and that the poor were simply acting in self-defense.[47]

Such attitudes were carried across the Atlantic, and rapidly became incorporated into the liberal-republican mainstream. During the 1806 trial of Philadelphia's journeymen shoemakers on common-law charges of conspiracy to raise their wages, Duane did indeed support the workers. But this was partly because of his general opposition to common-law precedents in the United States, and partly because he believed it was unfair to punish journeymen for combining without taking similar action against "the *combination of masters*." He did not, in fact, endorse the principle of collective bargaining; like other radical republicans, Duane believed that equality before the law and the operation of the open market would remove the need for combinations. At the very same time that he was fighting against the "monopoly" of the Bank of the United States during the winter of 1810–11, Duane was also locked in conflict with his own journeymen printers who had "*struck for wages*." Refusing to compromise, he waited them out for several months, while employing "raw boys" as replacement labor. It is difficult, under these circumstances, to see Duane as the voice of a developing working-class consciousness in America.[48]

An equally revealing view of United Irish attitudes toward trade unions comes from the trial of the journeymen shoemakers of New York in 1809, on similar charges of combining for the closed shop and higher wages. One of the prosecutors was Thomas Emmet; his old friend and political ally William Sampson acted for the defense. In Emmet's view, combinations violated both the public good and private rights. Any workers who formed themselves into a trade union and threatened strike action, he declared, were elevating private interests over the general welfare. Just as there were laws against forestalling and engrossing to protect the community from unscrupulous merchants, Emmet argued, there should be strong action against conspiracies of equally unscrupulous workers. In this way, customary "moral economy" notions were used to justify repressive legislation against trade unions. Combinations also trampled on the freedom of those individuals who wished to keep working, Emmet continued; as such, they were "most tyrannical violations of private right." Both the general welfare and individual freedom, he concluded, must be safeguarded from "the extortions of the conspirators."[49]

For the defense, Sampson sympathized with the journeymen's plight, and complained about the injustice of a situation in which merchants could meet "to settle the markets" while journeymen were "indicted for combining against starvation." But he did not challenge the basic assumptions of Emmet's position, and actually seems to have shared them. "If the butchers and bakers combine, the one not to kill, and the other not to bake; they, and not the community, will starve for that," Sampson argued in his summation; "and if the evil requires a law we shall have a legislature to provide one in due time." The central thrust of his argument was that the journeymen had been charged under the English common law and that the common law was inapplicable in the United States. Rather than asserting the primacy of collective over individual rights, or advancing "the first argument in American law for the closed union shop," Sampson insisted that the "single question" on which the trial hinged was "whether the law of England was to govern this case." Emmet replied that such a question should be settled in the legislature rather than a court of law, and the judge agreed; the journeymen were found guilty, but received only a nominal fine.[50]

As Richard Twomey has shown, the arguments of both Emmet and Sampson demonstrate their common hostility to any manifestations of class conflict within the "productive classes." The United Irishmen were Paineite individualists, who wanted to build a relatively egalitarian democracy of useful citizens, characterized by freedom of thought, economic opportunity, low taxes and lack of deference. There was no place in this vision for trade unions, which by their very nature contradicted the social ideal for which the radicals strove. Although the United Irishmen wanted to improve the condition of the poor, they maintained that combinations were not the answer; like Paine himself, they believed that the best way to raise wages was to let the principles of the free market operate with minimal governmental interference.[51]

Nevertheless, the democratic ideology of the United Irishmen could move in different and unanticipated directions when it was transposed onto the increasingly industrial and class-conscious world of nineteenth-century America. On the one hand, the emphasis on limited government, low taxes and free enterprise pointed toward middle-class liberalism; on the other, the egalitarian outlook and the vague but powerful sense of conflict between the "productive" and "parasitic" members of society fed into an emerging working-class movement. The very notion of the "productive" classes was profoundly ambiguous; like a concertina, it could be expanded or contracted according to the melody that was being played. In the hands of most United Irish leaders, it was pulled out to incorporate not only laborers, artisans and farmers, but also manufacturers, merchants and professional men. For Duane and his Irish followers in Southwark and the Northern Liberties, in contrast, it was squeezed in to become part of a "small producer" consciousness. And within this consciousness, democratic republicanism glissaded during the 1820s into trade-union, communitarian and nascent socialist movements that found expression in the Working Men's Party before becoming absorbed into Jacksonianism.[52]

There can be little doubt that many of those immigrants who traveled by steerage and who formed the United Irish political constituency in America participated in working-class republican politics. It was no coincidence that a radical Irish artisan stronghold such as the Northern Liberties supported both Duane's Old School Democrats and the Working Men's Party that emerged from the Old School in 1828. There was, indeed, a very real sense in which the district had become "Duane's quarter." Common to both parties was a deep hostility to the banking and paper money systems, which were associated with an aristocracy of wealth in a republic supposedly of equals. Similar views were expressed in New York by the "lower orders" who broke into MacNeven's house and terrified his family in 1834 after he had publicly opposed Jackson's attack on the Bank of the United States. But while there was a growing gap between middle-class and working-class Irish republicans, it should also be remembered that even a radical populist such as Duane stopped short of endorsing the Working Men's Party. Although he influenced many of its leaders and agreed with many of its ideas, Duane refused to join the organization on the grounds that its class-based politics were incompatible with his vision of a harmonious, class-free society of useful citizens.[53]

This vision, it is clear, was very much confined to white males. Although they were generally opposed to slavery in principle, the United Irishmen did not in practice want to share the continent with African Americans; radicals such as Carey and Binns supported the mass deportation of slaves and free blacks from America to Africa. To create the democratic republican utopia, trade unions would be suppressed, African Americans would be removed, and Native Americans would become assimilated. Women, in contrast, were viewed as subordinate partners in the democratic republican project, and their domestic functions were extended to embrace the political education of their husbands and children.

Within these core views, there were significant differences of opinion and outlook among the United Irishmen. Emmet defended fugitive slaves, while Blennerhassett owned slaves; Rowan was much more critical of white attitudes toward Native Americans than was Burk; Warden had more advanced views about the education of women than did Sampson. In this sense, there is much validity in Smyth's view that United Irish social attitudes were "unformed and contradictory."

On balance, though, the United Irishmen were much less radical on social issues than they were on the question of political change. This does not mean, however, that they can be neatly categorized as social conservatives. If some Americans were further to the left on questions of race, gender and class, there were many more who were further to the right. And in some areas, such as prison reform, the United Irishmen were at the forefront of the reform movement; they had, after all, considerable personal experience of the conditions of life in jail.[54] Rather than judging them as social conservatives, it would be more accurate to view the United Irishmen as egalitarian democrats whose social attitudes spanned the spectrum of American life but whose center of gravity was somewhat to the left of center. Apart from anything else, this testifies to their own assimilation to the dominant values of white male American society, with all its limitations and blindspots.

CHAPTER EIGHT

The Cause of Ireland

The history of Irish-American nationalism usually begins with the Great Famine of 1846–51, or at the very earliest with the influx of Catholic immigrants during the 1820s. Because the Famine produced a fundamental quantitative and qualitative shift in Irish migration to the United States, and because Irish-American nationalism has generally been associated with Catholicism, the United Irishmen have largely been written out of the picture. Such an approach not only underestimates the importance of the United Irish émigrés in the context of their own time but also ignores the underlying continuities in the history of Irish America. In fact, Irish-American nationalism originated between 1795 and 1812, and was pioneered by republican Protestants and Catholics whose common commitment to Irish independence transcended the divisions that arose among them over specifically American issues.

The United Irishmen in the United States acted as an American link between Irish revolutionaries and their French allies, and organized shipments of weapons and ammunition for the movement back home. They contributed to the formation of a distinct Irish identity in the United States by establishing emigration and patriotic societies, promoting Irish culture, and supplying their fellow countrymen with news about political events in the Old Country. At the same time, they communicated their case for Irish independence to an American audience with an impressive output of books, pamphlets and newspaper articles. The central contours of Irish-American nationalist ideology had already been mapped out well before the mass migration that occurred later in the nineteenth century.

"A kind of seditious convention is now forming in America," Leonard McNally informed the Chief Secretary of Ireland in 1795, "composed of

Hamilton Rowan, Napper Tandy, Doctor Reynolds, Wolfe Tone and other fugitives from Ireland. These men have it in their power, and no doubt it is their wish to give every possible information and assistance to France." His concern was well placed. Just before Tone left for America, he had been briefed by the Ulster radicals about their preparations for a French invasion of Ireland. In Philadelphia, he contacted the French minister Pierre Adet, and eventually persuaded him to support a mission to France. At the beginning of 1796, Tone traveled to Paris, carrying a letter of introduction from Rowan to James Monroe, the American minister; through Monroe, Tone established the connections with the Directory that culminated in the invasion attempts of 1796 and 1798.[1]

Meanwhile, Tandy had formed a close friendship with Governor Thomas Mifflin of Pennsylvania, who provided him with a separate entrée to Adet. "I have become extremely intimate with the French Minister," he boasted to his friends back home. Tandy began to request "a most *particular* and *minute* account" of Irish affairs from his correspondents in Dublin, so that the information could be transmitted through Adet to Paris. During the summer of 1796, he informed the United Irish leaders in Dublin that the French were preparing to invade, and commented that "I hope to be again in my own country with honor." In May, 1797, Tandy left Philadelphia for Cuxhaven; while Tone had traveled under the alias of "Smith," Tandy adopted the equally unimaginative one of "Jones." It did not work; British spies tracked his movements to Paris, where he became one of Tone's principal rivals in the attempt to win French support for an Irish revolution.[2]

Tone and Tandy were clearly the major figures in McNally's "seditious convention." Reynolds, as has been seen, became increasingly drawn into American politics, although he strongly supported a French expedition to Ireland. Rowan, in contrast, distanced himself from revolutionary politics. Not only was he dispirited; his mind was "much agitated" by letters from his wife urging him to seek a pardon from the government, and he began to isolate himself from United Irish circles in the autumn of 1796. His colleagues feared that he was deserting the cause, and even suspected that he had become an informer.[3]

Rowan's alienation from the Irish revolutionaries in America increased after the Rising of 1798, when he came to the conclusion that union with Britain would benefit Ireland. Such a policy, Rowan believed, would short-circuit the power of the Protestant Ascendancy, put an end to parliamentary corruption in Dublin, and pave the way for economic and political progress. It was not a popular position: "I am almost sent to Coventry here by the Irish," he told his wife, "for my opinions concerning a union." They were probably glad to see him leave for Hamburg in 1800, and would not have been surprised to learn that he received a pardon three years later. But if he renounced revolution, Rowan remained a reformer; right up to the end of his life he continued to support radical causes, and participated in the campaign for Catholic Emancipation. His last public appearance was in 1829, when he was carried through the streets by an enthusiastic Dublin crowd after appearing at a reform meeting in the city. He was seventy-eight years old.[4]

The tension between Rowan and other leading United Irish émigrés was mirrored by less visible but equally serious splits within the rank-and-file. According to one observer, there were "great dissensions amongst the Passengers going out to America, many glorying in their Banishment and feeding their passions with the Ideas of a Return to Vengeance[,] others cursing their seducers and lamenting their Folly." The two sides "were with difficulty kept from fighting." Among the militants, a significant minority sailed straight back across the Atlantic. "Numbers have returned in every vessel," it was reported; they included people like the mysterious "Mr. Monk," who wound up plotting revolution among the United Irish community in Manchester. There were even rumors that an "army of American rebels," led by John Daly Burk, had landed at Galway Bay in 1797 to liberate the country.[5]

From the loyalist perspective, of course, the fundamental flaw in the government's policy of banishment was that the United Irish in America could regroup and reorganize themselves for the struggle at home. And indeed, the first recorded example of Irish-American ammunition running dates from this period. In May 1796, the government received information "that Powder came to Belfast from America, in flax seed casks." There was probably collusion from revolutionary sympathizers in the customs and excise service; "the revenue officer at Larne," noted General Lake, "is remarkably inattentive (if not more) & ought to be remov'd." The authorities were sufficiently alarmed to order that all suspicious American ships in Belfast Lough be monitored closely.[6]

Within the growing Irish community in America, the United Irishmen played a central role in helping immigrants adjust to their new environment while continuing to provide a connection with the concerns of the old. Through the ideological medium of democratic republicanism and the organizational structure of emigration and patriotic societies, the political refugees fostered a sense of identity that was simultaneously American and Irish, and that readily defined itself against aristocratic and imperialist Britain. In Philadelphia, Mathew Carey's Hibernian Society of 1790 had pointed the way; it replaced the older and more conservative Friendly Sons of St. Patrick, elbowed out Federalist Irish members like Thomas Fitzsimons, and funneled recently arrived immigrants into the city's emerging Republican Party. The radicals were effectively taking over the emigrant vote, and establishing themselves as the authentic voice of Irish America.[7]

As good Irish-American democrats, people like Carey actively encouraged Irish migration to the United States. The immigrants, Carey argued, would escape from poverty and oppression, enjoy the benefits of economic opportunity and liberty, and help to build the Empire of Liberty. "Worthless, disorderly characters" should be excluded; only those people who were known for their "sobriety, industry, and honesty" should be allowed into the country, he believed. Other radicals, such as John Chambers and Thomas Emmet, agreed that the most suitable immigrants were intelligent and industrious merchants, farmers and mechanics. John Caldwell wrote:

> It will readily be admitted that the most useful class of emigrants for these United States is that of the labourers and the middle rank of society, imbued with republican principles and determined to support the laws, constitution and institutions of their adopted country, without making invidious and almost always ill founded comparisons between the country they left and that which opened its arms for their hospitable reception.[8]

To attract ambitious and enterprising republican immigrants, the émigrés attempted to ensure that accurate information about the United States circulated in Ireland. After Rowan returned home, he was deluged with requests for advice about settling in the United States, and urged his American friends to inform prospective immigrants about practical matters such as soil conditions, transportation and the state of the economy. Carey argued that American agents should be sent to Ireland for the same purpose. Such information was clearly needed. After John Binns decided to go to the United States, he read everything he could find about the country, and wound up with totally misleading impressions. "I expected that among the people, even in the large towns," he wrote, "I should occasionally meet one of our red brethren with his squaw leaning lovingly on his arm. I expected that I should find the white men so plain and quakerly in their dress that I had the lace ripped from my neckerchiefs, and the ruffles from my shirts." Realizing that other immigrants could benefit from his experiences, he made a serious effort to help those who came after him.[9]

While Carey and Binns led the way in Philadelphia, Thomas O'Connor and William MacNeven played a similar role in New York. From the offices of the *Shamrock,* O'Connor supplied immigrants with information about the availability of work and land, as well as general information about the climate and conditions of the country. His newspaper recommended the Shamrock Friendly Society's "Hints to Emigrants," and emphasized the connection between economic opportunity and political liberty. The author of the pamphlet was MacNeven, who had been, in O'Connor's own words, "a member of nearly every society formed in this city, having for its object the honour and interest of his countrymen."[10]

Through such activities, the United Irishmen remained influential figures in the post-Napoleonic War period. During the winter of 1817–18, MacNeven participated in a colonization project for Irish immigrants. The idea was to obtain land in Illinois from the federal government and establish an exclusively

Irish settlement in the American West. In this way, impoverished Irish immigrants in the cities could be transformed into independent and productive citizens on the frontier. Along with MacNeven, the leaders of the scheme included Sampson, Chambers and Emmet; this was very much a United Irish affair. They formed the New York Irish Emigrant Society, elected Emmet as president, linked up with similar organizations in Philadelphia and Baltimore, and lobbied Congress. Even such mutually antagonistic groups as the Hibernian Provident Society and the Shamrock Friendly Society joined forces in support of the project. It was an impressive effort, but was not quite enough; with the southerners in the House of Representatives voting against the proposal, it failed by a margin of twelve votes. Despite periodic attempts to revive the idea of colonization, more traditional methods of helping Irish immigrants prevailed; they would be given economic information, financial assistance, and political advice, to protect them in an alien and sometimes a hostile environment.[11]

The need for protection became greater in the 1820s, when the growing numbers of Catholic immigrants ran up against ultra-Protestant opposition, in a conflict that in many respects reproduced the religious and economic battles back home. In 1824, Irish Protestants in New York celebrated the anniversary of the Battle of the Boyne by marching through the predominantly Catholic weaving district of Greenwich Village. As in Ireland, such an assertion of territorial supremacy produced immediate resistance; the Catholics came out fighting, and a major riot ensued. The United Irishmen strongly supported the Catholics against their Orange enemies. Emmet and Sampson helped to defend the Catholics in America, just as they had done in Ireland. Unless Orange Parades were banned, argued Emmet, they would bring discord and violence into American life; there was no room, he insisted, for such manifestations of intolerance and triumphalism in the New World. During the trial, Emmet took the opportunity to declare that "he had been, was, and ever should be, an United Irishman," and identified the enemies of Orangeism with the friends of America. "The highest aspiration and most fervent aspiration of the United Irishmen," he asserted, "was to make Ireland what America is—politically free." As a result of such actions and such language, Emmet became something of a folk hero within the city's Catholic Irish community; the same folktales that circulated about O'Connell in Ireland were told about Emmet in America.[12]

The United Irishmen were also active in patriotic clubs that fostered Irish nationalist sentiments in America. In many cases, there was no clear distinction between emigration societies and patriotic clubs. The Hibernian Provident Society of New York, for example, functioned as a charitable organization for Irish immigrants, a center of militant Irish-American nationalism, and, up to 1817, an arm of the Clintonian faction in state politics. Organized by transplanted revolutionaries from Belfast and adopting a constitution modeled on the American Society of United Irishmen in Philadelphia, it was established in 1801 to help Irishmen who were "forced by persecution, and the oppression of a tyrannic government to seek asylum in the United States."[13]

Accordingly, the Society toasted the memory of "those brave and patriotic Irishmen" who had died in the Rising of 1798, and anticipated the day when the "starving human property of George the 3d on the Island of Britain" would "partake of the spirit of their ancestors of the 17th century" and "avenge the injuries of mankind, by breaking their chains on the guilty heads of their blood-stained tyrants." In 1807, it welcomed Matilda Tone to America, and presented her son William with a sword in the "lively hope, that it may one day in his hand, avenge the wrongs of his country." "I am proud of belonging to a nation," she replied, "whose sons preserve, under every vicissitude of Fortune, a faithful attachment to their principles; and from whose firm and generous minds, neither persecution, exile, nor time, can obliterate the remembrance of those who have fallen, though ineffectually, in the cause of our country."[14]

Another magnet for United Irish émigrés in New York was the Friendly Sons of St. Patrick; its most prominent members included Caldwell, Emmet, MacNeven and O'Connor. The radicals appear to have been in a constant tug-of-war with the moderates in the organization. Before 1812, the radicals were in the minority; the fact that the society invited the unpopular British minister Francis James Jackson to the St. Patrick's Day dinner of 1810 indicates where the power lay. During and after the war, however, the balance tipped the other way, with the Emmet faction firmly in control. There was a noticeable softening of positions, even among the older hard-liners, by the late 1820s. In 1828, with Chambers in the chair, the Friendly Sons drank toasts not only to the memory of the recently deceased Emmet, who was described as a "brilliant star," but also to "The King of Great Britain and Ireland." Similarly, after Catholic Emancipation in 1829, the society decorated the walls with the names of heroes including not only Washington, Jackson and O'Connell but also George Canning and the Duke of Wellington. This was a broad church indeed.[15]

Among the other organizations that kept the old memories alive were the Baltimore Hibernian Society, led by the Ulster radicals John Campbell White and the Reverend William Crawford, and the Charleston Hibernian Society, which was founded by Presbyterian and Catholic United Irish refugees from the Rising of 1798. In the rapidly expanding town of Pittsburgh, Pennsylvania, according to one disgruntled Orangeman, "the Blagaird Runaway united Irish men make a Great fuss"; they held regular meetings that combined support for Simon Snyder's Republicans with attacks on "British tyranny" in Ireland and America. There was an equally strong Irish republican presence in Albany, New York, where the United Irish and Scotch Benevolent Society was formed in 1803. The vice-president was William McClelland, who had led the Islandmagee contingent to the battle of Antrim in 1798, and who returned to Ireland sometime before the War of 1812. News about his imaginative entrepreneurial activities continued to cross the Atlantic; in 1814, it was reported, he had actually managed to capture a mermaid and was making a tidy profit by charging people to see it. McClelland wound up as a successful Islandmagee businessman; it is not recorded what became of the mermaid.[16]

The Irish nationalism that found expression in these clubs also permeated the early American labor movement, where the highly politicized artisans who fled Ireland during the 1790s and early 1800s initiated a tough and durable tradition of working-class Irish-American republicanism. This was particularly the case in the textile sector, which contained significant numbers of handloom weavers from the north of Ireland. Attempting to protect their independent status from the twin threats of concentration and mechanization, they blended their radical political notions of democracy and equal rights with increasingly militant trade union organizations. In the process, many Irish artisans and laborers made direct connections between British tyranny in Ireland and employers' tyranny in America. During the 1820s and 1830s, they moved into the Democratic Party, and denounced the Whigs (the party to which the millowners belonged) as the "faithful allies of Great Britain and the corrupt tools of the British Bank of Philadelphia." At the same time, they strongly supported the movement for civil and religious liberty back in the Old Country; the battle for economic independence in America became inseparable from the battle for political independence in Ireland. Such an outlook anticipated later developments in the nineteenth-century labor movement, as post-Famine Irish immigrants became an increasingly important component of the workforce and Irish nationalism intersected with American reform movements. The most conspicuous case would be Patrick Ford's attempt to link Irish anti-landlordism with American social issues during the Land League agitation of the 1870s and 1880s.[17]

Another long-standing Irish-American tradition, but one which drew in all classes, was the St. Patrick's Day parade; under United Irish auspices, the celebrations acquired their distinctive political character. In Philadelphia in 1807, for example, Duane's Incorporated Benevolent Society of St. Patrick joined the Republican Greens in drink, song and revolutionary toasts. Along with enthusiastic declarations of support for the "sovereign people," the liberty of the press, and Thomas Jefferson, the marchers paid tribute to the martyrs and exiles of 1798, and looked forward to their ultimate victory. In New York, the Hibernian Provident Society finished its festivities in 1812 with a toast to "Ireland—A total separation from Britain, the sure mode of emancipation; repeal of partial grievances only retards her independence." And in Baltimore in 1803, a "band of patriotic and excellent musicians," playing the pipes, fiddles and flutes, paraded through the center of town amid shouts of "Erin go Bragh." Throughout the United States, celebrations of Irishness became closely connected with assertions of revolutionary republicanism, in an exuberant atmosphere of music, poetry and song.[18]

Irish cultural activities were not confined to St. Patrick's Day and other special events; music, poetry and song played an important role in sustaining a revolutionary Irish consciousness in the United States. Many of the United Irishmen who came to America were musicians themselves. Sampson kept himself sane in Portuguese prisons by playing the flute, and was also an accomplished fiddle player. Harman Blennerhassett also played the flute, and was described by one contemporary (who mistakenly believed that his name was "Blaney Hazzard") as "a sort of a quack & musician." MacNeven composed a song for St. Patrick's Day, and Chambers actively encouraged the "Collection of Irish Music" to arouse the "sleeping genius" of their native country.[19]

In the United States, the radicals continued to perform and publicize the songs and poems of the Irish democratic movement. Burk's *Time-Piece,* for example, reprinted pieces from the collection of subversive songs that had alarmed the authorities at Dublin Castle, *Paddy's Resource,* or "Paddy's Race-Horse," as it was affectionately known. (In the same spirit, one Irish American in Maryland named his racehorse, which was born in 1798, "NAPPER TANDY.") One of the most popular song-poems among the émigré community was William Drennan's "Erin," which he composed in 1795. Not only was this the piece that gave birth to the expression "the Emerald Isle"; it also contained the oft-quoted lines that connected Ireland's destiny with that of America:

> In her sun, in her soil, in her station thrice blest,
> With her back turned to Britain, her face to the West.

"It is one of those emanations of Genius, Intellect and Feeling," commented Carey in the *American Poetical Miscellany,* "which adorns the page of a generous and gallant Nation, at a period when the Moral and Political World was shaken to its centre."[20]

Other favorites were "The Grave of Russell" and "To the Memory of B. Teeling," which combined a tone of moral outrage toward Britain with the message that those who died for Ireland would inspire future generations to carry on the fight. One of the most popular poets was Edward Rushton, an English supporter of revolutionary Irish nationalism. His best-known piece was the mawkish "Mary Le More," about an attack on a woman in Munster; after burning her cabin and killing her father, the soldiers raped Mary and left her to wander through the land in grief and insanity. Although the poem is permeated by gloom and despair, there is also a call for revenge:

> O Ireland's fair daughters, your country's salvation,
> While the waves of old Ocean shall beat round your shore,
> Remember the wrongs of your long-shackl'd nation,
> Remember the woes of poor Mary le More.

And while your hearts swell, O, with spirits all fire,
Your lovers, your brothers, your husbands inspire,
Till the *Union* shall make all oppressors retire,
From the soil where now wanders poor *Mary le More.*

James Carey and Burk both printed the poem in their newspapers, and Mathew Carey included it in the *American Poetical Miscellany.* The words, commented Burk, "*exhibit a picture but too true, as every village in Ireland can bear testimony.*" Mathew Carey agreed, adding that "many of the images and lines are worthy the successor of *Homer,* of *Ossian,* and of *Milton.*"[21]

The theme of suffering, endurance, revenge and ultimate victory fused with the equally powerful "ancient splendour-present misery" motif that was transmitted from the Irish literary tradition to America during the late eighteenth and early nineteenth centuries. In this respect, Thomas Moore, despite his links with Britain and his negative remarks about the United States, became a major source of inspiration. "He has touched upon the ancient freedom and valor of the Sons of Erin," wrote one of his admirers in Binns's *Democratic Press,* "and upon their oppression and sufferings in the latter periods of their history." Central to this imagery was the harp, which symbolized the beauty and sophistication of ancient Irish culture, and which would be "new-strung" by the modern revolutionary movement. The implication was clear: Political independence would culminate in a cultural revival that would replace the degradation of conquest with the poetry of liberty.[22]

Within this outlook, the myth of Ossian played a pivotal role. In the 1760s, the Scottish antiquarian James Macpherson claimed to have discovered the lost epic poems of Ossian, son of Fingal, and located them within his own country's literary tradition. Despite, or possibly because of, the dubious quality of his claims, not to mention of the poetry itself, Macpherson successfully initiated one of the most powerful literary cults of the late eighteenth and early nineteenth centuries. The Irish intelligentsia were incensed. Ossian, they insisted, was actually an ancient Hibernian bard whose work had fallen victim to Scottish fraud and forgery, and who should be rescued from the clutches of the Caledonians. A Scottish-Irish cultural war was fought on the issue, in which each side sought to assert the supremacy of its own culture over the pretensions of the other.[23]

The conflict was carried over to America, where Burk took up the cause of his native country. Never doubting that Ossian was an actual rather than a mythic figure, and refusing to admit that the bards of Scotland and Ireland might have shared a common cultural heritage, he kicked and elbowed his way through the controversy, in characteristic fashion. The Scots, he maintained, had no culture whatsoever, except for a few Irish airs that they had plagiarized—an ironic charge indeed, given Burk's own track record. Scotland, Burk argued, was merely an "Irish colony," and its people had "minds deficient in inventive sagacity." Scots lacked creativity partly because they were too busy fighting each other, and had not time for the "arts of peace." Another reason was that there were too many mountains in Scotland; mountains, wrote Burk, fostered the hardy virtues, while "the muses have ever been wont to dwell in regions of balmy softness and luxuriant fertility."[24]

Burk's logic may have been eccentric, but his purpose was very serious: to detach the cult of Ossian from Scotland, claim it for Ireland, and boost his countrymen's self-respect and international reputation. There was also a significant revolutionary component to the recovery of Ossian; the United Irishmen in America frequently expressed their nationalist aspirations in Ossianic strains that echoed the language of Macpherson. A typical example ran:

> Sad is the sleep of Erin, and her dreams are troubled and gloomy. Her enemy has come! he has come in her hour of slumber, and his hand has stolen the emerald from her head; but Erin has not awakened—no! she still sleeps. Bloody is the field where she lies, and her garments are weeping with blood. . . . but Erin has not awakened—no! she still sleeps. A sigh comes on the breezes of the night—'tis the spirit of ORR. . . . Has Erin heard the voice of the Chief? has Erin awakened? no! she still sleeps. IRELAND AWAKE. At once the thunder of a thousand harps bursts upon the sleep of Erin. The storm whistles along the heath. . . . Erin arises in her strength. . . . Her eyes are lightnings; her voice is thunder; she sweeps like the whirlwind of the desert thro' the bloody ranks of the strangers, and Erin is *victorious, free,* and *independent!*

This style became a literary and oratorical model for Irish patriotic sentiments in early republican America, where it effectively tapped into contemporary romantic sensibilities, and combined images of ancient glory with the continuing struggle for Irish independence and regeneration.[25]

Much the same motivation lay behind the United Irishmen's writings about the Gaelic language, which was increasingly regarded as a source of pride rather than a sign of cultural backwardness. Following the lead of such enthusiastic amateur philologists as Charles Vallencey, Burk, McCreery and Sampson believed that "the celtic language used by the Irish is the most original and unmixed language in Europe," and convinced themselves that it was "the identical language of the ancient Carthaginians in the days of Hannibal." Reacting strongly against "the ignorant and provoking insults which the English have heaped upon the Irish," Sampson connected Gaelic with the biblical universal tongue that existed before Babel. Ancient Ireland, from this perspective, possessed a brilliant and sophisticated civilization while the English, with their mongrel tongue, were skulking around in the bushes and painting themselves blue. Had it not been for the English conquest, Sampson continued, Ireland would have been "an earthly paradise" instead of "the pre-eminent abode of misery." This was, in effect, a kind of inverted "barbarian" theory, with Ireland cast as the center of civilization and England as the land of savages. As such, it attempted to link cultural self-respect with United Irish nationalism in America.[26]

Along with these cultural and communal activities, the émigrés attempted to ensure that a steady stream of political information about Ireland continued to flow into America. Between 1792 and 1812, Irish radicals edited at least seventeen newspapers in the United States, all of which devoted significant space to Irish affairs. Driscol's *American Patriot* is a case in point. During the first three months of its existence, it was crammed with letters from Ireland, extracts from Irish newspapers, speeches, court cases and accounts of British atrocities; it was the first distinctively Irish-American newspaper in the country. Eight years later, the *Shamrock* took the process still further and catered exclusively to the radical Irish in America. Other Irish-American editors, such as Duane, Binns, Burk and the Careys, focused more on American issues, but shared the general aim of defending Irish revolutionary nationalism from its detractors in the United States.

Convinced that negative images of Irish democrats were the product of sinister British propaganda and news manipulation, the radical Irish journalists established their own channels of communication and publicized their own version of events. When news of the Rising of 1798 crossed the Atlantic, Irish newspaper editors cautioned their readers about the "mutilated and partially selected articles of foreign intelligence" coming into the country, and frequently refused to believe reports of republican defeats. Even after the Rising had been crushed, Irish-American journalists continued to exaggerate the strength of the revolutionary movement in Ireland. "The germ of revolt is making a secret, slow, and alarming progress," James Carey told his readers in 1799. "Revolutionary measures [are] persevered in with more secrecy and more success than ever," wrote Driscol the following year. Much of this was wishful thinking; nevertheless, in reacting against Tory propaganda, they wound up producing at least as much propaganda of their own.[27]

While United Irish newspaper editors and journalists attempted to reclaim the present, sometimes through dubious means, a significant number also set out to reclaim the past from the hostile interpretations of their conservative opponents. Birch, Burk, MacNeven, Sampson and Mathew Carey all wrote histories of Ireland that were intended to raise the reputation of their countrymen in America and provide intellectual ammunition for the struggle back home. All these writers had a strong sense of the practical significance of historical arguments. Carey, for example, regarded the publication of his *Vindiciae Hibernica* in 1819 as being "among the most important operations of my life," and devoted almost a fifth of his autobiography to a discussion of its arguments. One of its major aims, he wrote, was to strengthen the case for Catholic emancipation in Ireland. MacNeven, who had advised Carey about sources, expressed his "highest gratification" about the publication of the book. "History, or the present recollection of past events," MacNeven commented in 1825, "if properly applied would emancipate the Catholics, or, better still, emancipate the Irish."[28]

Within these "applied histories" of Anglo-Irish relations, the Rising of 1798 provided the filter through which the past was viewed. Writing immediately after the event, Birch and Burk reflected the passionate intensity and anger that it evoked; their style and tone are at least as revealing as their content. Both men produced their work in a hurry, and gave free rein to their feelings; Burk's work, in particular, contains outraged and indignant reports of British floggings, beatings, half-hangings and executions. Drawing on fellow exiles James Reynolds, Robert Orr, Thomas Robinson and Birch himself for information, Burk transformed the Rising into a gigantic morality play, in which a "brave, humane and persecuted people" were goaded into rebellion by a vicious government that continued the "*most grinding despotism of six hundred years.*" Significantly, the theatrical language of *Bunker-Hill* and *Female Patriotism* resurfaced in his historical writing; Burk's description of the Irish people awaiting the signal for revolution was pure melodrama, and his imagery about the patriots forming "*torrents of the mountains*" that swept away "*the straggling detachments of the royalists*" was drawn directly from his earlier plays. Even Burk's description of Father Murphy, the revolutionary priest from County Wexford, cast him in the same role as Joan D'Arc in *Female Patriotism,* as a leader who circulated reports of his own invulnerability as a matter of policy to raise the morale of his men.[29]

Burk's desire for revenge, which still has the capacity to unsettle modern historians, was palpable. "I would have retaliated on these ruffians to the utmost extent," he wrote after describing the murder of wounded patriots at Vinegar Hill. Lord Kingsborough, the colonel of the notorious North Cork militia, should have been "instantly put to death" when he was captured; no mercy should be shown to the oppressors of the people. Such sentiments struck a responsive chord among the Irish in America who had been driven out by repression, and who needed to vent the feelings that were born of frustration and helplessness and fury about the counter-revolutionary triumph in Ireland. Other United Irishmen, such as James Carey, helped to circulate the book; over thirty years later, Sampson consulted it for the additions he was making in the American edition of William Taylor's patriotic *History of Ireland.* In this way, Burk's work became incorporated into the nineteenth-century radical Irish-American historical tradition.[30]

Sampson had already contributed to that tradition in 1807 with the publication of his *Memoirs,* which contained not only an account of his personal vicissitudes but also a wide-ranging discussion of Irish history, culture and politics. The central argument of the book was that the United Irishmen were reformers who had been forced into revolution by "the cruelties inflicted upon the people." In his own case, this was almost certainly true. Sampson had attempted in Ireland to use the threat of popular revolution to push the government into reform, while simultaneously trying to control the more militant figures in the movement—a strategy that made him many enemies on both sides. "It required exile, and years of Persecution," commented David Bailie Warden, "to make him, what he now is, an advocate for the Independence of Ireland."[31]

There is no doubt that Sampson's experiences during and after 1798 embittered him, and that his book was written as an act of literary revenge against the British and Irish authorities. "It is very sharp," he told his wife. "You see they did not listen to me when I was moderate. We must see how this will do. I am sure they will repent having worn out my patience so perversely." His *Memoirs* did very well indeed. The book was popular in America, where Jefferson was among its many admirers, and was read in England with enthusiasm by leading radicals such as Horne Tooke and Francis Burdett; there was even talk of a French edition. The result was to reinforce the "reluctant revolutionaries" interpretation of the United Irishmen. By projecting his own political trajectory onto the movement as a whole, Sampson ignored the original revolutionary strain within United Irish radicalism, and pinned all the blame for violence on the shoulders of Britain. His argument struck the [illegible] within nationalist circles on both sides of the Atlantic, and particularly in Irish America.[32]

The belief that Britain bore exclusive responsibility for revolutionary violence in Ireland found further expression in MacNeven's *Pieces of Irish History*, a collection of documents that he had gathered for an intended full-scale history of Ireland. The Irish, MacNeven maintained, had been the victims of a sinister governmental "conspiracy" to foment a rebellion that would be used to justify the Act of Union. Lords Clare and Castlereagh, he wrote, "with cold-blooded artifice, stirred up an insurrection that was to supply the necessary pretext for effecting their nefarious design." His views fitted into a well-established United Irish interpretive framework. For example, as early as 1792, one correspondent in the *Dublin Evening Post* warned his readers that "wicked ministers, skilled in political intrigue," were "goading the people to outrage, that men of property and peace may take refuge even in the *curse* of an union rather than hazard the evils of anarchy, and the violence of a populace." The events of 1798–1800 only seemed to confirm this interpretation, and MacNeven's position soon assumed the character of a self-evident truth; the believers included such unlikely bedfellows as Daniel O'Connell and Karl Marx.[33]

Although MacNeven failed to complete his larger "history of the sufferings and struggles of the Irish Nation," he welcomed the news in 1818 that Mathew Carey was preparing a broadly similar work. "I am consoled," MacNeven told Carey, "in seeing it taken up by one who views the subject as I do." Ostensibly about the Irish insurrection of 1641, Carey's *Vindiciae Hibernica* was intended to debunk loyalist arguments that a bigoted and violent Catholic populace had massacred tens of thousands of innocent Protestant settlers. Influenced by John Curry's *Historical and Critical Review of the Civil Wars in Ireland,* which had played a crucial role in the political education of Thomas Emmet, Carey rejected the view that Catholics had conspired against Protestants in 1641, and showed that the number of Protestant deaths during the insurrection had been grossly inflated by pro-British historians.[34]

What is particularly striking about Carey's book is the way in which his arguments about 1641 corresponded with contemporary United Irish interpretations of 1798. All the principal tenets of his position—the view that the Catholic Irish were oppressed, that they were more the victims than the perpetrators of massacres, that the Anglo-Irish entertained policies of genocide, that the people were goaded into insurrection by a government bent on tightening its grip on Ireland, that the Irish were no more rebels than the Americans, and that Anglo-Irish histories were a tissue of lies and propaganda—had been applied by the United Irishmen to their own insurrection. It is no coincidence that Carey had first thought about writing such a book in the aftermath of the 1798 Rising. The time-frame was collapsed; this was contemporary history, with the purpose of bolstering the Irish character in America while undercutting anti-emancipation arguments in Britain and Ireland.

Nor was it without effect. In America, Carey's book was admired by his fellow Irish radicals, and caught the attention of Madison. "I have dipped enough into your research & observations," Madison told Carey, "to be satisfied of your success in showing that the Irish Nation has been as much traduced by the pen of History, as it has been scourged by the rod of power." And in Ireland, the *Vindiciae Hibernica* became part of a broad and assertive Catholic historiographical movement that accompanied the campaign for emancipation.[35]

While these radical histories of Ireland became part of the intellectual recovery from the defeat of 1798, the United Irishmen in America also continued to support the struggle back home in more tangible ways. There were close connections between the émigrés and the revolutionary nationalists in Ireland who were behind Robert Emmet's insurrection of 1803. Phineas Bond, the British consul at Philadelphia, passed on information to his government that "Pikes, as well as ball Cartridges, had been exported from hence to Ireland, some time before the late sanguinary Insurrection in Dublin." The details, though, remained elusive; the informer, commented Bond, "expressed great Dread of the United Irishmen, in and about this City, and was convinced it would cost Him his Life, if it should ever be said, that He had revealed any of their Schemes."[36]

Other reports from Ireland suggested that the "Irish Rebels in America" were still organizing meetings at New York in 1806 "for the purpose of Supplying these Traitors who should choose to return, with sufficient money to defray all expenses to Ireland, for the *very purpose* of organizing the people again, & exciting another *General Rebellion*." Meanwhile, Leonard McNally, who kept his finger on what was left of the revolutionary pulse in Dublin, suspected that the United Irish émigrés in Philadelphia and New York continued to provide a channel of information between France and Ireland; he was either unaware of the disillusionment with Napoleon that had set in, or chose not to believe it. As late as 1820, McNally was still corresponding with the United Irishmen in the United States, feigning friendship while seeking information. "My Irish friends in America often visit my imagination," he told Sampson, "and are often, very often remembered in my cups." In the 1790s, he had supplied a steady stream of information to Dublin Castle about his "Irish friends" in general and Sampson in particular.[37]

McNally's continuing interest in Irish-American nationalism is not as puzzling as it might appear. After the Napoleonic Wars, as Daniel O'Connell's campaign for Catholic emancipation gathered momentum, Irish immigrants in America continued to provide moral and monetary support for the movement back home. Some of the older radicals, however, initially felt that the Irish in Ireland were not sufficiently aggressive in their [illegible]. When the United Irish émigrés learned that the King's visit to Dublin in 1821 has produced popular celebrations that were full of "fawning and adulation," they were appalled. Catholic declarations of loyalty, they believed, would only perpetuate their "present inferior condition." Drawing on what proved to be wrong lessons from their own experience, the radicals insisted that only a combination of external danger and internal resistance would force Britain to repeal the last of its "Popery Laws." To believe otherwise, commented MacNeven, was to believe in miracles. Thus it had been in 1778 and 1782, when restrictions on Catholics had been eased during the American war; thus it had been in 1793, when Catholics had been granted the franchise during the French war; thus it had been in Canada, where concessions to the Catholics had been made to prevent the colony from joining the United States.[38]

In effect, MacNeven was reviving his old criticisms of the Catholic Committee's conciliatory strategy during the late eighteenth century, and trying to ensure that his countrymen did not repeat the same mistakes. Although MacNeven and his colleagues in New York attacked O'Connell for raising false hopes about emancipation and for ignoring the issue of independence, they nevertheless perceived revolutionary potential in the emerging grass-roots movement in Ireland. Accordingly, in 1825, they resolved to raise an American counterpart to O'Connell's Catholic rent, "in order to co-operate the more effectually with those illustrious individuals in Ireland, who are desirous to accomplish the emancipation of their Country."[39]

As far as the United Irishmen were concerned, Catholic emancipation was an issue that demanded the support of all Irishmen, whatever their religious persuasion. It was, argued Sampson, a question of justice rather than religion. "I am a Catholic in this respect," he said, "that I would not honor any community that would change its religion, and prove renegado through fear or compulsion. It is that terror, tyranny, and persecution, that has made the Population of Ireland so truly Catholic; and it is the knowledge of that sacrilege, that places an honest man, particularly an American, on the side of Catholic Ireland." In practice, however, the campaign naturally produced a growing identification between Catholicism and nationalism. The pro-emancipation Irish-American newspapers that emerged in the 1820s were clearly Catholic in character; organizers of emancipation meetings pointed out with pride that "none but Catholics took a share in the discussion." When the Friends of Ireland Society first met in Philadelphia in 1828 to raise funds for O'Connell, religious tensions surfaced immediately. Some Protestants objected to the Catholic character of the organization, and refused to donate funds to the cause. On the other hand, some Catholics wanted to exclude even sympathetic Protestants from the organization, on the grounds that Catholics should fight their own battles themselves. The United Irish leaders of the movement, however, managed to sustain a precarious unity at the top; the Catholic-Protestant alliance was symbolized in New York by the cooperation of MacNeven and Sampson, and in Philadelphia by the alliance of Carey and Binns.[40]

When news reached America in May 1829 that Catholic emancipation had been won, the veteran radicals were exuberant. "The Catholics are no longer serfs," declared Binns; "our bells are ringing a merry peal for *Catholic* Emancipation from the Steeple of a *Protestant* Episcopal Church." On July 14, at the end of an impassioned address to the "Catholic Association of the Friends of Ireland" in Philadelphia, he proposed a toast to "The 4th of July, 1776; the 14th of July, 1789; and the 13th of April, 1829—the anniversaries of the emancipation of the United States, France, and of Ireland." The sister organization in New York decided to apply the funds that had not yet been sent across the Atlantic to erect a monument to the memory of Thomas Emmet, who "did not live to behold the triumph of the Catholic cause, that happy accomplishment of one of the great measures to which he devoted fortune and life." After a history of unremitting failure in Ireland, the United Irishmen celebrated Catholic emancipation not only as a resounding symbolic success but also as a form of personal vindication.[41]

And yet, when the dust had settled, it remained clear that much work remained to be done; the Catholic Relief Act had actually restricted the franchise, and Ireland was still far from independence. "The Union has degraded Ireland," MacNeven had said in 1825; "and from the Peer to the Peasant, all are sick of it; let the Catholics join their Countrymen in demanding a repeal of that Act." In 1831, he reconstituted the Friends of Ireland as a repeal organization: "All America will soon resound with it," he told David Bailie Warden. Meanwhile, in Philadelphia, the Hibernian Society attracted a number of "physical force" republicans who wanted to resurrect the revolutionary tradition in Ireland. Carey strongly criticized this approach, on essentially pragmatic grounds. To advocate physical force from an American platform, he argued, would play into anti-Irish stereotypes in the United States and deter moderates from joining the society, without making any difference to the situation back home. Besides, he commented, there was "no want of 'physical force' in Ireland" itself. He himself would refuse to preside over such an organization; among the people who supported him in this stance was the former physical-force republican John Binns.[42]

By this time, MacNeven had also come to the conclusion that revolutionary violence was counterproductive; the achievement of Catholic emancipation by peaceful means in 1829 had forced him to reevaluate his earlier criticisms of O'Connell. "We must all prefer, to the most successful use of physical violence," he declared in his last public speech in 1837, "the moral, peaceful revolution which Mr. O'Connell is now effecting by the masterly employment of his powers acquired to his country since 1798." This was not, MacNeven insisted, a repudiation of the earlier United Irish strategy; during the 1790s, he argued, the option of moral force was simply not available, and armed revolution was the "one mode of redress" that was left. Toward the end of his life, however, it was clear that MacNeven had become an O'Connellite not simply in means but also in ends. By 1839, he was prepared to accept a settlement that stopped well short of separatist republicanism: "a domestic legislature for the business of the country, not extending to foreign policy, continuing to be a part of the English monarchy, subject to the King of England; no Church Establishment; no tithes." "All schemes for the advantage of Ireland, short of this," he added, "are futile."[43]

This flexibility of approach, informed by close contact with events in Ireland, runs counter to customary notions of the émigrés as people frozen in time, stuck forever in the 1790s. But their revolutionary republican background placed them on the radical edge of the O'Connellite movement. Just as MacNeven had criticized the strategy for Catholic emancipation in the mid-1820s, Sampson and Carey expressed similar doubts and misgivings about the Repeal movement during the following decade. In both cases, the émigrés were more militant than the reformers back home. Not surprisingly, O'Connell's critical comments in 1841 about the United Irishmen as "weak and wicked men who considered force and sanguinary violence as part of their resources for ameliorating our institutions" were greeted in Irish-American radical circles with a mixture of shock and anger, although even here, an aging MacNeven appeared much less upset by the remarks than were his younger admirers.[44]

More generally, the United Irishmen were closer to the spirit of Young

Ireland than to O'Connell, and those who lived long enough welcomed the resurgence of radicalism during the 1840s. After the failure of the Young Ireland insurrection of 1848, a new wave of exiled revolutionaries came into the United States, and breathed new life into the Irish-American nationalist tradition initiated by the United Irishmen. Among the recent émigrés was Thomas D'Arcy McGee, who had attempted to raise a contingent of Irish revolutionaries from Scotland to participate in the rising and had escaped arrest by disguising himself as a priest and taking ship to New York. When he visited Philadelphia, McGee made a point of visiting John Binns, one of the few surviving United Irishmen in the country. Their handshake symbolized the connection of the revolutionary Irish nationalist tradition in America, even though McGee would eventually move in a very different direction and wind up as a liberal-conservative Founding Father of Confederation in British North America.[45]

That, however, lay in the future. At the time, Binns supplied McGee with materials for his *History of the Irish Settlers in America*, which attempted to heighten the reputation of the Irish in the United States by demonstrating how they had contributed to the establishment of a free and progressive civilization in the New World. Shortly after their meeting, McGee pondered Edmund Spenser's comment that Ireland might be destined to stand as a judgment on England and eventually humble her powerful neighbor. Spenser's forebodings, he concluded, were now being realized through an Irish-American medium. "The Irish emigrate to America," he wrote, "and help to take this continent from England in 1775, as they now help to keep it anti-British in temper and policy."[46]

But there was another side to this, as well. Not only did the radical Irish contribute to anti-British sentiment in America; they also believed that the model and example of America would inspire the cause of nationalism back home. "I devoutly hope," Emmet wrote Carey in 1819, "that the propagation of truth & the extension of the principles of free Government, which America is teaching by her example, may yet produce the regeneration of our beloved Ireland." Although much wishful thinking was expressed on the subject, many Irish radicals did indeed look upon America as a City upon a Hill. In 1820, Robert Johnson wrote a gloomy letter to Carey about the "torpid" state of politics in his native country. "Yet we still hope," Johnson concluded; "and this hope is principally nourished by our anticipations of the progress of America, and the relative diminution of those who hate America." Or, as Thomas O'Connor put it, "the cause of Ireland is essentially the same as that of America."[47]

This belief not only meant that the United Irishmen could help the "cause of Ireland" by supplying money, morale, and (in the early years, at least) ammunition to their fellow nationalists at home; it also implied that they could strengthen nationalism in Ireland by demonstrating the viability of democratic and republican institutions in the United States. By their very immersion in American politics, culture, religion and society, they believed, the United Irishmen were actively contributing to the cause of their native country. In this sense, the wheel had turned full circle.

CONCLUSION

The Tradition of All the Dead Generations

In Ireland, the United Irishmen had been trapped by the contradiction of the necessary but impossible revolution. The status quo, they believed, was intolerable; the entire system of British rule, hereditary privilege and religious discrimination weighed down upon the country, preventing its people from realizing their full potential. Aristocracy, as John Chambers had remarked in 1792, was a yoke that the Irish would have around their necks for another century unless it was shaken off now. But the yoke proved too heavy to shift. Underestimating the repressive apparatus of the state and the strength of sectarianism in the country, the United Irishmen precipitated a civil war that blew up in their faces. Even had they succeeded in defeating the British in 1798, it is extremely unlikely that they would have been able to establish the non-sectarian, democratic republic that they desired. Had they won with the support of the French, they would have been absorbed into the Napoleonic imperialist system. Had they won without the support of the French, they would have been changed beyond recognition by their alliance with the Defenders.

The United Irish dilemma was broadly similar to that facing Francisco Goya in Spain during the Age of Revolution. During the late 1790s, in his *Caprichos* series, Goya produced an engraving that depicted a man who was asleep at his desk, slumped over his papers. Behind him, coming out of the shadows, a cluster of hideous shapes was emerging, strange bat-like creatures that were taking possession of the scene. "El sueño de la razon produce montruos," it was entitled; "the sleep of reason produces monsters." This was a meaning that the Irish democrats would have grasped immediately. But there was a hidden ambiguity in Goya's etching. The Spanish word for sleep, "sueño," is also the word for dream; the engraving could equally be translated as "the dream of reason produces monsters." And there is a sense in which this second meaning is particularly appropriate for the revolutionary ideology of the United Irishmen, as applied to the condition of their own country.[1]

From the United Irish perspective, Reason appeared as a kind of panacea for all political ills. More impressed with first principles than with probable consequences, the United Irishmen were convinced that the rights of man, freedom of expression and equality of opportunity would banish forever the monsters of hereditary rule, religious bigotry and oppressive taxation. The logic was linear, in a species of revolution by syllogism: Natural and civil rights formed the basis of legitimate government; existing regimes were based on power and precedent; therefore, such regimes were illegitimate, and must be replaced by ones that corresponded with correct political premises. Government should be stripped of the aura of mystery, majesty and awe, and be based on the practical wisdom of the people; it was, in the end, only a matter of common sense. Associated with this position was a powerful utopian strand that found expression in both secular and religious forms of millenarianism.

Precisely because the rewards promised to be so great, the ends apparently justified a variety of means; many [illegible] would [illegible] particular omelette. Convinced of their own "benevolence of intention," in MacNeven's phrase, the radicals believed that only ignorant or self-interested men could possibly oppose such a program. There was, within this position, considerable potential for intolerance in the name of liberty, lies in the name of truth, destruction in the name of utopia, monsters in the dream of reason. One thinks of Driscol's contemptuous dismissal of those who rejected his deism, Benjamin Binns's easy justification of deception in a good cause, or Tone's view that tens of thousands of lives were a cheap price for the emancipation of mankind. This, indeed, was one of the principal reasons for Edmund Burke's ferocious reaction against revolutionary ideology. "I have no great opinion," he wrote, "of that sublime, abstract, metaphysic reversionary, contingent humanity, which in *cold blood* can subject the *present time,* and those whom we *daily see and converse with,* to *immediate* calamities in favour of the *future and uncertain* benefit of persons who *only exist in an idea.*"[2]

The democratic views that Burke attacked were not, of course, confined to the United Irishmen; they were commonplace throughout the Atlantic world, and the Irish revolutionaries saw themselves as a local variant of a broader phenomenon. But if they were exponents of an apparently universalist ideology, they were also products of specific historical circumstances whose importance they underestimated. Their very call for their countrymen to "forget all former feuds," and to focus on future possibilities instead of brooding on past wrongs, actually testified to the strength of the historical forces that pressed down upon them. "The tradition of all the dead generations weighs like a nightmare on the brain of the living," Karl Marx would write; with their essentially ahistorical outlook, the United Irishmen wound up living through the very nightmare from which they were trying to awake.[3]

Not that they were blind to the problems of reconciling the ideal with the real. One of the most fascinating things about the United Irishmen is the degree of self-criticism that surfaced in their private correspondence. At times, their writings provide striking confirmations of the conservative case against the revolutionary movement. Thomas Emmet, for example, eventually came to accept the view that the United Irish alliance with France would be disastrous for the democratic republican cause; Napoleon, he believed, would have treated Ireland like a conquered country, and ruled it through an authoritarian Catholic establishment. Agonizing about the relationship between ends and means, John Caldwell displayed deep misgivings about the Defender alliance, and deplored the "many instances of depravity and wickedness and departure from the unerring rule of right" that occurred within the revolutionary movement. "Alas," he wrote, "I had too many convincing proofs as we proceeded of what would have been the ultimate fate of such men as William Sinclaire [*sic*], Robert Simms, and hundreds of others, without character, whose names I forbear to mention, had we succeeded in accomplishing the object of our wishes, the liberty of our country."[4]

Other United Irishmen expressed grave reservations about the elitism and factionalism that characterized the organization. Drennan's comment that many of his fellow radicals talked like open-minded democrats but acted like intolerant aristocrats was amply illustrated by the careers of such Irish-American radicals as Burk, Driscol and Duane. As Brendan Behan later remarked, the first item on the agenda of any nationalist meeting is usually the split; within the United Irish movement, there were regular denunciations of the "spirit of faction," in which each side accused the other of apostasy. Arthur O'Connor, for example, attacked Emmet and his supporters as Maratists who claimed to hold a monopoly on patriotism, refused to tolerate differences, and would plunge the country into a bloodbath to get their way; there is nothing to distinguish this position from the High Tory arguments of William Cobbett. Yet O'Connor was totally oblivious to the way in which he himself exhibited the very traits that he attacked in others. He saw himself as a man who was not "capable of entertaining hatred," while pouring out hatred of his enemies in a stream of incoherent rage. Had they been in power, O'Connor and his supporters would played the role of Jacobins, Emmet and his supporters would have been the Girondins, and each side would accused the other of being sans-culottes. It was exactly this kind of factional conflict, experienced repeatedly in Ireland, France and America, that drove Hamilton Rowan out of revolutionary politics altogether.[5]

There was, within the movement, a sense that the revolutionary tactics could backfire, that an Irish revolution could devour its own children, and that a combination of intolerance, arrogance and internecine conflict could cause the revolution to self-destruct. Countering this was a continuing belief that democratic republicanism nevertheless remained the best prospect of liberating humanity from monarchical and aristocratic oppression in general, and liberating Ireland from British rule in particular. Caldwell wrote:

> Even under the conviction that there are bad, designing and wicked men insidiously professing our opinions and offering themselves if needs be as sacrifices at the shrine of liberty, a virtuous and patriotic man will not on that account withdraw himself from doing his part for the general weal, or refuse his aid to the salvation of his country tho he may keep himself aloof from the contagion of personal intercourse with the loathesome objects with whom he may for a time be partially associated.[6]

The "salvation of the country," together with a deep-rooted hatred of British rule in Ireland, took precedence over all the doubts and misgivings and fears, and prevented the United Irishmen from facing the logic of their own internal critique.

In America, of course, they ordered things differently. Here the United Irishmen's commitment to the rights of man, their utopianism and their Anglophobia could be given free rein. The ideas were the same, but the context was radically altered; the émigrés transmitted their beliefs, values and attitudes to the United States, where they became transmuted into a hyperpatriotic form of American nationalism. Although the United Irishmen continued to generate considerable controversy, they moved with remarkable rapidity into the Jeffersonian mainstream. By the War of 1812, they had established political strongholds in the mid-Atlantic states, formed networks throughout the length and breadth of the country, made substantial contributions to journalism and education in the United States, and emerged as forceful and dynamic figures in the cultural, religious and social life of the new republic.

Striving for acceptance and respectability, they became sufficiently acculturated to adopt white images of the Native Americans as savages who had the potential to be "civilized," and to accept the view that slavery was an acceptable price that other people paid for the greater good of national unity. Some became slaveowners themselves; others looked forward to the day when all blacks in America would be deported to Africa. Battling manifestations of American nativism, the United Irishmen formed immigrant support groups, became leaders of the growing Irish community in the United States, and made Irishness appear synonymous with radical republicanism. Defining Americanism primarily in ideological terms, they viewed themselves as being among the most dedicated democrats, and thus among the most dedicated Americans, in the world. In the United States, they were convinced, they were working with the grain of history; not surprisingly, they emerged as some of the strongest supporters of the rising American empire. It is no coincidence that it was one of their successors, the Irish-American journalist John O'Sullivan, who coined the phrase "manifest destiny."

Their views on democracy, commerce and nationalism were already becoming part of the American political culture, as was their utopian and Anglophobic cast of mind; this, indeed, is a major reason why the United Irishmen were able to fit into their new environment so quickly. But the fact that their political outlook had been formed in Ireland meant that they injected a distinct tone into American politics. The United Irishmen not only developed sophisticated electoral machines in the mid-Atlantic states but also energized democratic political movements throughout the country; in the process, radical American politics began to acquire Irish inflections.

At one level, this process was readily recognizable; it took its most obvious form in the argument that the causes of Ireland and the United States were identical, and in the frequently expressed belief that the Federalists were the American equivalent of the Orangemen and should be treated accordingly. At another level, it was much more subtle and difficult to detect. Burk's *Bunker-Hill,* or his *History of Virginia,* seem at first glance to have nothing whatsoever to do with Ireland; in fact, they were strongly influenced by his experiences as a revolutionary in Cork and Dublin. McCreery's "The American Star," one of the most popular songs of the War of 1812, apparently had no Irish connection; in fact, the American words were set to an Irish tune. Birch's ferocious attack on the religious revivalists of western Pennsylvania appears to be solely connected to American circumstances; in fact, it can also be understood as a continuation of his earlier, equally vitriolic battle with the Seceders in County Down. Whether consciously expressed or unconsciously absorbed, their experiences in Ireland provided the conceptual filter through which the United Irishmen viewed politics in America. It could hardly have been otherwise.

In part, this was a matter of political style. The belief that the ends justified the means was carried over from Irish to American politics, where it fitted easily with existing practices. Duane, for example, had no compunction about forging documents or spreading lies for the higher purpose of winning an election. "Morality," he said on one occasion, "is not a necessary qualification in a legislator." John Binns paid him back in kind, while other Irish radicals, such as the editors of Baltimore's *American Patriot,* attempted to discredit their rivals by smearing them as Orangemen or denouncing them as informers. Such tactics were not, of course, the exclusive property of the United Irishmen; native-born American politicians across the political spectrum could be equally unscrupulous, and leading anti-Republicans such as Cobbett and Fenno twisted the truth whenever it suited them.

More closely connected to the radical political culture in Ireland was the United Irish tendency to see politics as a zero-sum game, in which compromise was regarded as victory or defeat in disguise. Convinced that they were locked in a life-or-death struggle that paralleled their battles with the

Orangemen back home, many United Irishmen believed that their Federalist enemies should be crushed rather than conciliated. Not all the émigrés felt this way; Mathew Carey in Philadelphia increasingly came to seek the political middle ground, as did Emmet, Sampson and MacNeven in New York. Generally speaking, it was those radicals who had been closest in spirit to the militant O'Connorite wing of the United movement in Ireland, such as Binns, Burk, Driscol and Reynolds, who were most likely to demand that American conservatives should be tarred and feathered or even hanged for voicing criticisms of Jefferson.

Such militancy was fed by the utopian element in United Irish politics, which was also transmitted across the Atlantic. Extreme circumstances had produced extreme reactions; apocalyptic visions of the world flourished in an atmosphere of terror and counter-terror. With the defeat of the democratic movement and the exodus of émigrés to America, a kind of double exceptionalism emerged. If the Irish were the most oppressed people ever, the United States was perceived as "a Real Republican government and the Best in the Woreld," as one émigré from north Antrim put it. The transatlantic voyage had become a journey from dystopia to utopia.[7]

Democratic republicanism had assumed the character of a secular religion; the United Irishmen were true believers who came to see America as the Promised Land. Virtually every émigré who left written records spoke in glowing terms about the United States as the land of liberty. Tone called it the best government under heaven; Burk believed that man was free from the moment he set foot on American soil; Warden felt that he was living in a wonderful country; Binns rejoiced that he was making a new start in the new world. For radical Presbyterian ministers such as Birch and John Glendy, the United States was not merely ushering in a secular utopia, but fulfilling a divine purpose; in the wilderness of America, believed Birch, the millennium was at hand. These arguments chimed with a political and religious culture already steeped in imagery of the City upon a Hill. Not the least of the United Irish contributions to the United States was to bolster the country's sense of mission, its belief that it was the political, social, economic, religious and moral center of the universe.

Above all, though, the United Irishmen sustained and strengthened the Anglophobic strain within American political life. In Ireland, Tone's view that England was "the never-failing source of all our political evils" had become deeply ingrained in United Irish politics.[8] England did, indeed, have much to answer for; such sentiments did not simply spring out of thin air. But by externalizing all Irish political conflict and projecting it onto England, the radicals ignored the breadth and depth of internal divisions among the Irish, while simultaneously absolving themselves of responsibility for their own actions. The Irish people who opposed the democratic republican movement, on this reading of reality, were merely dupes of Britain. By the same reasoning, revolutionary atrocities were viewed as the regrettable but inevitable products of imperialist oppression; the government, according to this view, was only reaping what it had sowed.

In America, such Anglophobia meshed with existing anti-British traditions that the United Irishmen made every effort to resuscitate. Time and again, Irish radicals reminded Americans of British atrocities during the War of Independence; there were frequent references to the mass execution of prisoners on the Jersey prison-ship, the transformation of churches into stables, barracks and play-houses in Boston and New York, and the killing of Washington's guards in their beds at Valley Forge. Just as the United Irishmen argued that their countrymen had been deliberately goaded into insurrection by the British, they maintained that the same conspiracy had been employed against the Americans, only to be defeated by the patriotic colonists. And just as the United Irish leaders were betrayed by false promises of amnesty by the British government in 1798, they wrote, Christopher Gadsden and the citizens of Charleston had experienced a similar fate at the hands of Lord Cornwallis during the American war.[9] From Birch's sermons to Burk's plays, from Sampson's memoirs to Driscol's newspaper articles, the same message was constantly repeated: Britain was a kind of political Antichrist, using every means at its disposal to crush liberty wherever and whenever it appeared.

Exactly the same reasoning was applied to American politics. When Tone told Thomas Russell that the Irish in Pennsylvania were boorish and ignorant blackguards, he had no hesitation in laying the blame at Britain's feet; having been corrupted by British oppression, he wrote, they had not learned how to live as free men. When Irish radicals encountered American Federalists, a reflex response kicked in; the Federalists were regarded as puppets of the British government, which was supposedly adopting the same divide-and-rule tactics that had served it so well in Ireland. The possibility that Federalism might actually have indigenous American roots was given short shrift, if indeed it was considered at all. On the same grounds, British machinations were blamed for outbreaks of American nativism. Just as British agents had spread stereotypes in Europe about the "ignorant Yankee," it was argued, they were now doing the same thing in America about the "stupid Paddy"; there were regular complaints, none of which was substantiated, that British spies were being paid to promote negative images of the Irish in the United States. So pervasive was United Irish Anglophobia that the British were even blamed for the persistence of slavery in republican America. Similarly, Native American attacks on white settlers were seen as products of British manipulation rather than as reactions to the westward march of the American empire. D'Arcy McGee was right; the United Irishmen had been remarkably successful in keeping anti-British feelings alive and well in the United States.

When McGee expressed this view, the next generation of Irish republicans was already establishing itself in the country. In the aftermath of the abortive rising of 1848, revolutionary nationalists such as John Mitchel, John O'Mahony and Michael Doheny found a receptive audience in the United States among the vast numbers of Famine immigrants who had flooded into the country. Intensely Anglophobic, they formed the Fenian Brotherhood in 1858, and perpetuated a strain of nationalism that was in many respects much more militant than its counterpart back in Ireland, but that was also a continuation of the United Irish tradition in America. The central tenets and tactics of American Fenians—including not only Anglophobia and separatist nationalism, but also fundraising, arms running, and the belief that Ireland could be liberated through an American-based attack on Canada—followed principles and practices that had been well established by the United Irish émigrés who had come to America between 1795 and 1812. Irish-American nationalism began during the late eighteenth and early nineteenth centuries; its first exponents were United Irishmen. And the tradition of the dead generations continues to press on the brain of the living.

Notes

Frequently cited sources have been identified by the following abbreviations.

GUS	*Gazette of the United States*
HO	Home Office Papers, Public Record Office, London
HSP	Historical Society of Pennsylvania, Philadelphia
PG	*Porcupine's Gazette*
PRONI	Public Record Office, Northern Ireland
RP	Rebellion Papers, National Archives, Ireland
WMQ	*William and Mary Quarterly*, 3d Series

Introduction. The Most God-Provoking Democrats on This Side of Hell

1. Uriah Tracy to Oliver Wolcott, August 7, 1800, in *Memoirs of the Administrations of Washington and John Adams, Edited from the Papers of Oliver Wolcott, Secretary of the Treasury*, ed. George Gibbs (1846; New York, 1971), vol. 2, p. 399.

2. Rufus King to the Duke of Portland, September 13, 1798, in *The Life and Correspondence of Rufus King: Comprising His Letters, Private and Official, His Public Documents, and His Speeches*, ed. Charles R. King (New York, 1971), vol. 2, p. 640.

3. Hans-Jurgen Grabbe, "European Immigration to the United States in the Early National Period, 1783–1820," *Proceedings of the American Philosophical Society* 133 (June 1989), p. 194.

4. _____ to George Ivie, New York, August 1, 1797, RP 620/32/4.

5. Edward C. Carter II, "A 'Wild Irishman' under Every Federalist's Bed: Naturalization in Philadelphia, 1789–1806," *Pennsylvania Magazine of History and Biography* 94 (July 1970), p. 333, n. 6.

6. For examples of the myth, see John Caldwell to Robert Simms, October 18, 1802, Emigrant Letters to Robert Simms, PRONI, T 1815, and David Noel Doyle, *Ireland, Irishmen and Revolutionary America* (Cork and Dublin, 1981), p. 224. The

revisionist view is presented by Donald Harman Akenson, *Being Had: Historians, Evidence, and the Irish in North America* (Port Credit, Ontario, 1985), pp. 37–75, and Akenson, *The Irish Diaspora: A Primer* (Toronto and Belfast, 1993), pp. 217–69.

7. Richard Twomey, *Jacobins and Jeffersonians: Anglo-American Radicalism in the United States, 1790–1820* (New York, 1989); Michael Durey, "Transatlantic Patriotism: Political Exiles and America in the Age of Revolutions," in *Artisans, Peasants and Proletarians, 1760–1860: Essays Presented to Gwyn A. Williams*, ed. Clive Emsley and James Walvin (London, 1985), pp. 7–31, and Durey, "Thomas Paine's Apostles: Radical Emigrés and the Triumph of Jeffersonian Republicanism," *WMQ* 44 (1987), pp. 661–88.

8. *GUS*, August 15, 1800.

9. John Daly Burk, *History of the Late War in Ireland* (Philadelphia, 1799), pp. 101, 135; *Shamrock*, January 25, 1817.

10. David Bailie Warden, *A Chorographical and Statistical Description of the District of Columbia* (Paris, 1816), p. 27.

11. Thomas Ledlie Birch, *Seemingly Experimental Religion* (Washington, Pennsylvania, 1806), p. 31; *Washington Reporter*, June 26, 1823.

12. There has been considerable controversy within American historiography over the significance of classical republicanism in the early national period; see, for example, Robert Shalhope, "Republicanism and Early American Historiography," *WMQ* 36 (April 1982), pp. 334–56. In my view, the most convincing contributions to the debate are Joyce Appleby, *Capitalism and a New Social Order* (New York, 1984), and John R. Nelson, Jr., *Liberty and Property: Political Economy and Policymaking in the New Nation, 1789–1812* (Baltimore, 1987), both of which argue for the primacy of the liberal tradition over classical republicanism.

13. On classical republicanism within Ireland, see Ian McBride, "William Drennan and the Dissenting Tradition," in *The United Irishmen: Republicanism, Radicalism and Rebellion*, ed. David Dickson, Dáire Keogh and Kevin Whelan (Dublin, 1993), pp. 56–57, and Ian McBride, "The School of Virtue: Francis Hutcheson, Irish Presbyterians and the Scottish Enlightenment," in *Political Thought in Ireland since the Seventeenth Century*, ed. D. George Boyce, Robert Eccleshall, and Vincent Geoghegan (London, 1993), pp. 86–92.

14. John Chambers to Mathew Carey, September 4, 1795, Lea and Febiger Collection, HSP; John Chambers to Robert Simms, May 25, 1821, Emigrant Letters to Robert Simms, PRONI, T 1815. See also Chambers to Mathew Carey, August 2, 1794, Lea and Febiger Collection, HSP.

15. George Cuming to Robert Simms, Emigrant Letters to Robert Simms, PRONI, T 1815; Archibald Hamilton Rowan to Caesar Rodney, February 27, 1816, and February 21, 1817, Gratz Collection, HSP; David Bailie Warden, *A Statistical, Political, and Historical Account of the United States of North America; From the Period of their First Colonization to the Present Day* (Edinburgh, 1819), vol. 3, p. 476.

16. Warden, *Statistical, Political, and Historical Account*, vol. 1, pp. xlviii–xlix.

17. *Constitutional Diary*, December 17, 1799.

18. *Polar Star*, December 13, December 22, 1796; John Binns to John Sergeant, January 17, 1834, Society Collection, HSP; *New York Evening Post*, November 11, 1809; Warden to Joel Barlow, January 1, 1810 (misdated by Warden as 1809), David Bailie Warden Papers, Maryland Historical Society, MS. 871.

19. See, for example, Thomas Ledlie Birch, *Letter from an Irish Emigrant, to his*

Friend in the United States (New York, 1798), p. 1; *Time-Piece,* June 13, 1798; John Daly Burk to Oliver Phelps, November 1796, Phelps and Gorham Papers, Box 23, New York State Library; [New York] *Evening Post,* April 11, 1807; William James MacNeven, *Pieces of Irish History* (New York, 1807), pp. 295–96.

20. Twomey, *Jacobins and Jeffersonians,* pp. 171–213.

21. Richard R. Madden, *The United Irishmen: Their Lives and Times,* 3 vols., 2d ed. (Dublin, 1858).

22. Madden, *United Irishmen,* vol. 3, p. 42.

23. See William Sampson to Grace Sampson, July 4, 1807, Papers of William Sampson, Library of Congress ("I do not like to be of any society"), and David Bailie Warden Papers, Maryland Historical Society, MS. 871, Register A, pp. 32–33, c. 1809 ("What a singular fate was his! To be proscribed as a United Irishman altho' he had never joined that association").

24. *Democratic Press,* June 10, 1807

Chapter 1. A Green Bough

1. Marianne Elliott, *Partners in Revolution: The United Irishmen and France* (New Haven and London, 1982), pp. 23–24; Robert Simms, "Declarations and Resolutions of the Society of United Irishmen of Belfast," October 1791, in William Theobald [illegible] *Star,* November 16, 1796; Birch, *Letter from an Irish Emigrant,* p. 5; Burk, *History of the Late War,* p. 15; John Binns, *Recollections of the Life of John Binns* (Philadelphia, 1854), pp. 52–53, 65–66; *Dublin Evening Post,* October 30, 1792.

2. For an excellent study that argues against a straightforward dichotomy between "reformist" and "revolutionary" phases of the United Irish movement, see Jim Smyth, *The Men of No Property: Irish Radicals and Popular Politics in the Late Eighteenth Century* (Houndmills, 1992), esp. pp. 79–99, 139–42.

3. William Drennan to William Bruce, February 7, 1784, PRONI, D 553/20; Drennan to William Bruce, n.d. [1790], PRONI, D 553/70; Drennan to Samuel McTier, May 21, 1791, in *The Drennan Letters,* ed. D. A. Chart (Belfast, 1931), pp. 54–55; Drennan to Samuel McTier, December 1791, *Drennan Letters,* p. 69; "Diary of Wolfe Tone," in Tone, *Life of Theobald Wolfe Tone,* vol. 1, p. 141; A. T. Q. Stewart, *A Deeper Silence* (London, 1993), pp. 149–63. For Tone's public position, see "A Letter to the Editor of Faulkner's Journal," in Tone, *Life of Theobald Wolfe Tone,* vol. 1, pp. 495–510; for his private views, see Wolfe Tone to Thomas Russell, [July] 9, 1791, Royal Irish Academy, 23/K/53 (6). See also JW [Leonard McNally] to ——, February 4, 1797, RP 620/10/121/49.

4. Louis M. Cullen, "The Internal Politics of the United Irishmen," in *The United Irishmen,* ed. Dickson, Keogh, and Whelan, p. 179; Drennan to Samuel McTier, February 5, 1791, *Drennan Letters,* p. 53; Drennan to Samuel McTier, September 1, 1793, *Drennan Letters,* p. 171; *Polar Star,* October 13, 1796; *Time-Piece,* August 14, 1798; Burk, *History of the Late War,* p. 16; *Polar Star,* November 16, 1796; John Caldwell, "Particulars of a North County Irish Family," PRONI, T 3541/5/3, p. 3.

5. Thomas Addis Emmet, "Part of an Essay Towards the History of Ireland," in MacNeven, *Pieces of Irish History,* p. 14; Drennan to William Bruce [n.d., 1791], PRONI, D 553/72; Ian McBride, "William Drennan and the Dissenting Tradition," in *The United Irishmen,* ed. Dickson, Keogh, and Whelan, pp. 49–61; Archibald

Hamilton Rowan to John Jebb, March 5, 1785, in *Autobiography of Archibald Hamilton Rowan,* ed. William Drummond (Dublin, 1840), pp. 127–29; John Jebb to Rowan, September 29, 1785, in *Autobiography,* ed. Drummond, p. 131.

6. Quoted in Thomas Pakenham, *The Year of Liberty: The History of the Great Irish Rebellion of 1798* (London, 1969; rpt. 1972), frontispiece.

7. Denis Gwynn, *The Struggle for Catholic Emancipation* (London, 1928), p. 29; James G. Leyburn, *The Scotch-Irish: A Social History* (Chapel Hill, 1962), p. 305; John Caldwell, "Particulars," PRONI, T 3541/5/3, pp. 4, 24; William Steel Dickson, *A Narrative of the Confinement and Exile of William Steel Dickson, D.D.* (Dublin, 1812), p. 7; *Northern Star,* November 17, 1792; Edward William Harcourt, ed., *The Harcourt Papers* (Oxford, n.d.), vol. 9, p. 363; "Memorial of Archibald Hamilton Rowan," 18 Vendemiaire, Year III (October 9, 1794), *Correspondance Politique Angleterre,* vol. 588, f. 274, Archives des Affairs Etrangers, Quai D'Orsay, Paris.

8. Caldwell, "Particulars," p. 4; see also Jonathan Powell, "Presbyterian Loyalists," *Journal of Presbyterian History* 57 (1979), pp. 135–60.

9. Maurice Bric, "Ireland, Irishmen, and the Broadening of the Late-Eighteenth-Century Philadelphia Polity" (Ph.D. diss., Johns Hopkins University, 1990), pp. 89–91.

10. Bric, "Ireland, Irishmen," pp. 92–97; Maurice O'Connell, *Irish Politics and Social Conflict in the Age of the American Revolution* (Philadelphia, 1965), pp. 32–33.

11. On the Whiteboys, see Maureen Wall, "The Whiteboys," in *Secret Societies in Ireland,* ed. T. D. Williams (Dublin, 1973), pp. 13–25, and James S. Donnelly, Jr., "The Whiteboy Movement, 1761–5," *Irish Historical Studies* 21 (1978), pp. 20–54.

12. See, for example, Caldwell, "Particulars," p. 26, and Bric, "Ireland, Irishmen," p. 97.

13. Dickson, *Narrative,* p. 10. On the political influence of the Volunteers, see Stewart, *A Deeper Silence,* pp. 21–22, 30–64, and P. D. H. Smyth, "The Volunteers and Parliament, 1779–84," in *Penal Era and Golden Age: Essays in Irish History, 1690–1800,* ed. T. Bartlett and D. W. Hayton (Belfast, 1979), pp. 113–36.

14. Henry Grattan, ed., *The Speeches of the Right Honourable Henry Grattan* (London, 1822), vol. 1, p. 123.

15. Rupert J. Coughlan, *Napper Tandy* (Dublin, 1976), p. 32; Benjamin Binns to R. R. Madden, May 24, 1843, Madden Papers, Trinity College Dublin, 873/451/7; Sir Jonah Barrington, *Historic Memoirs of Ireland* (London, 1835), vol. 1, p. 164; Rowan, "Memorial," f. 274; Harold Nicolson, *The Desire to Please: A Story of Hamilton Rowan and the United Irishmen* (London, 1943), pp. 77–83; Caldwell, "Particulars," p. 63.

16. The best treatment of Carey's career is Edward C. Carter II, "The Political Activities of Mathew Carey, Nationalist, 1760–1814" (Ph.D. diss., Bryn Mawr College, 1962).

17. The pamphlet, which was not actually published in Ireland, is printed in Mathew Carey, *Miscellaneous Essays* (Philadelphia, 1830), p. 452; see also Mathew Carey, *Autobiography* (1833–34; New York, 1942), pp. 4–5.

18. *The Volunteers Journal,* January 2, 1784, March 26, 1784, April 5, 1784, April 16, 1784, April 21, 1784; Carey, *Autobiography,* pp. 8–9.

19. Dáire Keogh, *The French Disease: The Catholic Church and Irish Radicalism, 1790–1800* (Blackrock, 1993), pp. 48–50; Eamon O'Flaherty, "Irish Catholics and the French Revolution," in *Ireland and the French Revolution,* ed. Hugh Gough and David Dickson (Blackrock, 1990), pp. 52–67; Smyth, *Men of No Property,* pp. 59–61; John

Chambers to Mathew Carey, April 12, 1792, Lea and Febiger Collection, HSP; Jane Maryanne MacNeven, "Memoir," in Madden, *United Irishmen,* vol. 3, p. 201.

20. Nicolson, *Desire to Please,* pp. 95–98; Drennan to Samuel McTier, March 3, 1792, April 28, 1792, April 2, 1793, *Drennan Letters,* pp. 86–87, 149; Michael Durey, "The Dublin Society of United Irishmen and the Politics of the Carey-Drennan Dispute, 1792–1796," *Historical Journal* 37 (1994), pp. 94, 104–5; Coughlan, *Napper Tandy,* pp. 49, 52, 95–96.

21. Emmet, "Part of an Essay," in MacNeven, *Pieces of Irish History,* p. 57; Elliott, *Partners in Revolution,* p. 42; Smyth, *Men of No Property,* p. 70; Coughlan, *Napper Tandy,* pp. 97–100; Samuel McSkimin, *Annals of Ulster* (Belfast, 1906), p. 24.

22. Elliott, *Partners in Revolution,* pp. 37–39.

23. Emmet, "Part of an Essay," in MacNeven, *Pieces of Irish History,* p. 59; *Dublin Evening Post,* March 28, 1793; Drennan to Samuel McTier, March 26, 1793, March 30, 1793, January 17, 1794, *Drennan Letters,* pp. 144–45, 146, 180; RP 620/20/54.

24. Emmet, "Part of an Essay," in MacNeven, *Pieces of Irish History,* pp. 97, 109; Thomas P. Robinson, "The Life of Thomas Addis Emmet" (Ph.D. diss., New York University, 1955), p. 79.

25. The best general treatment of United Irish attempts to bring about a French invasion is Elliott, *Partners in Revolution.*

26. J .J. St. Mark, "The Oswald Mission to Ireland from America: 20 February to 8 June 1794," *Éire-Ireland* [illegible] (Summer [illegible]), pp. 25–[illegible]; Elliott, *Partners in Revolution,* pp. 60–61; Rowan, "Memorial of Archibald Hamilton Rowan," f. 275.

27. _____ to _____, February 1, 1794, RP 620/21/27; Rowan, "Memorial," ff. 276–77; Emmet, "Part of an Essay," in MacNeven, *Pieces of Irish History,* pp. 86–87; Martha McTier to William Drennan, August 3, 1794, *Drennan Letters,* p. 213.

28. Elliott, *Partners in Revolution,* pp. 64–67; Robinson, "Life of Thomas Addis Emmet," pp. 59–61. The account of Rowan's escape is based on Rowan, "Memorial," f. 278; for a slightly different version, see *Autobiography of Archibald Hamilton Rowan,* ed. Drummond, pp. 213–16, and Nicolson, *Desire to Please,* pp. 128–35. The event rapidly acquired folkloric dimensions; see Binns, *Recollections,* pp. 26–28. On the charge against Reynolds, see Drennan to Samuel McTier, May 14, 1794, *Drennan Letters,* p. 201; the report that he hung George III in effigy is in *PG,* February 2, 1798.

29. "Autobiography of Theobald Wolfe Tone," in Tone, *Life of Theobald Wolfe Tone,* vol. 1, p. 128; Marianne Elliott, *Wolfe Tone: Prophet of Irish Independence* (New Haven and London, 1989), pp. 242–45, 251–52, 258; Nicolson, *Desire to Please,* pp. 124–25.

30. William Sampson, *Memoirs of William Sampson* (New York, 1807), p. 36; James A. L. Whittier, ed., *Speeches of John Philpot Curran* (Chicago, 1877), pp. 154–74.

31. Smyth, *Men of No Property,* pp. 100–20; Nancy J. Curtin, *The United Irishmen: Popular Politics in Ulster and Dublin, 1791–1798* (New York, 1994), pp. 148–65; David W. Miller, *Peep o'Day Boys and Defenders: Selected Documents on the County Armagh Disturbances, 1784–96* (Belfast, 1990); Louis M. Cullen, "The Political Structures of the Defenders," in *Ireland and the French Revolution,* ed. Gough and Dickson, pp. 117–38.

32. Michael Durey, "Irish Deism and Jefferson's Republic: Denis Driscol in Ireland and America, 1793–1810," *Éire-Ireland* 25 (Winter 1990), pp. 61–62. John Daly Burk, "Defence on a Charge of Deism and Republicanism, before the Board of Trinity College, Dublin," in *Polar Star,* October 16–26, 1796; see esp. October 19 and

October 21, 1796. For Burk's relation to Edmund Burke, see *Augusta Chronicle,* November 11, 1809.

33. "Extracts from Letters &c in the Office of the Chief Secretary, relative to the Societies of United Irishmen," HO 100/58/187, 100/58/189–90; *American Patriot,* October 11, 1803; *Augusta Chronicle,* November 11, 1809; Burk, *History of the Late War,* pp. 44–45; *Dublin Evening Post,* December 29, 31, 1795; Joseph I. Shulim, "John Daly Burk: Irish Revolutionist and American Patriot," *Transactions of the American Philosophical Society* 54, pt. 6 (October 1964), p. 9. See also Drennan to Samuel McTier, c. October 1794, *Drennan Letters,* pp. 214–15, and *Northern Star,* February 1, 1792.

34. Burk, *History of the Late War,* pp. 45, 47, 50; *Dublin Evening Post,* December 29, 31, 1795; Shulim, "John Daly Burk," p. 9.

35. "Comparison of the plan, general objects & views of the United Irishmen and Defenders," July 1795, HO 100/58/178; John Chambers to Mathew Carey, April 12, 1792, Lea and Febiger Collection, HSP; Emmet, "Part of an Essay," in MacNeven, *Pieces of Irish History,* pp. 90–92; "The Examination of Thomas Addis Emmet, Before the Secret Committee of the House of Commons, August 14, 1798," in MacNeven, *Pieces of Irish History,* p. 269; Smyth, *Men of No Property,* p. 183; Thomas Reynolds, Jr., *Life of Thomas Reynolds* (London, 1839), vol. 1, p. 169. See also _____ to _____, March 3, Dublin, 1797[?], RP 620/14/218/5: "Defenderism though not confined to the Lower Orders, was nearly so. But now it has spread through the mercantile and higher classes, and has even infected some of the noble blood of the country."

36. William MacNeven, "An Account of the Treaty Between the United Irishmen and the Anglo Irish Government in 1798," in MacNeven, *Pieces of Irish History,* p. 171; *Memoire, or, Detailed Statement of the Origin and Progress of the Irish Union* (London, 1802), pp. 70, 73–74; Robinson, "Life of Thomas Addis Emmet," pp. 73, 86; William Doyle, *The Oxford History of the French Revolution* (Oxford, 1990), pp. 341–68, 419; "Substance of Thomas Addis Emmet's Examination, Before the Secret Committee of the House of Commons, August 10, 1798," in MacNeven, *Pieces of Irish History,* p. 257; "Examination of William James MacNeven, Before the Secret Committee of the House of Lords, August 7, 1978," in MacNeven, *Pieces of Irish History,* p. 239. See also Joseph James St. Mark, "The Red Shamrock: United Irishmen and Revolution, 1795–1803" (Ph.D. diss., Georgetown University, 1974).

37. Wolfe Tone, "Journal," in Tone, *Life of Theobald Wolfe Tone,* vol. 2, pp. 255–69; Pakenham, *Year of Liberty,* pp. 17–19; Marianne Elliott, "The Role of Ireland in French War Strategy, 1796–98," in Gough and Dickson, eds., *Ireland and the French Revolution,* pp. 202–19.

38. Martha McTier to William Drennan, c. March 1797, *Drennan Letters,* p. 255.

39. Benjamin Binns to R. R. Madden, May 24, 1843, Madden Papers, Trinity College Dublin, 873/451/7; G. F. Hill to E. Cooke, July 11 [1797?], RP 620/31/216.

40. JW [McNally] to _____, May 14, 1797, RP 620/10/121/56; Robinson, "Life of Thomas Addis Emmet," pp. 87; "Substance of Thomas Addis Emmet's Examination, Before the Secret Committee of the House of Commons, August 10, 1798," in MacNeven, *Pieces of Irish History,* p. 260; Madden, *United Irishmen,* vol. 3, pp. 215–16.

41. JW [McNally] to Edward Cooke, January 7, 1798, RP 620/36/277.

42. Elliott, *Partners in Revolution,* pp. 133, 172–73; JW [McNally] to Edward Cooke, January 7, 1798, RP 620/36/277.

43. Binns, *Recollections,* pp. 24–26, 30–33, 42–43, 47, 54–56, 66, 69–72.

44. Benjamin Binns to R. R. Madden, May 24, 1843, Madden Papers, 873/451/2; James Coigly, *The Life of the Rev. James Coigly* (London, 1798), pp. 15–18; Elliott, *Partners in Revolution,* pp. 146–47; Roger Wells, *Insurrection: The British Experience, 1795–1803* (Gloucester, 1983), pp. 70–71; "Examination of William White," RP 620/18A/11.

45. Elliott, *Partners in Revolution,* pp. 175, 179; Wells, *Insurrection,* pp. 121–24; Benjamin Binns to R. R. Madden, May 24, 1843, Madden Papers, 873/451/3; Binns, *Recollections,* pp. 88–91; JW [McNally] to Edward Cooke, February 5, 1797, RP 620/36/277; Charles Greville to Thomas Pelham, RP 620/30/27.

46. Binns, *Recollections,* pp. 100–39; JW [McNally] to ____, January 11, 1797, RP 620/10/121/45; T. B. Howell, *A Complete Collection of State Trials* (London, 1819), vol. 26, pp. 1324–25; Benjamin Binns to R. R. Madden, May 24, 1843, Madden Papers, 843/451/8; Elliott, *Partners in Revolution,* pp. 182–89.

47. Pakenham, *Year of Liberty,* pp. 32–36, 56–58, 60.

48. HO 76/14; Pakenham, *Year of Liberty,* pp. 93–94.

49. HO 76/14; William Sampson, *An Appeal from William Sampson, Esq., Barrister at Law, to The Public* (n.p., 1798), pp. 4–6, RP 620/43/7; *Dublin Evening Post,* [illegible]; JW [McNally] to ____, February 1, [illegible], RP 620/10/121/49; RP 620/28/14/6; RP 620/37/162; Sampson, *Memoirs,* pp. 9, 344–45.

50. Madden, *United Irishmen,* vol. 3, pp. 15–19, 269–87; Caldwell, "Particulars," p. 70; Thomas Robinson to Archibald Hamilton Rowan, November 25, 1825, in *Autobiography of Archibald Hamilton Rowan,* ed. Drummond, p. 427.

51. Pakenham, *Year of Liberty,* pp. 63–73, 82–87; Cullen, "The Internal Politics of the United Irishmen," in *The United Irishmen,* ed. Dickson, Keogh, and Whelan, pp. 195–96.

52. Elliott, *Partners in Revolution,* p. 166; Pakenham, *Year of Liberty,* pp. 163, 192, 198–99, 208, 257; R. F. Foster, *Modern Ireland, 1600–1972* (Harmondsworth, 1988), p. 280; Doyle, *Oxford History of the French Revolution,* p. 343.

53. The best accounts are Pakenham, *Year of Liberty,* and Daniel Gahan, *The People's Rising: Wexford, 1798* (Dublin, 1995).

54. Charles Dickson, *Revolt in the North: Antrim and Down in 1798* (Dublin and London, 1960); A. T. Q. Stewart, *The Summer Soldiers: The 1798 Rebellion in Antrim and Down* (Belfast, 1995).

55. Quoted in Pakenham, *Year of Liberty,* pp. 306–7.

56. Pakenham, *Year of Liberty,* pp. 298–328; Jean-Paul Bertaud, "Forgotten Soldiers: The Expedition of General Humbert to Ireland in 1978," in *Ireland and the French Revolution,* ed. Gough and Dickson, pp. 220–28. For a brilliant fictional account of these events, see Thomas Flanagan, *The Year of the French* (New York, 1979).

57. William Sampson to ____, September 12, 1798 [Enclosure of the Agreement], RP 620/40/65; "Offer of the State Prisoners in Dublin" (August, 1798), RP 620/39/231; Samuel Neilson, *Brief Statement of a Negociation Between Certain United Irishmen and the Irish Government, in July, 1798* (New York, 1802).

58. MacNeven to Cornwallis, October 11, 1798, RP 620/15/5/4; Emmet to ____, October 11, 1798, RP 620/15/2/13.

59. Castlereagh to Sampson, September 18, 1798, RP 620/40/65; Emmet to ——, March 18, 1799, RP 620/15/2/18. See also Castlereagh to Henry Jackson, September 13, 1798, RP 620/8/85/25, which clearly indicates that the government had no problem in sending a state prisoner to America if Rufus King approved.

60. Caldwell, "Particulars," pp. 107–10; "Court Martial of Richard Caldwell, Coleraine, July 13–14, 1798," RP 620/2/8/8; RP 620/3/51/5; John Parks to John Caldwell, July 1798, Caldwell Papers, PRONI, T 3541/1/1, T 3541/1/2, T 3541/1/3, T 3541/5/2; "To His excellency Charles Marquis Cornwallis Lieutenant General and Governor General of Ireland—The Humble Petition of John Caldwell . . . ," T 3541/6/2.

61. David Bailie Warden, "Preface" to H. Grégoire, *An Enquiry Concerning the Intellectual Moral Faculties and Literature of Negroes* (Brooklyn, 1810), p. 9; "Porter MS," PRONI, D 3579/2, p. 9; HO 77/45–46; [David Bailie Warden], "A Narrative of the Principal Proceedings of the Republican Army of the County of Down, during the late Insurrection," RP 620/4/41, pp. 5–11; Cleland Papers, PRONI, D 714/3/30; Francis C. Haber, "David Bailie Warden, A Bibliographical Sketch of America's Cultural Ambassador in France, 1804–45," *Institut Français de Washington* (1954), p. 2.

62. Caldwell, "Particulars," pp. 95, 98, 106; Cleland Papers, PRONI, D 714/2/14; Tennent Papers, D 1748/A/3/9/14, D 1748/A/3/9/15.

63. Caldwell, "Particulars," pp. 116–17; Warden to ——, c. December 1799—January 1800, David Bailie Warden Papers, Maryland Historical Society, MS 871; Birch, *Letter from an Irish Emigrant,* pp. 32–34; Dickson, *Narrative,* p. 101.

64. "Answer of the Belfast Prisoners—to the offer of being banished," August 24, 1798, RP 620/39/203.

65. Campbell, "Sketches of the History of Presbyterians in Ireland," p. 100.

66. Martha McTier to William Drennan, c. December 24, 1802, *Drennan Letters,* p. 323; see also Drennan to Martha McTier, June, 1801, *Drennan Letters,* p. 311, and Martha McTier to William Drennan, August 2, 1803, *Drennan Letters,* p. 326.

67. Norman Vance, "Celts, Carthaginians and Constitutions: Anglo-Irish Literary Relations, 1780–1820," *Irish Historical Studies* 87 (March 1981), pp. 216–38; Gráinne Yeats, *The Harp of Ireland: The Belfast Harpers' Festival, 1792 and the Saving of Ireland's Harp Music by Edward Bunting* (Belfast, 1992), pp. 10–22; Mary Helen Thuente, *The Harp Re-strung: The United Irishmen and the Rise of Irish Literary Nationalism* (Syracuse, 1994).

68. David W. Miller, "Presbyterianism and 'Modernization' in Ulster," *Past and Present* 80 (1978), pp. 66–90; James S. Donnelly, Jr., "Pastorini and Captain Rock: Millenarianism and Sectarianism in the Rockite Movement of 1821–4," in *Irish Peasants: Violence and Political Unrest, 1780–1914,* ed. Samuel Clark and James S. Donnelly, Jr. (Madison, 1983).

69. "Substance of Thomas Addis Emmet's Examination, Before the Secret Committee of the House of Commons, August 10, 1798," in MacNeven, *Pieces of Irish History,* p. 265; MacNeven, "Statistical Essay, on the Population and Resources of Ireland," in *Pieces of Irish History,* pp. 297–302; [MacNeven], *An Argument for Independence, in Opposition to an Union. Addressed to All His Countrymen. By an Irish Catholic* (Dublin, 1799).

70. Caldwell, "Particulars," p. 118; John Parks to John Caldwell, September 10, 1799, Caldwell Papers, PRONI, T 3541/1/12.

71. John Chambers to Mathew Carey, March 26, 1794, Lea and Febiger Collection, HSP.

72. See, for example, James Pollock to Lord Downshire, April 12, 1798, Downshire Papers, PRONI, D 607/F/137, and Lord Downshire to Edward Cooke, May 18, 1798, RP 620/37/102

Chapter 2. Hordes of Wild Irishmen

1. Tone to Thomas Russell, August 7, 1795, Sirr Papers, Trinity College Dublin, 868/2/2–3; Tone to Thomas Russell, October 25, 1795, Sirr Papers, 868/2/13–15.

2. Tone to Thomas Russell, October 25, 1795, Sirr Papers, 860/2/13–15.

3. Wolfe Tone, "Autobiography," Papers of Theobald Wolfe Tone, Trinity College Dublin, 2046, Notebook 3, p. 32.

4. For Reynolds's image of America, see "The Society of United Irishmen of Dublin, to Joseph Priestley, L.L.D.," broadsheet, PRONI, T 965/4; Reynolds is identified as the author, along with J. Donovan, in *American Patriot,* June 21, 1803; for his involvement in American politics, see Rowan to Mrs. Rowan, September 7, 1795, and September 21, 1795, in *Autobiography of Archibald Hamilton Rowan,* ed. Drummond, pp. 283–84.

5. Rowan to Mrs. Rowan, January 19, 1796, and April 16, 1796, in *Autobiography of Archibald Hamilton Rowan,* ed. Drummond, pp. [illegible], [illegible].

6. *Autobiography of Archibald Hamilton Rowan,* ed. Drummond, pp. 237–38, 240–41; Rowan to Mrs. Rowan, 1795, in *Autobiography,* ed. Drummond, p. 266; Memorial of Archibald Hamilton Rowan, 18 Vendemiaire, Year III (October 9, 1794), *Correspondance Politique Angleterre,* vol. 588, f. 280, Archives des Affairs Etrangers, Quai D'Orsay, Paris; Nicolson, *Desire to Please,* p. 151.

7. Rowan to Mrs. Rowan, February 20, 1796, April 16, 1796, May 4, 1796, November 1, 1796, in *Autobiography of Archibald Hamilton Rowan,* ed. Drummond, pp. 289, 294–95, 300, 306–7; JW [McNally] to Edward Cooke, September 16, 1796, RP 620/36/277; Mrs. Rowan to Rowan, May 1, 1799, in *Autobiography,* ed. Drummond, p. 336.

8. Durey, "Transatlantic Patriotism," p. 12; see also John Caldwell to Robert Simms, October 18, 1802, "Emigrant Letters to Robert Simms," PRONI, T 1815.

9. JW [McNally] to Edward Cooke, July 26, 1796, RP 620/36/277. It should be noted that Tone and Tandy did not get along; according to William Drennan, "Tone does not like Tandy"; see Drennan to Samuel McTier, April 25, 1792, *Drennan Letters,* p. 87. The common experience of exile in America brought them temporarily together. In his "Autobiography," Tone wrote of "my old friend and fellow-sufferer James Napper Tandy"; see Papers of Theobald Wolfe Tone, 2046, Notebook 3, p. 40. In France, however, the old animosities resurfaced, with disruptive consequences for the United Irish movement; see Elliott, *Partners in Revolution,* pp. 170–71.

10. *Polar Star,* October 6, October 12, November 19, 1796.

11. The literature on this subject is, of course, vast. On the high political stakes of the 1790s, see John R. Howe, Jr., "Republican Thought and the Political Violence of the 1790s," *American Quarterly* 19 (1967), pp. 147–65. For an excellent account of the "high politics" of the decade, see Stanley Elkins and Eric McKitrick, *The Age of*

Federalism: The Early American Republic, 1788–1800 (New York, 1993). The political economy of the Federalists and Republicans is perceptively discussed in Nelson, *Liberty and Property.* See also John C. Miller, *The Federalist Era* (New York, 1960), and Richard Buel, *Securing the Revolution: Ideology in American Politics, 1789–1815* (Ithaca, 1972).

12. Appleby, *Capitalism and a New Social Order,* pp. 25–50; William Bruce Wheeler, "Urban Politics in Nature's Republic: The Development of Political Parties in the Seaport Cities in the Federalist Era" (Ph.D. diss., University of Virginia, 1967), pp. 114, 277, 403–12.

13. Eugene P. Link, *Democratic-Republican Societies, 1790–1800* (New York, 1942); Philip S. Foner, ed., *The Democratic-Republican Societies, 1790–1800: A Documentary Source-Book* (Westport, Conn., 1976); "They Steer to Liberty's Shore," Library of Congress, Pennsylvania Broadsides, August, 1793; Wheeler, "Urban Politics," p. 259; Doyle, *Ireland, Irishmen and Revolutionary America,* p. 190; Roland Baumann, "The Democratic-Republicans of Philadelphia: The Origins, 1776–1797" (Ph.D. diss., Pennsylvania State University, 1970)," pp. 493–506.

14. Samuel Flagg Bemis, *Jay's Treaty: A Study in Commerce and Diplomacy* (New York, 1924); Jerald A. Combs, *The Jay Treaty: Political Battleground of the Founding Fathers* (Berkeley, 1970); for contemporary Republican criticisms of the Treaty, see [Alexander Dallas], *Letters of Franklin on the Conduct of the Executive* (Philadelphia, 1795).

15. Oliver Wolcott to Mrs. Wolcott, July 26, 1795, in Gibbs, ed., *Memoirs of the Administrations of Washington and Adams,* vol. 1, p. 218; *Autobiography of Archibald Hamilton Rowan,* ed. Drummond, p. 326; *PG,* February 17, 1798; Baumann, "Democratic-Republicans of Philadelphia," p. 128; Mathew Carey to Daniel McCurtin, May 25, 1796, Carey Letterbook, Lea and Febiger Collection, HSP; Miller, *Federalist Era,* p. 168.

16. Kim Tousley Phillips, *William Duane, Radical Journalist in the Age of Jefferson* (New York and London, 1989), pp. 4–46; Harman Blennerhassett, "Journal," August 23, 1807, in *The Blennerhassett Papers,* ed. William H. Safford (Cincinnati, 1864); *Aurora,* May 18, 1799.

17. Carey, *Autobiography,* p. 40; Jeffery A. Smith, *Franklin and Bache: Envisioning the Enlightened Republic* (New York, 1990), pp. 139–47; Jasper Dwight [William Duane], *A Letter to George Washington* (Philadelphia, 1796), pp. 6, 11, 19–21, 34, 47–48; *Aurora,* March 6, 1797; for Reynolds's authorship of the article in question, see James Tagg, *Benjamin Franklin Bache and the Philadelphia Aurora* (Philadelphia, 1991), pp. 285–86, 305.

18. Carey, *Autobiography,* p. 40. For examples of pro-Washington sentiments among United Irish émigrés, see *Polar Star,* October 7, 1796; *Time-Piece,* July 11, 1798; Birch, *Seemingly Experimental Religion,* p. 8; Caldwell, "Particulars," p. 27; David Bailie Warden to _____, December 20, 1799, January 24, 1800, Warden Papers, Maryland Historical Society, MS. 871.

19. Carter, "A 'Wild Irishman' Under Every Federalist's Bed," pp. 343–45; Wheeler, "Urban Politics," pp. 104, 107; Alfred F. Young, *The Democratic Republicans of New York* (Chapel Hill, 1967), pp. 476–95; Carey, *Autobiography,* p. 13; Carter, "Political Activities of Mathew Carey," pp. 58–59, 61, 79, 84, 89, 235; JW [McNally] to _____, October 1, 1796, RP 620/10/121/37; *Polar Star,* October 7, 1796, October 13, 1796, November 1, 1796, November 19, 1796, December 13, 1796.

20. _____ to George Ivie, August 1, 1797, RP 620/32/4; *Aurora*, February 22, 26, 1798; Bric, "Ireland, Irishmen," pp. 526–29.

21. *Aurora*, January 30, 1800; William Cobbett, "Detection of a Conspiracy, Formed by the United Irishmen" (Philadelphia, 1798), in *Peter Porcupine in America: Pamphlets on Republicanism and Revolution*, ed. David A. Wilson (Ithaca, 1994), p. 251.

22. *GUS*, December 18, 1798, December 20, 1798, December 22, 1798, December 26, 1798; Mathew Carey, *A Plumb Pudding for the Humane, Chaste, Valiant, Enlightened Peter Porcupine* (Philadelphia, 1799); John Chambers to Carey, March 26, 1794, April 2, 1794, May 24, 1795, Lea and Febiger Collection, HSP; Daniel McCurtin to Carey, April 12, 1796, Lea and Febiger Collection, HSP; James Reynolds to Carey, May 13, 1799, Lea and Febiger Collection, HSP; Carter, "Political Activities of Mathew Carey," pp. 262–63; *PG*, December 27, 1798, December 28, 1798; Samuel Wylie to David Bailie Warden, November 15, 1809, Warden Papers, Maryland Historical Society, MS. 871.

23. Cobbett, "Detection of a Conspiracy," pp. 243–48; *PG*, December 21, 1798, December 26, 1798; Smyth, *Men of No Property*, pp. 86–88; *Dublin Evening Post*, April 23, 1793; Drennan to Samuel McTier, May 21, 1793, *Drennan Letters*, p. 54; Nancy J. Curtin, "Symbols and Rituals of United Irish Mobilization," in *Ireland and the French Revolution*, ed. Gough and Dickson, pp. 68–82; John Durkin to Mathew Carey, n.d. [illegible], Lea and Febiger Collection, HSP; [illegible] Caldwell, "Particulars," pp. 129, 132.

24. Cobbett, "Detection of a Conspiracy," p. 246; *Carey's United States Recorder*, May 19, 1798.

25. On the XYZ affair and the American war fever, see Miller, *Federalist Era*, pp. 210–14; Elkins and McKitrick, *Age of Federalism*, pp. 549–79, 581–88, 595–99.

26. Cobbett, "Detection of a Conspiracy," pp. 246–49, 251–54; *PG*, December 26, 1798; *GUS*, November 26, 1798, December 18, 1798.

27. Benjamin Binns to R. R. Madden, May 24, 1851, Madden Papers, Trinity College Dublin, 873/451/5; Cobbett, "Detection of a Conspiracy," p. 247; *GUS*, October 29, 1798.

28. James Morton Smith, *Freedom's Fetters: The Alien and Sedition Laws and American Civil Liberties* (Ithaca, 1956), pp. 163–64; William Loughton Smith to James McHenry, February 2, 1799, James McHenry Papers, Library of Congress, Container 7; *Carey's United States Recorder*, August 25, 1798; *GUS*, December 18, 1798; *PG*, December 24, 1798; Pickering to John Adams, July 24, 1799, in *The Works of John Adams*, ed. Charles Francis Adams (Boston, 1854), vol. 9, p. 4.

29. *GUS*, November 19, 1798, December 11, 1798; *PG*, January 28, 1799. It is unlikely that Burk would have been unaware of LeBlanc's plan to assassinate John Cockayne in 1795; see *Dublin Evening Post*, December 29, 1795, and, more generally, Burk, *History of the Late War*, pp. 47, 90, 112–13. See also *American Patriot*, February 24, 1803, and Binns, *Recollections*, pp. 55–56.

30. Bric, "Ireland, Irishmen," pp. 44–45; William Cobbett, *A Bone to Gnaw, for the Democrats, Part II* (Philadelphia, 1795), pp. 11–12; *GUS*, December 18, 1798, March 7, 1799.

31. Hugh Gaine, "Journal," October 13, 1798, in *The Journals of Hugh Gaine, Printer*, ed. Paul Leicester Ford (New York, 1902), vol. 2, p. 209; see also vol. 1, pp. 64–65.

32. *GUS,* November 22, December 18, 1798; for the Irish original, see Smyth, *Men of No Property,* pp. 112–13.

33. *GUS,* November 21, 1798; see also *GUS,* November 22, 1798, *Aurora,* November 20, 1798, and *PG,* November 21, 1798.

34. Smith, *Freedom's Fetters,* esp. pp. 22–34, 50–93; John C. Miller, *Crisis in Freedom: The Alien and Sedition Acts* (Boston, 1952); Elkins and McKitrick, *Age of Federalism,* pp. 590–93; *Debates and Proceedings of Congress,* 5th Congress, Session 1, July 1, 1797, col. 30.

35. *PG,* November 9, 1798, December 24, 1798.

36. Shulim, "John Daly Burk," pp. 19, 22–23; *Time-Piece,* June 22, June 29, July 27, July 30, August 1, August 6, August 25, 1798. On Smith, see R. Troup to Rufus King, July 10, 1798, in *Life and Correspondence of Rufus King,* ed. King, vol. 2, p. 364.

37. *Time-Piece,* June 1, June 13, June 27, July 2, July 30, 1798.

38. *Commercial Advertiser,* July 6, 1798; Smith, *Freedom's Fetters,* pp. 210–11; *Time-Piece,* July 13, July 30, 1798. For Burk's denials, see *Time-Piece,* June 27, July 6, 1798.

39. Smith, *Freedom's Fetters,* p. 209; *Time-Piece,* July 6, July 9, July 25, 1798; John Burk, *An Oration, Delivered on the Fourth of March, 1803, at the Court-House, in Petersburg: To Celebrate the Election of Thomas Jefferson, and the Triumph of Republicanism* (Petersburg, 1803), pp. 12, 14–15; *Richmond Enquirer,* March 11, 1808; *Aurora,* December 11, 1798; Burk, *History of the Late War,* p. 30.

40. *Commercial Advertiser,* July 16, 1798; *Time-Piece,* July 25, 1798, August 18, 1798; Shulim, "John Daly Burk," pp. 30–31; Smith, *Freedom's Fetters,* pp. 214–19; Burk to Thomas Jefferson, [June 19, 1801], in *WMQ,* 2d series, vol. 5 (January 1925), p. 100.

41. *Carey's United States Recorder,* May 10, May 19, May 22, 1798; *Aurora,* August 14, 1798.

42. *Carey's United States Recorder,* May 10, May 15, 1798.

43. Rowan to Mrs. Rowan, July 20, 1798, in *Autobiography of Archibald Hamilton Rowan,* ed. Drummond, p. 323.

44. Daniel McCurtin to Mathew Carey, June 13, 1798, Lea and Febiger Collection, HSP.

45. *Time-Piece,* August 8, 1798; *Aurora,* August 14, 1798; *GUS,* December 21, 1798; Carey, *A Plumb Pudding,* pp. 33–34, 40.

46. *A Memorial. To the Senate and House of Representatives. The Respectful Memorial of the Subscribers, Natives of Ireland, Residing Within the United States of America* (n.p., n.d. [Philadelphia, 1798]), pp. 1–5.

47. *Memorial,* pp. 4–6; [Continental Congress], *An Address . . . to the People of Ireland* (Philadelphia, 1775), p. 10.

48. William Duane, *A Report of the Extraordinary Transactions which took place at Philadelphia, in February 1799* (Philadelphia, 1799), pp. 3–12, 16–17; *PG,* February 12, February 14, 1799.

49. Duane, *Extraordinary Transactions,* pp. 14–15, 18–35, 37.

50. *GUS,* February 11, 12, 1799.

51. Duane, *Extraordinary Transactions,* pp. 7, 15–17; *GUS,* February 11, 1799.

52. *GUS,* March 29, 30, April 1, May 15, 16, 1799; Phillips, *William Duane,* pp. 70–75.

53. Robert Liston to Grenville, May 29, 1799, Foreign Office Papers, 5/25; *Au-*

rora, July 24, 1799, February 19, March 25, 27, 1800; Smith, *Freedom's Fetters,* pp. 277–306; Phillips, *William Duane,* pp. 76–91; John Adams to Christopher Gadsden, April 16, 1801, in *Works of John Adams,* ed. Adams, vol. 9, p. 584; see also Adams to Benjamin Stoddert, March 31, 1801, vol. 9, p. 582.

54. See, for example, Robert Liston to Grenville, November 5, 1799, Foreign Office Papers, 5/25; *GUS,* November 22, 1799.

55. Quoted in Carter, "Political Activities of Mathew Carey," pp. 265–66.

Chapter 3. The Land of Liberty

1. Chambers to Mathew Carey, September 3, 1805, Lea and Febiger Collection, HSP; Chambers to Robert Simms, May 9, 1806, PRONI, T 1815; Thomas Bailey to David Bailie Warden, November 28, 1809, Warden Papers, Maryland Historical Society, MS. 871. For Chambers's role in the Society of United Irishmen, see JW [McNally] to ____, March 24, 1797, RP 620/10/121/52; JW to ____, June 20, 1797, RP 620/10/121/68; JW to ____, September 10, 1797, RP 620/10/121/75; JW to Edward Cooke, December 7, 1797, RP 620/36/277.

2. Thomas Emmet to Robert Simms, June 1, 1805, PRONI, T 1815; Emmet to Archibald Hamilton Rowan, July 8, 1802, in *Autobiography of Archibald Hamilton Rowan,* ed. Drummond, p. 469; Emmet to John [Emmet], March 31, 1803, RP [illegible]; Robinson, "Life of Thomas Addis Emmet," pp. 198–99, 207; Deasmumhan Ó Raghallaigh, "William James MacNeven," *Studies: An Irish Quarterly Review* 30 (1941), pp. 247–59; Madden, *United Irishmen,* vol. 3, p. 204.

3. Portland to Cornwallis, March 20, 1799, RP 620/18A/1; Sampson, *Memoirs;* Sampson to Grace Sampson, July 8, 1806, July 18, 1806, October 15, 1806, September 5, 1808, November 6, 1808, December 24, 1809, Papers of William Sampson, Library of Congress.

4. Caldwell, "Particulars," pp. 18, 130, 151; Warden to ____, n.d. [December 1799–January 1800], Warden to ____, April 20, 1800, Warden to ____, April 28, 1800, Warden Papers, Maryland Historical Society, MS. 871; Warden, *Statistical, Political, and Historical Account,* vol. 3, pp. 488–91.

5. George Cuming to Charles Cutts, May 21, 1813, in "Correspondence Relating to Aliens, Enemy and Neutral," Naval Records Collection, Record Group #45, Subject File, US Navy, 1775–1910, RN, 1812–15, National Archives, Washington; Cuming to Robert Simms, May 9, August 13, 1805, PRONI, T 1815; *The Irish Magazine, or Monthly Asylum for Neglected Biography,* January 1810, pp. 32–33; W. S. Smith, *Memories of '98* (Belfast, 1895), pp. 37–39.

6. "Report on the United Britons," January 12, 1799, RP 620/18A/14; *Republican Argus,* January 13, 1803; Binns, *Recollections,* p. 197.

7. Henry Jackson to Rufus King, July 22, 1799, and Rufus King to Henry Jackson, August 28, 1799, in *Life and Correspondence of Rufus King,* ed. King, vol. 2, pp. 645–47; John Campbell White to Robert Simms, November 16, December 4, 1804, PRONI, T 1815. On D'Evereux (frequently spelled Devereux), see Binns, *Recollections,* pp. 317–38, and Eric T. D. Lambert, "Note," in *The Correspondence of Daniel O'Connell,* ed. Maurice R. O'Connell (Shannon, 1972), vol. 2, p. 208.

8. On Driscol and the United Irishmen in Cork, see "Extracts from Letters &c in the Office of the Chief Secretary, relative to the Societies of United Irishmen," HO/58/187; JW [McNally] to ____, September 13, 1795, RP 620/10/121/28;

Isaac Heron to ____, January 2, 1797, RP 620/28/15; Denis Driscol to Edward Cooke, May 4, 1799, RP 620/47/5; for his general career, see Durey, "Irish Deism and Jefferson's Republic," pp. 56–76.

9. Edward A. Wyatt, "John Daly Burk: Patriot-Playwright-Historian," *Southern Sketches* 7 (Charlottesville, Va., 1936), pp. 19, 30; see also Burk, *History of the Late War,* "Appendix," pp. 10, 37–38; Madden, *United Irishmen,* vol. 3, p. 279; Archibald Hamilton Rowan to James Monroe, February 13, 1800, Gratz Collection, HSP.

10. See Chapter 6.

11. Ronald Ray Swick, "Harman Blennerhassett: An Irish Aristocrat on the American Frontier" (Ph.D. diss., Miami University, 1978); Henry Marie Brackenridge, *Recollections of Persons and Places in the West* (Pittsburgh, 1834), pp. 181–82; *The Blennerhassett Papers,* ed. Safford, for the view that Burr did not intend to dismember the union, see Milton Lomask, *Aaron Burr: The Conspiracy and Years of Exile, 1805–1836* (New York, 1982).

12. *American Patriot,* September 25, 1802.

13. *Temple of Reason,* January 24, 1801; *American Patriot,* October 2, October 9, 1802, March 8, 1803; Burk, *An Oration, Delivered on the Fourth of March, 1803,* p. 12; Duane to James Madison, December 1, 1809, "Letters of William Duane," *Massachusetts Historical Society,* 2d ser., 20 (May 1906), p. 315; William Duane, *Politics for American Farmers* (Washington, 1807), p. 22.

14. Duane to Jefferson, June 10, 1801, "Letters of William Duane," p. 265; *Temple of Reason,* September 2, 1801; *American Patriot,* September 25, 1802, February 1, 1803.

15. *GUS,* March 9, 11, 1801; see also *Aurora,* March 6, 1801.

16. Sanford W. Higginbotham, *The Keystone in the Democratic Arch: Pennsylvania Politics 1800–1816* (Harrisburg, 1952), pp. 18, 100–101, 137; Phillips, *William Duane,* pp. 191–216; Binns, *Recollections,* p. 196.

17. John Caldwell to Robert Simms, October 18, 1802, PRONI, T 1815; *American Patriot,* January 27, March 8, March 24, March 26, 1803; *Evening Post,* April 28, 1802; Frank George Franklin, *The Legislative History of Naturalization in the United States from the Revolutionary War to 1861* (Chicago, 1906), pp. 97–116.

18. *Aurora,* January 30, February 28, 1805; Twomey, *Jacobins and Jeffersonians,* pp. 111–15; Phillips, *William Duane,* pp. 177–79; Higginbotham, *Keystone in the Democratic Arch,* pp. 49–58, 80–81.

19. Higginbotham, *Keystone in the Democratic Arch,* pp. 89–93; Carter, "Political Activities of Mathew Carey," pp. 274–75; Binns, *Recollections,* pp. 177–79, 185–91; *Washington Reporter,* August 22, September 19, October 17, 1808.

20. "Address of the Hibernian Provident Society," *Evening Post,* April 20, 1807; William Sampson to Grace Sampson, July 4, 1807, Papers of William Sampson, Library of Congress; John D. Crimmins, *St. Patrick's Day: Its Celebration in New York and other American Places, 1737–1845* (New York, 1902), pp. 112–16, 145–46, 340; Richard C. Murphy and Lawrence J. Mannion, *The History of the Friendly Sons of Saint Patrick in the City of New York, 1784 to 1955* (New York, 1962), p. 130; Robinson, "Life of Thomas Addis Emmet," pp. 228–29; Steven E. Siry, *De Witt Clinton and the American Political Economy: Sectionalism, Politics, and Republican Ideology, 1787–1828* (New York, 1989), pp. 89–90, 120–22. See also Harvey Strum, "Federalist Hibernophobes in New York, 1807," *Éire-Ireland* 16 (Winter 1981), pp. 7–13.

21. *Evening Post,* April 4, 1807; King to Henry Jackson, August 28, 1799, in *Life and Correspondence of Rufus King,* ed. King, vol. 2, p. 647; Emmet to King, April 9, 1807, in MacNeven, *Pieces of Irish History,* p. 294.

22. Emmet to King, April 9, 1807, in MacNeven, *Pieces of Irish History,* pp. 291–92; see also Emmet to _____, October 11, 1798, RP 620/15/2/13.

23. *Washington Reporter,* November 13, 1809.

24. King to Mr. Gore, April 10, 1807, in *Life and Correspondence of Rufus King,* ed. King, vol. 5, p. 24; "Address to the Public," in *Life and Correspondence of Rufus King,* ed. King, vol. 5, pp. 24–27; *Evening Post,* April 9, 1807.

25. *Evening Post,* April 9, 10, 11, 16, 24, 1807; *Morning Chronicle,* April 6, 22, 25, 1807; *Weekly Inspector,* April 25, 1807. This was not the first time that Jackson had used the letter against King; in 1803, Jackson gave a copy of the letter to Duane, who published it in his newspaper. See *Aurora,* February 17, 1803.

26. *Morning Chronicle,* April 10, April 28, 1807; *Evening Post,* April 6, 7, 16, 17, 1807; *Weekly Inspector,* April 11, 1807; Strum, "Federalist Hibernophobes in New York," p. 7.

27. *Evening Post,* April 4, 25, 1807.

28. *Morning Chronicle,* April 10, 28, 1807; see also April 22, 28, May 4, 1807. For similar examples outside New York, see *Petersburg Intelligencer,* August 19, September 16, 1806.

29. *Morning Chronicle,* April [illegible], 1807; *People's Friend,* April 6, 7, [illegible], 1807.

30. *People's Friend,* May 2, 1807.

31. *Evening Post,* May 1, 1807; Robinson, "Life of Thomas Addis Emmet," p. 258; Emmet to John Patten, July 11, 1807, in Madden, *United Irishmen,* vol. 3, p. 158; Emmet to Robert Simms, November 2, 1807, PRONI, T 1815; King to David Ogden, April 19, 1806, in *Life and Correspondence of Rufus King,* ed. King, vol. 5, p. 531.

32. William Sampson, *A Faithful Report of the Trial of Hurdy Gurdy* (Belfast, 1794), which parodied the trial in 1792 of the owners of the *Northern Star.* See Samuel McSkimin, *Annals of Ulster* (Belfast, 1906), p. 27. Durey, "Irish Deism and Jefferson's Republic," p. 60; Phillips, *William Duane,* pp. 175–77.

33. *Aurora,* January 30, 1800; William Sampson, *An Anniversary Discourse, Delivered Before the Historical Society of New-York . . . ; Showing the Origin, Progress, Antiquities, Curiosities, and Nature of the Common Law* (New York, 1824), p. 57; see also William Duane, *An Epitome of the Arts and Sciences* (Philadelphia, 1811), p. 196, and *American Patriot,* February 8, 1803.

34. Elizabeth K. Henderson, "The Attack on the Judiciary in Pennsylvania, 1800–1810," *Pennsylvania Magazine of History and Biography* 61 (April 1937), pp. 113–36; William Sampson, *Trial of the Journeymen Cordwainers of the City of New York for a Conspiracy to Raise their Wages* (New York, 1810), pp. 94–104; Robinson, "Life of Thomas Addis Emmet," p. 360.

35. Warden, *Statistical, Political, and Historical Account,* vol. 1, p. lv; see also Duane, *Epitome of the Arts and Sciences,* p. 211.

36. Warden, *Statistical, Political, and Historical Account,* vol. 1, p. lvi; William Sampson, *The Catholic Question in America. Whether a Roman Catholic Clergyman be in any case compellable to disclose the secrets of Auricular Confession. Decided at the Court of General Sessions, in the City of New-York* (New York, 1813), pp. 56, 65–68, 76–78, 83, 92, 107.

37. Roderick S. French, "Elihu Palmer, Radical Deist, Radical Republican: A Reconsideration of American Free Thought," *Studies in Eighteenth-Century Culture* 8 (1979), pp. 87–108; *Temple of Reason,* November 8, 15, 29, 1800.

38. John Wood, *A Full Exposition on the Clintonian Faction, and the Society of the Columbian Illuminati* (Newark, 1802), pp. 28, 41–43; Durey, "Irish Deism and Jefferson's Republic," p. 67; *GUS,* January 15, 1799; Wyatt, "John Daly Burk," p. 17; Burk may also have written the positive review of Paine's *Age of Reason* in the *Dublin Evening Post,* May 13, 1794.

39. *Temple of Reason,* April 22, 1801; *Augusta Chronicle,* May 19, 1804.

40. *Temple of Reason,* December 6, 1800, May 27, 1801.

41. Wood, *Full Exposition,* p. 45; *Augusta Chronicle,* August 18, 1810.

42. Eric Foner, *Tom Paine and Revolutionary America* (New York, 1976), pp. 257, 266–68.

43. Drennan to Mrs. McTier, October 27, 1802, *Drennan Letters,* p. 321; Duane to Jefferson, July 23, 1809, January 23, 1809, "Letters of William Duane," pp. 313–14.

44. Duane to Caesar Rodney, January 28, 1807, Gratz Collection, HSP; Phillips, *William Duane,* p. 2; *Temple of Reason,* January 24, July 1, December 23, 1801; Carter, "Political Activities of Mathew Carey," p. 123; Binns, *Recollections,* pp. 42, 62, 154, 185–90; Shulim, "John Daly Burk," p. 51.

45. Burk to Jefferson [1801], in *WMQ,* 2d series, 5 (January 1925), pp. 98, 102; Carter, "Political Activities of Mathew Carey," pp. 267–71; Phillips, *William Duane,* pp. 131–39.

46. Higginbotham, *Keystone in the Democratic Arch,* pp. 136–38; Binns, *Recollections,* p. 197; *Democratic Press,* May 15, 1807.

47. John Binns, *Six Letters on the Intrigues, Apostacy and Ambition of Doctor Michael Leib* (Philadelphia, 1807), pp. 23–24; *Aurora,* October 20, 1807.

48. Higginbotham, *Keystone in the Democratic Arch,* p. 202; Binns, *Recollections,* pp. 310–17; John Binns, *Trial of Edward Lyon, for Subornation of Perjury* (Philadelphia, 1817).

49. Phillips, *William Duane,* p. 294; Ronald Schultz, *The Republic of Labor: Philadelphia Artisans and the Politics of Class, 1720–1830* (New York, 1993), pp. 183–91.

50. Phillips, *William Duane,* pp. 284–85; Higginbotham, *Keystone in the Democratic Arch,* pp. 215–16.

51. Higginbotham, *Keystone in the Democratic Arch,* pp. 227–31; Phillips, *William Duane,* pp. 288–314.

52. George Cuming to Robert Simms, January 18, 1816, PRONI, T 1815; for political conflicts in New York, see Alvin Kass, *Politics in New York State, 1800–1830* (Syracuse, 1965), and Robinson, "Life of Thomas Addis Emmet," pp. 99–300, 314, 318–26.

53. Duane to Warden, April 6, 1811, July 11, 1811, Warden Papers, Library of Congress.

Chapter 4. Humbling the British Tyrant

1. Binns, *Recollections,* pp. 163–64.

2. A. L. Burt, *The United States, Great Britain and British North America* (New Haven, 1940), pp. 210–55; Nelson, *Liberty and Property,* pp. 135–38, 143–49, 173–75; Bradford Perkins, ed., *The Causes of the War of 1812: National Honor or National*

Interest? (New York, 1962); Marshall Smelser, *The Democratic Republic, 1801–1815* (New York, 1968); David Bailie Warden to Van Willinck, August 14, 1810, Register C, pp. 43–44, Warden Papers, MS. 871, Maryland Historical Society.

3. Higginbotham, *Keystone in the Democratic Arch,* pp. 145–47, 174, 176, 178–79; Burk, "Oration," *Richmond Enquirer,* March 11, 1808.

4. George Cuming to Robert Simms, May 10, 1806, John Chambers to Robert Simms, December 21, 1807, PRONI, T 1815; Burk, "Oration," *Richmond Enquirer,* March 11, 1808; Binns, *Recollections,* p. 198; Sampson to Grace Sampson, July 4, 1807, Sampson Papers, Library of Congress; Sampson, *Memoirs,* p. 369; Emmet to Robert Simms, November 2, 1807, PRONI, T 1815; *Augusta Chronicle,* July 11, 1807.

5. *Augusta Chronicle,* August 8, 29, 1807; *Petersburg Intelligencer,* June 3, 1806; Wyatt, "John Daly Burk," p. 16; *Shamrock,* December 15, 1810; *Aurora,* July 9, 1807.

6. *Temple of Reason,* January 10, 1801; Binns, *Recollections,* p. 199; Warden, *Statistical, Political, and Historical Account,* vol. 3, p. 496.

7. John Chambers to Robert Simms, May 24, 1811, PRONI, T 1815; *Shamrock,* July 6, July 13, August 10, 1811.

8. *Shamrock,* July 13, 1811, June 20, 1812; *Washington Reporter,* August 26, 1811.

9. *Washington Reporter,* July 22, 1811.

10. Higginbotham, *Keystone in the Democratic Arch,* p. 166; Nelson, *Liberty and Property,* p. 170; [illegible]

11. *Petersburg Intelligencer,* February 14, 1806; MacNeven, *An Argument for Independence,* p. 23.

12. William Duane, *The Mississippi Question Fairly Stated* (Washington, 1807), pp. 8–10, 20, 37–56; Duane, *Politics for American Farmers,* pp. 8–10, 20, 37–56.

13. Nelson, *Liberty and Property,* pp. 150–61; Carter, "Political Activities of Mathew Carey," p. 25.

14. Nelson, *Liberty and Property,* pp. 41–47, 85–86; Jacob E. Cooke, *Tench Coxe and the Early Republic* (Charlottesville, Va., 1978); Carter, "Political Activities of Mathew Carey," pp. 143–44; *Volunteers Journal,* April 21, 1784; Binns to Coxe, February 9, 1809, n.d. [1810?], October 11, 1810, July 18, 1811, October 1, 1811, October 2, 1814, Tench Coxe Papers, HSP; *Democratic Press,* May 13, 1817; Binns, *Recollections,* pp. 165–66.

15. Duane, *Politics for American Farmers,* p. 62; *Augusta Chronicle,* February 4, 1809; *Richmond Enquirer,* March 11, 1808; Shulim, "John Daly Burk," pp. 50–51.

16. Warden, *Statistical, Political, and Historical Account,* vol. 3, p. 492; Duane to Thomas Jefferson, August 11, 1814, "Letters of William Duane," p. 371.

17. Phillips, *William Duane,* p. 395; Higginbotham, *Keystone in the Democratic Arch,* pp. 246–47, 254; *Aurora,* May 27, August 8, November 7, 8, 9, 1811, February 24, 1812; *Democratic Press,* February 18, 1812; Binns, *Recollections,* pp. 211–12; Crimmins, *St. Patrick's Day,* p. 139.

18. *Shamrock,* March 9, December 14, 1811; June 20, 1812.

19. William James MacNeven, *Of the Nature and Functions of Army Staff* (New York, 1812), pp. iii–v, vii–viii, 15.

20. Duane to Jefferson, received December 5, 1807, "Letters of William Duane," p. 305; Duane to Henry Dearborn, July 27, 1809, "Letters of William Duane"; William Duane, *The American Military Library; or, Compendium of the Modern Tactics* (Philadelphia, 1809); William Duane, *A Hand Book for Infantry* (Philadelphia, 1812);

William Duane, *A Hand Book for Riflemen* (Philadelphia, 1812); William Duane, *A Hand Book for Cavalry* (Philadelphia, 1814); *Shamrock,* September 14, 1814; Higginbotham, *Keystone in the Democratic Arch,* p. 276; Binns, *Recollections,* p. 207; Binns to Charles Jared Ingersoll, May 31, June 9, June 23, July 11, 1813, Charles Jared Ingersoll Correspondence, HSP.

21. Caldwell, "Particulars," pp. 5, 145, 154; Caldwell Papers, PRONI, T 3541/5/2.

22. *Shamrock,* August 29, September 19, 26, November 28, December 19, 1812; Murphy and Mannion, *The History of the Society of the Friendly Sons of St. Patrick,* pp. 13, 230.

23. *Shamrock,* August 6, 13, 20, 27, 1814; April 26, 1817.

24. See, for example, *Shamrock,* January 23, 1813.

25. Mathew Carey to James Madison, August 1, 1812, August 12, 1812, January 25, 1813, Papers of James Madison, Library of Congress; for similar statements by Federalists in 1798, see Miller, *Crisis in Freedom,* pp. 11–15, 32–35.

26. Carey to Madison, August 1, 12, 1812, December 15, 1813, October 14, 30, 1814, November 16, 1814; Madison to Carey, January 28, 1815, Papers of James Madison, Library of Congress.

27. Mathew Carey, *The Olive Branch: or Faults on Both Sides, Federal and Democratic* (Philadelphia, 1814), pp. 5, 26; Carter, "Political Activities of Mathew Carey," p. 317; Sampson to Carey, February 15, 1815, Edward Carey Gardiner Collection, HSP.

28. Binns, *Recollections,* pp. 213–18; *Shamrock,* March 6, 1813.

29. Madison to Binns, February 11, 1813, Papers of James Madison, Library of Congress; Binns, *Recollections,* pp. 219–20; Thomas D'Arcy McGee, *A History of the Irish Settlers in North America, From the Earliest Period to the Census of 1850* (Boston, 1855), p. 105.

30. Alien Enemies Proclamation, Department of State, February 23, 1813, "Correspondence Relating to Aliens," Naval Records Collection; *Shamrock,* March 4, 1813.

31. Petition of Thomas Burke, n.d., "Correspondence Relating to Aliens," Naval Records Collection.

32. James Frazer to John Eppinger, March 29, 1813; Petition of John McClintock, December 18, 1813, "Correspondence Relating to Aliens," Naval Records Collection.

33. See, for example, Binns to James Monroe, March 24, 1813; Petition of John Taylor to James Madison, March 12, 1813 (for the testimonial of Emmet); Duane to James Monroe, April 10, 1813; Petition of James McCall, April 1, 1813 (for the testimonial of Cuming); Cuming to Dr. Nicholas, May 21, 1813, and John Morgan to John Mason, May 24, 1814 (for the testimonial of Sampson), in "Correspondence Relating to Aliens," Naval Records Collection.

34. *Shamrock,* March 13, 1813, June 18, 1814; on the "emigration-as-exile" motif, see Kerby Miller, *Emigrants and Exiles: Ireland and the Irish Exodus to North America* (New York, 1985).

35. John Chambers to Robert Simms, "Emigrant Letters to Robert Simms," March 10, 1815, PRONI, T 1815; Richard Rush to Richard Bache, August 4, 1818, Society Collection, HSP. See also Binns, *Recollections,* pp. 242–43; Warden, "Of the Probable Duration of the American Government," n.d., c. 1815, Warden Papers, Library of Congress, and Warden, *Statistical, Political, and Historical Account,* vol. 1, p. lxiii.

36. Duane to Warden, May 7, 1821, Papers of David Bailie Warden, Maryland Historical Society, MS. 871.

37. Binns to John Sergeant, January 17, 1834, Society Collection, HSP; Binns, *Recollections,* pp. 246–57.

38. Carey, *Autobiography,* pp. 101–3, 124; Mathew Carey, *Maxims for the Promotion of the Wealth of Nations* (Philadelphia, 1830), pp. iii–v; Mathew Carey, *Thirteen Essays on the Policy of Manufacturing in this Country* (Philadelphia, 1830), pp. 2–6; Carter, "Political Activities of Mathew Carey," pp. ii, vi.

39. Sampson to Grace Sampson, February 4, 1817, Sampson Papers, Library of Congress; Sampson to Mathew Carey, February 15, 1817, April 23, 1817, Lea and Febiger Collection, HSP; "Circular," Committee of Correspondence for the Promotion of Domestic Manufactures in New York, April 24, 1817, Sampson Papers, Library of Congress; Sampson to Tench Coxe, February 8, 1819, Tench Coxe Papers, HSP.

40. Jefferson to Sampson, January 26, 1817, Papers of Thomas Jefferson, Library of Congress; see also Jefferson to Warden, June 6, 1817, Papers of David Bailie Warden, Maryland Historical Society, MS. 871.

41. *Shamrock,* May 4, 1816; Crimmins, *St. Patrick's Day,* pp. 174–77; Robinson, "Life of Thomas Addis Emmet," pp. 328–29. On Irish canal workers in North America, see Peter Way, *Common Labour: Workers and the Digging of North American Canals, 1780–1860* (Cambridge, 1993), pp. 76–104.

42. Crimmins, *St. Patrick's Day,* p. 136; "Anti-Monopoly," in [William Duane], *Observations on the Principles and Operation of Banking; with Strictures on the Opposition of the Bank of Philadelphia* (Philadelphia, [illegible]), pp. 10–18; Duane to Madison, December 5, 1809, "Letters of William Duane," p. 330; *Aurora,* November 8, December 25, 1810; Duane to Warden, April 6, 1811, Warden Papers, Library of Congress.

43. Mathew Carey, *Desultory Reflections upon the Ruinous Consequences of a Non-Renewal of the Charter of the Bank of the United States* (Philadelphia, 1810), pp. 3, 6–7, 20, 22–23; Mathew Carey, *Nine Letters to Dr. Adam Seybert, Representative in Congress for the City of Philadelphia* (Philadelphia, 1810), p. 24; Carey, *Autobiography,* pp. 48, 53–56; Carter, "Political Activities of Mathew Carey," pp. 292–98.

44. Carey, *Desultory Reflections,* p. 6; Binns, *Recollections,* p. 233; MacNeven to Warden, 1825, Warden Papers, Library of Congress; Robinson, "Life of Thomas Addis Emmet," p. 344; Madden, *United Irishmen,* vol. 3, pp. 207, 233–38; see also Binns to John Sergeant, January 17, 1834, Society Collection, HSP.

45. Duane to Warden, May 10, 1819, David Bailie Warden Papers, Maryland Historical Society, MS. 871; Phillips, *William Duane,* pp. 473–82.

46. Warden, *Statistical, Political, and Historical Account,* vol. 3, pp. 230, 262–63; 280.

47. Warden, *Statistical, Political, and Historical Account,* vol. 1, p. 7; vol. 3, p. 220; Chambers to Robert Simms, May 25, 1821, January 1, 1822, "Emigrant Letters to Robert Simms," PRONI, T 1815; Binns, *Recollections,* pp. 73–74.

48. Warden, *Statistical, Political, and Historical Account,* vol. 1, p. lx; Robinson, "Life of Thomas Addis Emmet," pp. 362–67; Binns to John Sergeant, January 17, 1834, Society Collection, HSP; Mathew Carey, *Prospects on and Beyond the Rubicon* (Philadelphia, 1830), pp. 1–2.

49. Carey, *Prospects on the Rubicon,* p. 1.

50. Phillips, *William Duane,* p. 450; Samuel Cooper to George Bryan, August 14, 1823, George Bryan Papers, HSP; Binns, *Recollections,* pp. 327–30.

51. Binns, *Recollections,* pp. 333–35. On the Philadelphia riots of 1844, see Michael

Feldberg, *The Philadelphia Riots of 1844: A Study of Ethnic Conflict* (Westport, Conn., 1975).

52. Warden, "Of the Probable Duration of the American Government," pp. 2, 6–9; Warden, *Statistical, Political, and Historical Account,* vol. 1, pp. lviii–lxi

Chapter 5. Marching to Irish Music

1. Noah Webster, "Remarks on the Manners, Government, and Debt of the United States," in Webster, *A Collection of Essays and Fugitiv Writings. On Moral, Historical, Political and Literary Subjects* (Boston, 1790), p. 84; Noah Webster, *Dissertations on the English Language: with Notes, Historical and Critical* (Boston, 1789); Benjamin Rush, *A Plan for the Establishment of Public Schools and the Diffusion of Knowledge in Pennsylvania* (Philadelphia, 1786), p. 27.

2. William Thornton, *Cadmus: or, a Treatise on the Elements of Written Language* (Philadelphia, 1793); Gwyn A. Williams, *The Search for Beulah Land: The Welsh and the Atlantic Revolution* (New York, 1980); Thuente, *The Harp Re-strung.*

3. Phillips, *William Duane,* p. 483; David Bailie Warden, *A Sermon, on the Advantages of Education* (Kingston, N.Y., 1802), p. 13; Warden, "On the Probable Duration of the American Government," p. 9, Warden Papers, Library of Congress; Mathew Carey, "To the Public" (Philadelphia, 1830), p. 1.

4. *American Patriot,* September 4, 1802; Carey, "To the Public," p. 1; Warden, *Chorographical and Statistical Description of the District of Columbia,* pp. 79–80; Samuel Knox, *An Essay, on the Means of Improving Public Education* (Fredericktown, 1803), p. 13.

5. Duane to Jefferson, August 17, 1810, "Letters of William Duane," pp. 341–42.

6. Duane, *Epitome of the Arts and Sciences,* pp. ix, xi–xii, 4, 70, 188–96, 201–2, 204–5, 211.

7. Warden, *A Sermon, on the Advantages of Education,* pp. 17, 21; Haber, "David Bailie Warden," pp. 3–4; Caldwell, "Particulars," p. 131; "Report from Kingston Academy, October 2, 1802," Newspaper Clipping, Warden Papers, Maryland Historical Society, MS. 871; Warden to Jefferson, December 4, 1807, Warden Papers, Maryland Historical Society, Register A, pp. 9–10.

8. *PG,* November 8, December 27, 29, 1798; Samuel Wylie to Warden, November 15, 1809, Warden Papers, Maryland Historical Society; Doyle, *Ireland, Irishmen and Revolutionary America,* p. 200.

9. Doyle, *Ireland, Irishmen and Revolutionary America,* pp. 206–7; McGee, *History of the Irish Settlers in North America,* pp. 83–84.

10. Mathew Carey, "Address to the Printers and Booksellers throughout the United States" (Broadside, 1801); Carey, *Autobiography,* p. 50; Carter, "Political Activities of Mathew Carey," pp. 106–7.

11. John Burk, *The History of Virginia, from its First Settlement to the Present Day* (Petersburg, Va., 1804–1805), vol. 1, p. 301; *Time-Piece,* October 9, 1797, June 8, July 30, 1798.

12. Burk to Jefferson, June 19, 1801, Papers of Thomas Jefferson, Library of Congress; Wyatt, "John Daly Burk," p. 20; Lyon G. Tyler, *The Letters and Times of the Tylers* (Richmond, 1884), vol. 1, p. 193.

13. Richard Beale Davis, *Literature and Society in Early Virginia, 1608–1840* (Baton Rouge, 1973), pp. 230–31; Michael Kraus, *A History of American History*

(New York, 1937), pp. 146–47; Burk to Jefferson, February 2, 1803, May 26, 1805, Jefferson to Burk, February 21, 1803, June 1, 1805, Papers of Thomas Jefferson, Library of Congress; *American Patriot,* February 15, 1803; Burk, *History of the Late War,* p. 7; Burk, *History of Virginia,* vol. 1, pp. i–iii.

14. Donald MacCartney, "The Writing of History in Ireland, 1800–1830," *Irish Historical Studies* 10 (September 1957), pp. 347–62; Burk, *History of the Late War,* pp. 7, 31, 74–75, 86, 98, 136.

15. Burk, *History of Virginia,* vol. 2, pp. 155–94, esp. pp. 160, 168, 193; Wilcomb E. Washburn, *The Governor and the Rebel: A History of Bacon's Rebellion in Virginia* (Chapel Hill, 1957), pp. 10–12; Stephen Saunders Webb, *1676, The End of American Independence* (New York, 1984).

16. Burk, *History of the Late War,* pp. 10–13, 136; Burk, *History of Virginia,* vol. 2, pp. 168–69, 194, 200; Washburn, *The Governor and the Rebel,* p. 165.

17. Burk, *History of the Late War,* p. iv; *Polar Star,* November 16, 1796.

18. Burk, *History of Virginia,* vol. 1, pp. 3–6, 69, 231, 299–300, 302, 315.

19. Burk, *History of Virginia,* vol. 1, pp. 302–4; vol. 2, pp. 67, 75–76, 130, 233; vol. 3, p. 468; for United Irish attitudes to African Americans and Native Americans, see Chap. 7.

20. *Petersburg Intelligencer,* August 19, 1806; *Augusta Chronicle,* November 11, 1809; Davis, *Literature and Society in Early Virginia,* p. 230; for a less flattering view of Burk's *History of Virginia,* see [illegible]

21. [Boston] *Independent Chronicle and Universal Advertiser,* February 16, 1797; Shulim, "John Daly Burk," p. 19; James Leith, *Media and Revolution: Moulding a New Citizenry in France during the Terror* (Toronto, 1968), pp. 32–42; Rush, *Plan for the Establishment of Public Schools,* pp. 26–27; Appleby, *Capitalism and a New Social Order,* p. 71; *Freeman's Journal,* April 11, 1784.

22. Carey, *Autobiography,* pp. 17–18; *American Patriot,* May 12, 1803; *Polar Star,* November 3, 1796; *Petersburg Republican,* April 30, 1807.

23. John Burk, *Bunker-Hill; or the Death of General Warren* (New York, 1797), p. 54.

24. Joseph T. Buckingham, *Specimens of Newspaper Literature: With Personal Memoirs, Anecdotes, and Reminiscences* (Boston, 1850), vol. 2, p. 300; Burk, *Bunker-Hill,* pp. 9–10, 20; Pakenham, *Year of Liberty,* p. 202.

25. Burk, *Bunker-Hill,* pp. 37, 52–53; Shulim, "John Daly Burk," p. 19; *New-York Gazette and General Advertiser,* September 8, 1797.

26. Burk to John Hodgkinson, 1797, in William Dunlap, *History of the American Theatre* (1832; New York, 1963), vol. 1, pp. 313–15; Dunlap, *History of the American Theatre,* vol. 1, p. 316.

27. Dunlap, *History of the American Theatre,* vol. 1, pp. 371–72; William Dunlap, *Diary of William Dunlap (1766–1839): The Memoirs of a Dramatist, Theatrical Manager, Painter, Critic, Novelist and Historian* (1930; New York, 1969), vol. 1, p. 144; Arthur Hobson Quinn, *A History of the American Drama From the Beginning to the Civil War* (New York, 1923), p. 126; [Boston] *Independent Chronicle,* February 16, 23, 1797; *American Patriot,* April 12, 1803.

28. John Burk, *Female Patriotism, or the Death of Joan D'Arc* (New York, 1798), pp. 4, 12, 40.

29. Burk, *Female Patriotism,* pp. 8, 19, 21.

30. Burk, *Female Patriotism,* pp. 23, 39.

31. *Time-Piece,* April 11, 1798; Dunlap, *Diary of William Dunlap,* April 17, 1798, vol. 1, p. 244; Dunlap, *History of the American Theatre,* vol. 2, p. 26; Shulim, "John Daly Burk," pp. 21–22.

32. Edward A. Wyatt, IV, "Three Petersburg Theatres," *WMQ,* 2d ser., 21 (April 1941), pp. 83–110; William Godwin, *St. Leon* (London, 1799; rpt. Oxford, 1994); John Burk, *Bethlem Gabor, Lord of Transylvania, or, The Man Hating Palatine* (Petersburg, 1807).

33. Wyatt, "Three Petersburg Theatres," p. 94; Burk, *Bethlem Gabor,* esp. p. 49.

34. Burk, *Bethlem Gabor,* p. 11; *Female Patriotism,* p. 40.

35. Burk, *Bethlem Gabor,* pp. 46–47.

36. Webster, "On the Education of Youth in America," in *Collection of Essays and Fugitiv Writings,* p. 26; Rush, *Plan for the Establishment of Public Schools,* p. 24; Yeats, *Harp of Ireland,* pp. 10–22; Vance, "Celts, Carthaginians and Constitutions," p. 228; Lord Castlereagh to ____ [1798], McCance Collection, D 272/3/23, PRONI; Thuente, *The Harp Re-strung,* pp. 54–57, 125–69; JW [McNally] to ____, February 12, 1797; *Irish Times,* December 18, 1996.

37. John Melish, *Travels through the United States of America* (London, 1818), p. 163; see also Warden, *Statistical, Political, and Historical Account,* vol. 2, p. 186.

38. Wyatt, "John Daly Burk," pp. 19–20; *Petersburg Intelligencer,* October 17, 1806.

39. *Shamrock,* December 15, 1810, August 12, 1812, June 18, 1814; *Augusta Chronicle,* November 11, 1809.

Chapter 6. Signs of the Times

1. Ebenezer Baldwin, *The Duty of Rejoicing under Calamities and Afflictions* (New York, 1776), pp. 38–40.

2. Nathan O. Hatch, *The Sacred Cause of Liberty: Republican Thought and the Millennium in Revolutionary New England* (New Haven, 1977); Ruth H. Bloch, *Visionary Republic: Millennial Themes in American Thought, 1756–1800* (Cambridge, 1985); Binns, *Recollections,* pp. 47–51; Jack Fruchtman, Jr., "The Apocalyptic Politics of Richard Price and Joseph Priestley: A Study in Late Eighteenth-Century English Republican Millennialism," *Transactions of the American Philosophical Society* 73 (1983), pp. 1–125.

3. McBride, "William Drennan," p. 55; James S. Donnelly, Jr., "Propagating the Cause of the United Irishmen," *Studies* 69 (Spring 1980), pp. 15–21; Smyth, *Men of No Property,* p. 170; A. C. Hamilton to ____, March 2, 1797, RP 620/29/8; Miller, "Presbyterianism and 'Modernization' in Ulster," pp. 69–90.

4. *Time-Piece,* August 16, 1798; *Temple of Reason,* December 20, 1800.

5. Brendan Clifford, ed., *The Causes Of The Rebellion in Ireland (1798) And Other Writings by Rev. Thomas Ledlie Birch, United Irishman* (Belfast, 1991); John B. Boles, *The Great Revival* (Lexington, Ky., 1972), p. 99; *Dictionary of National Biography* (Oxford, 1917), vol. 2, p. 532; Thomas Witherow, *Historical and Literary Memorials of Presbyterianism in Ireland (1731–1800)* (London and Belfast, 1880), p. 286; *Northern Star,* January 14, 1792. The best account of Birch's Irish career is Aiken McClelland, "Thomas Ledlie Birch, United Irishman," *Belfast Natural History and Philosophical Society Proceedings,* 2d ser., 7 (1965), pp. 24–35.

6. S. A. Grave, *The Scottish Philosophy of Common Sense* (Oxford, 1960); William G. Lehmann, *John Millar of Glasgow, 1735–1801* (Cambridge, 1960); McBride, "School of Virtue," pp. 73–99; Reid to Andrew Skene, November 14, 1764, in William Hamilton, ed., *The Works of Thomas Reid, D.D., Now Fully Collected, with Selections from his Unpublished Letters,* 2d ed. (Edinburgh, 1849), pp. 40–43; W. Innes Addison, *A Roll of Graduates of the University of Glasgow, 1727 to 1897* (Glasgow, 1898); James Seaton Reid, *History of the Presbyterian Church in Ireland* (Belfast, 1867), vol. 3, pp. 294–301.

7. "An Autobiographical Sketch of Andrew Craig, 1754–1833. Presbyterian Minister of Lisburn," *Ulster Journal of Archaeology* 14 (May–August 1908), p. 51; Birch, *Seemingly Experimental Religion,* pp. 33–54. Birch was a member of the Presbytery of Belfast, which subscribed to the Westminster Confession of Faith; see Peter Brooke, *Ulster Presbyterianism: The Historical Perspective, 1650–1970* (New York, 1987), p. 130. For Miller's analysis, see his "Presbyterianism and 'Modernization' in Ulster," pp. 77–80.

8. McClelland, "Thomas Ledlie Birch," p. 27; *Northern Star,* November 17, 1792; Birch, *Letter from an Irish Emigrant,* pp. 3–4; for Birch's role in the publication of the Yankee Club's correspondence with Washington, see *Belfast Mercury,* October 5, 1784.

9. Birch, *Letter from an Irish Emigrant,* pp. 5–6, 24–25, 27; *Northern Star,* February 1, 1792, July 28, 1792, June 29, 1795, October 14, 1796.

10. [illegible] *Christians, and Especially Ministers to be Exemplary in Their Lives* (Belfast, 1794); for an accessible, but abridged, modern publication, see Clifford, *Causes of the Rebellion,* pp. 28–37.

11. Birch, *Obligation upon Christians,* pp. 13, 15–19.

12. Birch, *Obligation upon Christians,* pp. 26–29.

13. Birch, *Obligation upon Christians,* pp. 29–31.

14. McClelland, "Thomas Ledlie Birch," p. 26; *Records of the General Synod of Ulster, 1691–1820* (Belfast, 1890–98), vol. 3, p. 172; David Stewart, *The Seceders in Ireland, with Annals of their Congregations* (Belfast, 1950).

15. Birch, *Obligation upon Christians,* p. 32; Thomas Birch, *Physicians Languishing Under Disease* (Belfast, 1796), pp. 7, 23–24.

16. Birch, *Physicians Languishing Under Disease,* pp. 19–20, 28–29, 35–37, 41–42, 47.

17. *Belfast News-Letter,* November 17, 1797, April 16, 1798; Birch, *Letter from an Irish Emigrant,* pp. 37–46; Thomas Lane to Lord Downshire, May 1, 1797 [misdated 1798?], Downshire Papers, PRONI, D 607/E/255; Thomas Lane to Lord Downshire, October 1, 1797, Downshire Papers, PRONI, D 607/E319.

18. McClelland, "Thomas Ledlie Birch," pp. 30–31; Stewart, *Summer Soldiers,* pp. 182–83; Birch, *Letter from an Irish Emigrant,* pp. 10–12, 39; "Court Martial," June 18–20, 1798, RP 620/2/9/5, p. 4.

19. Stewart, *Summer Soldiers,* pp. 222–29; Birch, *Letter from an Irish Emigrant,* p. 22.

20. "Court Martial," RP 620/2/9/5; George Stephenson to Lord Downshire, June 17, 1798, Downshire Papers, PRONI, D 607/F/251; Thomas Lane to Lord Downshire, June 19, 1798, Downshire Papers, PRONI, D 607/F/255.

21. "Court Martial," RP 620/2/9/5, pp. 17–18; Dickson, *Revolt in the North,* p. 144; T. G. F. Patterson, "Lisburn and Neighbourhood in 1798," *Ulster Journal of*

Archaeology, 3d ser., 1 (1938), p. 198; Caldwell, "Particulars," p. 87; ____ to the Rev. Forster Archer, n.d. [June, 1798], RP 620/38/202.

22. Patterson, "Lisburn and Neighbourhood," p. 198; Birch, *Letter from an Irish Emigrant,* pp. 23–24, 32–34.

23. *Washington Reporter,* May 21, 1810; *Shamrock,* March 30, 1811; John Glendy to Thomas Jefferson, December 5, 1801, February 28, 1805, March 3, 1805, September 28, 1815, Papers of Thomas Jefferson, Library of Congress; Miller, "Presbyterianism and 'Modernization' in Ulster," pp. 77–78; Stewart, *Summer Soldiers,* pp. 191–92, 234.

24. *Records of the General Synod,* vol. 3, pp. 208–12.

25. Dickson, *Narrative of the Confinement and Exile,* p. 240; David Warden, "A Farewell Address to the Junto of the Presbytery of Bangor" (Glasgow, 1798), in W. T. Latimer, "David Bailie Warden, Patriot 1798," *Ulster Journal of Archaeology,* 2d ser., 13 (1907), pp. 33–38.

26. *Minutes of the General Assembly of the Presbyterian Church in the United States of America, 1798–1820* (Philadelphia, 1847), p. 152.

27. *Minutes of the General Assembly,* pp. 152–53; see also p. 181.

28. *Minutes of the General Assembly,* pp. 148–49, 172–73, 179–80, 202; "Minutes of the Baltimore Presbytery," Presbyterian Historical Society, Philadelphia, p. 8.

29. Birch, *Seemingly Experimental Religion,* pp. 32–34; Samuel Miller, *A Sermon, Preached in New-York, July 4th, 1793* (New York, 1793); Samuel Miller, *A Sermon, Delivered May 9, 1798* (New York, 1798); B. C. Lane, "Democracy and the Ruling Eldership," (Ph.D. diss., Princeton Theological Seminary, 1976). On Kelburn, see Stewart, *A Deeper Silence,* pp. 54, 133, 155, 179; Stewart, *Summer Soldiers,* pp. 13, 56, 244, 248; Sinclair Kelburn, *The Divinity of Our Lord Jesus Christ* (Philadelphia, 1795); on Henry, see McClelland, "Thomas Ledlie Birch," p. 33.

30. Birch, *Seemingly Experimental Religion,* p. 31; *Letter from an Irish Emigrant,* pp. 1, 26–27, 55.

31. Birch, *Seemingly Experimental Religion,* p. 6.

32. Birch, *Letter from an Irish Emigrant,* p. 53; Birch, *Seemingly Experimental Religion,* pp. 7, 31.

33. Birch, *Seemingly Experimental Religion,* pp. 7–10.

34. Birch, *Seemingly Experimental Religion,* pp. 7, 10–11.

35. Birch, *Seemingly Experimental Religion,* pp. 12, 14–18.

36. Birch, *Seemingly Experimental Religion,* pp. 19–21.

37. Birch, *Seemingly Experimental Religion,* pp. 7–8.

38. Bloch, *Visionary Republic;* Michael Barkun, *Crucible of the Millennium: The Burned-Over District of New York in the 1840s* (Syracuse, 1986); Paul Boyer, *When Time Shall Be No More* (Cambridge, Mass., 1992).

39. William Woodward, *Surprising Accounts of the Revival of Religion* (Philadelphia, 1802), pp. 53–54; Birch, *Seemingly Experimental Religion,* pp. 31, 64–65; "Records of the Ohio Presbytery," vol. 1 (1793–1806), pp. 66, 70–73, Presbyterian Historical Society, Philadelphia; *Minutes of the General Assembly,* pp. 213, 218–19.

40. Birch, *Seemingly Experimental Religion,* pp. 74, 105; "Records of the Ohio Presbytery," pp. 78–79, 81, 86–87.

41. "Records of the Ohio Presbytery," pp. 98–108; pp. 110, 112–13, 118–19, 152–56; Birch to Ashbel Green, July 14, 1802, Gratz Collection, HSP; *Washington*

Reporter, October 3, 1808; Horace Binney, *Report of Cases Adjudged in the Supreme Court of Pennsylvania* (Philadelphia, 1809), vol. 1, pp. 178–88.

42. *Minutes of the General Assembly,* pp. 271–73; Birch to Ashbel Green, May 27, May 31, 1803, Gratz Collection, HSP.

43. Joseph Smith, *Old Redstone, or Historical Sketches of Western Presbyterianism, its Early Ministers, its Perilous Times and its First Records* (Philadelphia, 1854), p. 195; "Records of the Ohio Presbytery," p. 98; Thomas Lane to Lord Downshire, October 1, 1797, Downshire Papers, D 607/E/319, PRONI; Thomas Lane to Lord Downshire, June 19, 1798, D 607/F/255, PRONI.

44. Catharine C. Cleveland, *The Great Revival in the West, 1797–1805* (Chicago, 1916; Gloucester, Mass., 1959); Paul K. Conkin, *Cane Ridge: America's Pentecost* (Madison, 1990); see also Boles, *The Great Revival,* while keeping in mind Boles's misplacement of Birch as a pro-revivalist preacher.

45. Birch, *Seemingly Experimental Religion,* pp. 51, 55; Birch to Ashbel Green, July 14, 1802, Gratz Collection, HSP. Birch was not impressed with the view that the West produced better ministers. "Almighty God," he commented, "is no respecter of persons or places." Nevertheless, his own belief that the gospel traveled from east to west and that western Pennsylvania would be the site of the Second Coming was strikingly similar to the revivalist view that he so easily dismissed. In both cases, there was a sense of the purity of the primitive, and that the West was uncorrupted by civilization.

46. *Minutes of the General Assembly,* p. [illegible]; [illegible] pp. 120–47; Birch, *Seemingly Experimental Religion,* p. 54.

47. Birch, *Seemingly Experimental Religion,* pp. 48–53.

48. Birch, *Seemingly Experimental Religion,* pp. 65, 100, 112; "Records of the Ohio Presbytery," p. 102; *Washington Reporter,* September 19, October 3, 1808, January 30, 1809, August 6, 1810.

49. Birch, *Seemingly Experimental Religion,* pp. 5, 12, 91.

50. *Minutes of the General Assembly,* pp. 430–31, 456; "Minutes of Baltimore Presbytery," Presbyterian Historical Society, Philadelphia, p. 8; *Records of the General Synod of Ulster,* vol. 3, p. 152; Smith, *Old Redstone,* pp. 196–200.

51. *Washington Reporter,* November 26, 1810.

52. *Washington Reporter,* October 8, 15, 22, November 26, 1810.

53. *Washington Reporter,* November 26, 1810.

54. *Washington Reporter,* November 26, 1810.

55. Crimmins, *St. Patrick's Day,* p. 130; *Washington Reporter,* October 11, December 13, 1813, February 20, 1815 (I have inferred from the style and substance of an article on the battle of New Orleans by "A Presbyterian" that Birch was the author); *Minutes of the General Assembly,* p. 517; McClelland, "Thomas Ledlie Birch," p. 35.

Chapter 7. No Excluded Class

1. Elliott, *Partners in Revolution,* p. 27; Smyth, *Men of No Property,* pp. 164–68.

2. Burk, *History of Virginia,* vol. 2, p. 109; Warden, *Statistical, Political, and Historical Account,* vol. 1, pp. l–li, lvi, lxiii; Warden, "On the Probable Duration of the American Government," pp. 6–7.

3. Crimmins, *St. Patrick's Day,* p. 137; *Shamrock,* December 14, 1811; Birch, *Letter from an Irish Emigrant,* p. 4.

4. Warden, "Translator's Preface" to H. Grégoire, *An Enquiry Concerning the Intellectual Moral Faculties and Literature of Negroes,* p. 9; Stewart, *A Deeper Silence,* p. 154; Drennan to Samuel McTier, February 3, 1792, *Drennan Letters,* p. 80.

5. *Shamrock,* December 29, 1810; Crimmins, *St. Patrick's Day,* pp. 117, 161.

6. Emmet to Joseph McCormick [Cormick?], January 28, 1805, in Dr. Thomas Addis Emmet, *Memoir of Thomas Addis and Robert Emmet* (New York, 1915), vol. 1, p. 227; Robinson, "Life of Thomas Addis Emmet," pp. 231, 313; cf. Foster, *Modern Ireland,* p. 265; Warden, *Statistical, Political, and Historical Account,* vol. 1, p. xl.

7. Burk, *History of Virginia,* vol. 1, pp. 211–13.

8. *American Patriot,* October 2, 1802.

9. *American Patriot,* November 13, 1802; *Augusta Chronicle,* January 28, 1804.

10. *Augusta Chronicle,* September 26, 1807, March 11, 1809; cf. *American Patriot,* March 17, 1803.

11. *Blennerhassett Papers,* ed. Safford, pp. 284, 315, 522; Binns, *Recollections,* p. 264; Durey, "Irish Deism and Jefferson's Republic," p. 75, n. 71; for a recent discussion of Binns's attitudes toward African Americans, see Noel Ignatiev, *How the Irish Became White* (New York, 1995), pp. 62–75.

12. Duane to Jefferson, August 11, 1814, "Letters of William Duane," p. 374.

13. Duane to Jefferson, August 11, 1814, "Letters of William Duane," pp. 373–74.

14. Cobbett, "Detection of a Conspiracy," p. 251; *PG,* August 15, 1797, June 11, 1798.

15. Liam Kennedy, *Colonialism, Religion and Nationalism in Ireland* (Belfast, 1996), pp. 182–223; *Shamrock,* June 20, 1812.

16. Carey, *Olive Branch,* p. 187.

17. Mathew Carey, "Slave Labour Employed in Manufactures," in *Miscellaneous Essays* (Philadelphia, 1830), pp. 232–34; Carey, *Autobiography,* p. 131.

18. Burk, *History of Virginia,* vol. 1, p. 212; Warden, *Statistical, Political, and Historical Account,* vol. 3, p. 211; Mathew Carey, "Emancipation of the Slaves in the United States," in *Miscellaneous Essays,* p. 224.

19. Carey, "Emancipation of the Slaves," pp. 225–26; Mathew Carey, "African Colonization," in *Miscellaneous Essays,* p. 218.

20. Emmet, "Part of an Essay," in MacNeven, *Pieces of Irish History,* p. 2.

21. *American Patriot,* February 10, 17, 1803; Warden, *Statistical, Political, and Historical Account,* vol. 1, pp. xl–xli, vol. 3, p. 211; Carey, *Autobiography,* p. 21; Carey, "African Colonization," pp. 214–22.

22. Binns, *Recollections,* pp. 261–64.

23. *American Patriot,* October 2, 1802; Carey, "Emancipation of the Slaves," pp. 230–31; Thomas Jefferson, *Notes on the State of Virginia,* ed. William Peden (London, 1787; New York, 1982), pp. 137–43.

24. Binns, *Recollections,* pp. 322–25.

25. Madden, *United Irishmen,* vol. 3, p. 17.

26. Warden, *Statistical, Political, and Historical Account,* vol. 1, p. 7; vol. 3, pp. 461, 527–88; Burk, *History of Virginia,* vol. 3, pp. 44–45; Phillips, *William Duane,* p. 25; Duane to Jefferson, January 7, 1802, "Letters of William Duane," pp. 273–74.

27. Burk, *An Oration, Delivered on the Fourth of March, 1803,* p. 6; Rowan to Mrs. Rowan, February 20, 1796, in *Autobiography of Archibald Hamilton Rowan,* ed. Drummond, p. 291.

28. Jefferson to Warden, December 29, 1813, Warden Papers, Maryland Historical Society, MS. 873; Warden, *Statistical, Political, and Historical Account,* vol. 3, p. 505.

29. Burk, *History of Virginia,* vol. 1, pp. 51, 140, 202; vol. 2, pp. 210–11, 216; vol. 3, pp. 13–14, 30–43.

30. Burk, *History of Virginia,* vol. 1, pp. 99, 139, 240–41, 249–51.

31. Burk, *History of Virginia,* vol. 1, p. 308.

32. Burk, *History of Virginia,* vol. 1, pp. 20–23, 31; Burk, *An Oration, Delivered on the Fourth of March, 1803,* p. 6.

33. *Aurora,* January 20, 1790; Wilson, ed., *Peter Porcupine in America,* pp. 27, 47, 89–90, 119–20, 130–31.

34. Burk, *Female Patriotism,* p. 16.

35. Burk, *Female Patriotism,* p. 24.

36. Burk, *History of Virginia,* vol. 2, p. 210.

37. Linda K. Kerber, "The Republican Mother: Women and the Enlightenment—An American Perspective," *American Quarterly* 27 (1976), pp. 187–205; Linda Kerber, *Women of the Republic: Intellect and Ideology in Revolutionary America* (Chapel Hill, 1980); Jan Lewis, "The Republican Wife: Virtue and Seduction in the Early Republic," *WMQ* 44 (October 1987), pp. 689–721.

38. Warden, *A Sermon, on the Advantages of Education,* pp. 8–9; Warden, *Chorographical and Statistical Description of the District of Columbia,* pp. 97–99, 182; Duane, *Epitome of the Arts and Sciences,* p. xii.

39. Mathew Carey, *Address to the Wealthy of the Land, Ladies as well as Gentlemen, on the Character, Conduct, Situation, and Prospects, of those whose Sole Dependence for Subsistence, is on the Labour of their Hands* (Philadelphia, 1831).

40. Carey, *Address to the Wealthy of the Land,* pp. v–vii, 2, 9, 12.

41. Carey, *Address to the Wealthy of the Land,* pp. vii, 25–26.

42. Sampson to Carey, May 31, 1831, Edward Carey Gardiner Collection, HSP.

43. Durey, "Irish Deism and Jefferson's Republic," p. 63; *American Patriot,* January 25, 1803.

44. *Dublin Evening Post,* September 24, 1793, December 19, 1795; Burk, *History of Virginia,* vol. 2, p. 31; *Polar Star,* October 24, November 7, 1796; *American Patriot,* February 19, 1803.

45. Burk, *History of Virginia,* vol. 1, pp. 171–72; Burk, *An Oration, Delivered on the Fourth of March, 1803,* p. 5; *Temple of Reason,* June 3, 1801. For a different interpretation of Driscol's attitude to private property, see Durey, "Irish Deism and Jefferson's Republic," p. 71, and Twomey, *Jacobins and Jeffersonians,* pp. 97–98.

46. *American Patriot,* January 11, 25, 1803; *Augusta Chronicle,* August 18, 1810; Duane, *Politics for American Farmers,* pp. 4, 6, 82–83; Duane, *Epitome of the Arts and Sciences,* p. 70; Duane, *Observations on the Principles and Operation of Banking,* p. 15; Schultz, *Republic of Labor,* pp. 150–58.

47. Smyth, *Men of No Property,* pp. 124, 145; Durey, "The Dublin Society of United Irishmen," p. 94.

48. *Aurora,* March 31, 1806; Duane to Jefferson, October 29, 1810, March 15, 1811, "Letters of William Duane," pp. 342, 345; Christopher L. Tomlins, *Law, Labor, and Ideology in the Early American Republic* (Cambridge, 1993), pp. 131–38. For a different view, see Schultz, *Republic of Labor,* pp. 159–64.

49. William Sampson, *Trial of the Journeymen Cordwainers,* pp. 88–89, 104–6.

50. Sampson, *Trial of the Journeymen Cordwainers,* pp. 6, 11–12, 46–47, 94, 95–104, 140, 155, 164–65, 168; Twomey, *Jacobins and Jeffersonians,* pp. 204–5; for the view that Sampson was arguing for the closed shop, see Doyle, *Ireland, Irishmen and Revolutionary America,* p. 218.

51. Twomey, *Jacobins and Jeffersonians,* pp. 171–213; Thomas Paine, *Rights of Man, Part 2,* in *The Complete Writings of Thomas Paine,* ed. Philip S. Foner (New York, 1945), vol. 1, pp. 439–40; see also David A. Wilson, *Paine and Cobbett: The Transatlantic Connection* (Montreal, 1988), p. 75.

52. Schultz, *Republic of Labor,* pp. 181–238; see also Bruce Laurie, *Artisans into Workers: Labor in Nineteenth-Century America* (New York, 1989), and Edward Pessen, *Most Uncommon Jacksonians: The Radical Leaders of the Early Labor Movement* (New York, 1967).

53. Phillips, *William Duane,* pp. 610–15.

54. See, for example, Binns, *Recollections,* pp. 278–80; Warden, *Statistical, Political, and Historical Account,* vol. 1, p. 514, vol. 2, pp. 77–78.

Chapter 8. The Cause of Ireland

1. JW [McNally] to T. Pelham, September 17, 1795, RP 620/10/121/29; Emmet, "Part of an Essay," in MacNeven, *Pieces of Irish History,* pp. 129–32; St. Mark, "Red Shamrock," p. 43; Elliott, *Wolfe Tone,* pp. 260–78, 281, 286–87.

2. JW [McNally] to Edward Cooke, June 6, July 26, 1796, RP 620/36/277; JW to ____, October 1, 1796, RP 620/10/121/37; JW to ____, October 19, 1796, RP 620/10/121/40; JW to ____, October 19, 1796, RP 620/10/121/39; JW to ____, January 17, 1797, RP 620/10/121/47; JW to ____, July 3, 1797, RP 620/10/121/69; Mr. Harward to Lord Grenville, June 2, 1797, RP 620/31/61; Elliott, *Wolfe Tone,* pp. 365–68.

3. JW [McNally] to ____, October 1, 1796, RP 620/10/121/37; Rowan to the Rev. George Potts, 1802, Gratz Collection, HSP; JW [McNally] to Edward Cooke, September 16, 1796, RP 620/36/277; JW to ____, October 24, 1796, RP 620/10/121/40; JW to ____, January 17, 1797, RP 620/10/121/47; JW to ____, July 24, 1797, RP 620/10/121/70; JW to Edward Cooke, September 25, 1797, RP 620/36/277.

4. *Autobiography of Hamilton Rowan,* ed. Drummond, pp. 340, 342, 385–87, 399–413, 431–32; Rowan to Pierce Butler, May 4, 1804, HSP; Rowan to Caesar Rodney, May 16, 1815, Gratz Collection, HSP.

5. Henry Alexander to ____, April 15, 1798, RP 620/36/174; Charles Greville to Thomas Pelham, May 23, 1797, RP 620/30/158; *Augusta Chronicle,* November 11, 1809.

6. James Durham to Rev. Clotworthy Soden, May 29, 1796, RP 620/23/129; General Lake to ____, January 9, 1797, RP 620/28/75; see also RP 620/26/24.

7. Carey, *Autobiography,* p. 29; Carter, "Political Activities of Mathew Carey," p. 194; Bric, "Ireland, Irishmen," pp. 415–25.

8. Mathew Carey, "Emigration from Ireland, and Immigration to the United States," in *Miscellaneous Essays,* pp. 321–25; *Shamrock,* August 17, 1816; Chambers to Robert Simms, June 6, 1818, PRONI, T 1815; Robinson, "Life of Thomas Addis Emmet," pp. 279–83; Caldwell, "Particulars," p. 158.

9. Rowan to John Dickinson, September 9, 1803, Maria Dickinson Logan Family Papers, HSP; Carey, "Emigration from Ireland," in *Miscellaneous Essays,* p. 322; Binns, *Recollections,* p. 73.

10. *Shamrock,* August 17, 1816; "Hints, by the Shamroc [*sic*] Society, New-York, to Emigrants from Europe," in Melish, *Travels through the United States of America,* pp. 625–39; Madden, *United Irishmen,* vol. 3, p. 233.

11. Robinson, "Life of Thomas Addis Emmet," pp. 289–96; Madden, *United Irishmen,* vol. 3, p. 232; Murphy and Mannion, *History of the Friendly Sons of St. Patrick,* pp. 186, 243; Chambers to Robert Simms, June 6, 1818, PRONI, T 1815.

12. Robinson, "Life of Thomas Addis Emmet," pp. 301–6; see also Sean O'Sullivan, *Folktales of Ireland* (Chicago, 1966), pp. 233–34.

13. William Sampson to Grace Sampson, July 4, 1807, Sampson Papers, Library of Congress; Crimmins, *St. Patrick's Day,* pp. 145–46.

14. Sampson, *Memoirs,* pp. 415–16; Crimmins, *St. Patrick's Day,* pp. 108–10, 112.

15. Crimmins, *St. Patrick's Day,* pp. 57–65; Murphy and Mannion, *History of the Friendly Sons of St. Patrick,* pp. 166–68, 174–78, 194, 219; Caldwell, "Particulars," p. 155.

16. *Shamrock,* March 30, 1811, December 24, 1814; A. H. Mitchell, *History of the Hibernian Society of Charleston* (Charleston, 1981); New York *Evening Post,* April 9, 1807; William Heazelton to John Greeves, May 29, 1814, PRONI, D 592/16 (with thanks to Kerby Miller for supplying this reference); *Washington Reporter,* September 19, 1808; *American Patriot,* January 15, 1803; see also Donald Harman Akenson, *Between Two Revolutions: Islandmagee, County Antrim 1798–1920* (Port Credit, Ontario, 1979), p. 20.

17. Howard Harris, "'The Eagle to Watch and the Harp to Tune the Nation': Irish Immigrants, Politics and Early Industrialization in Paterson, New Jersey, 1824–1836," *Journal of Social History* 23 (Spring 1980), pp. 575–97; Cynthia J. Shelton, *The Mills of Manayunk: Industrialization and Social Conflict in the Philadelphia Region, 1787–1837* (Baltimore, 1986); Robert Sean Wilentz, "Industrializing America and the Irish: Towards the New Departure," *Labor History* 20 (Fall 1979), pp. 579–95; Eric Foner, *Politics and Ideology in the Age of the Civil War* (New York, 1980), pp. 157–200.

18. *Aurora,* March 19, 1807; *Shamrock,* April 4, 1812; *American Patriot,* March 19, 1803; see also Crimmins, *St. Patrick's Day.*

19. Sampson, *Memoirs of William Sampson,* pp. 140, 270; Thomas Rodney, "Diary," September 24, 1803, in Rodney Family Papers, Library of Congress; Armistead C. Gordon, *Virginian Writers of Fugitive Verse* (New York, 1923), pp. 76–77; *Shamrock,* March 16, 1811; Chambers to Robert Simms, June 17, 1807, PRONI, T 1815.

20. *Time-Piece,* August 3, 6, 8, 1798; *Augusta Chronicle,* March 30, 1805; *The American Poetical Miscellany* (Philadelphia, 1809), p. 59; [William MacNeven], *Meeting of Irishmen in New York [From the American Truth Teller.] To the People of Ireland* (New York, 1825), frontispiece; R. R. Madden, *Literary Remains of the United Irishmen* (Dublin, 1887), pp. 37–42; Thuente, *The Harp Re-strung,* pp. 239–41.

21. *Washington Reporter,* September 10, 1810; *Time-Piece,* August 18, 1798; *American Poetical Miscellany,* pp. 77–81, 247–48.

22. MacCartney, "The Writing of History in Ireland," pp. 359–61; *Augusta Chronicle,* November 11, 1809 (reprinting an article from the *Democratic Press*); *Washington Reporter,* November 7, 1808, October 8, 1810; *Shamrock,* December 15, 1810.

23. The literature on the Ossianic revival is vast; see Malcolm Chapman, *The Gaelic Vision in Scottish Culture* (London, 1978), Howard Gaskell, *Ossian Revisited* (Edinburgh, 1991), and Fiona J. Stafford, *The Sublime Savage: A Study of James Macpherson and the Poems of Ossian* (Edinburgh, 1988).

24. John Burk, "An Historical Essay on the Character and Antiquity of Irish Songs," in *The Enquirer* [Richmond], May 27, 1808.

25. Burk, "Erin," in *History of the Late War,* Appendix, p. 4; *Time-Piece,* June 13, 1798; *Washington Reporter,* September 18, 1809; "Memoir of Jane MacNeven," in Madden, *United Irishmen,* vol. 3, p. 204; see also Thuente, *The Harp Re-strung,* pp. 30–34, 81–87, 136, 247–48. William Orr had been executed for treason on suspect evidence in 1797, and became a symbol of British oppression in Ireland.

26. Burk, "Historical Essay," in *The Enquirer* [Richmond], May 27, 1808; *Shamrock,* December 15, 1810; Sampson, *Memoirs,* pp. 270–74, 280–81; W. C. Taylor, *History of Ireland, from the Anglo-Norman Invasion till the Union of the Country with Great Britain, with Additions by William Sampson,* vol. 2 (New York, 1833), p. 299.

27. *Time-Piece,* August 10, 14, 16, 30, 1798; *Constitutional Diary,* December 3, 1799; *Temple of Reason,* December 6, 1800, June 3, 1801.

28. Carey, *Autobiography,* pp. 58–61; MacNeven to Carey, May 4, December 8, 1818, February 24, April 12, 1819, Edward Carey Gardiner Collection, HSP; [MacNeven], *Meeting of Irishmen in New York,* pp. 9–11. Compare MacNeven's remark with A. T .Q. Stewart's observation that "to the Irish all History is Applied History," in Stewart, *The Narrow Ground: Aspects of Ulster, 1609–1969* (London, 1977), p. 16.

29. Burk, *History of the Late War,* pp. 73–75, 80–81, 86, 91, 114; Burk, *History of the Late War,* "Appendix," p. 10; *Aurora,* December 11, 1798; Martin Burke, "Piecing Together a Shattered Past: The Historical Writings of the United Irish Exiles in America," in *The United Irishmen,* ed. Dickson, Keogh and Whelan, pp. 299, 306; compare Burk's *History of the Late War,* pp. 129–31, 134, with Birch's *Letter from an Irish Emigrant,* pp. 10–13; compare Burk's *Bunker-Hill,* prologue, n.p., and *Female Patriotism,* pp. 8, 17, 19, with his *History of the Late War,* pp. 97, 114.

30. Burk, *History of the Late War,* pp. 87, 90, 110–13; Shulim, "John Daly Burk," p. 34, and Joseph I. Shulim, *Liberty, Equality, and Fraternity: Studies on the Era of the French Revolution and Napoleon* (New York, 1989), p. 80; *Constitutional Diary,* January 7, 1800; Sampson to Carey, May 31, 1830, Edward Carey Gardiner Collection, HSP; Taylor, *History of Ireland.*

31. Sampson, *Memoirs,* pp. 30, 33–34, 69; David Bailie Warden Papers, Maryland Historical Society, MS. 871, Register A, pp. 32–33.

32. Sampson to Grace Sampson, November 5, 1807, March 29, 1809, Sampson Papers, Library of Congress; John Chambers to Mathew Carey, December 7, 1807, Lea and Febiger Collection, HSP; Sampson to Thomas Jefferson, December 12, 1807 [misdated 1804 by Sampson], Jefferson to Sampson, December 20, 1807, Papers of Thomas Jefferson, Library of Congress. Sampson was ready to publish his *Memoirs* in 1806, but held back while his wife petitioned the British government to allow him to return. When the petition failed and he no longer had anything to lose, Sampson went straight to the printer with his manuscript. See Sampson to Grace Sampson, October 15, 1806, February 17, April 18, April 27, 1807.

33. MacNeven, *Pieces of Irish History,* pp. 170–71; *Dublin Evening Post,* November 10, 1792; Smyth, *Men of No Property,* p. 174.

34. *Augusta Chronicle,* July 26, 1806; MacNeven to Carey, May 4, 1818; Emmet to Carey, April 22, 1819, Edward Carey Gardiner Collection, HSP; Mathew Carey, *Vindiciae Hibernica: or, Ireland Vindicated: An Attempt to Develop and Expose a few of the Multifarious Errors and Falsehoods Respecting Ireland* (Philadelphia, 1819), pp. xiv–xix, 100, 183–84, 514; Carey, *Autobiography,* pp. 58–59.

35. Madison to Carey, February 11, 1820, *Papers of James Madison,* Library of Congress; MacCartney, "Writing of History," p. 361.

36. Phineas Bond to Lord Hawkesbury, December 14, 1803, Public Record Office, FO 5/39.

37. _____ to Henry Charles Sirr, July 24, 1806, RP 620/14/198/16; JW [McNally] to _____, January 6, 1806, RP 620/14/198/2; JW to _____, June 26, 1806, RP 620/14/198/8; Leonard MacNally [*sic*] to Sampson [1820], Dreer Collection, HSP; compare JW to _____, March 4, 1798, RP 620/10/121/93, and JW to _____, July 26, 1798, RP 620/10/121/121.

38. Jane MacNeven, "Memoir," in Madden, *United Irishmen,* vol. 3, p. 208; MacNeven to Carey, May 4, 1818; Arthur Daly to Carey, September 20, 1821, Edward Carey Gardiner Collection, HSP; John Chambers to Robert Simms, May 25, 1821, January 1, 1822, Emigrant Letters to Robert Simms, PRONI, T 1815; [MacNeven], *Meeting of Irishmen in New York,* pp. 9–12.

39. [MacNeven], *Meeting of Irishmen in New York,* pp. 11–12, 15–16.

40. [illegible] William Sampson," in [MacNeven], *Meeting of Irishmen in New York,* pp. 6–7; McGee, *History of the Irish Settlers in America,* p. 132; [MacNeven], *Meeting of Irishmen in New York,* p. 3; Jane MacNeven, "Memoir," in Madden, *United Irishmen,* vol. 3, p. 208; "Address of the Committee of Superintendence of the friends of Ireland," August 1828 [misdated 1829], Society Miscellaneous Collection, HSP.

41. *Democratic Press,* May 14, 1829; Binns, *Recollections,* pp. 307–10; Sampson to Rowan, April 29, 1829, in *Autobiography of Archibald Hamilton Rowan,* ed. Drummond, p. 472.

42. [MacNeven], *Meeting of Irishmen in New York,* p. 12; MacNeven to Warden, March 30, 1831, Warden Papers, Library of Congress; Carey to Members of the Hibernian Society, May 1, 1833, Society Small Collection, HSP.

43. Madden, *United Irishmen,* vol. 3, pp. 242–44.

44. Sampson to Carey, March 26, 1831, Edward Carey Gardiner Collection, HSP; John Chambers to Robert Simms, Emigrant Letters to Robert Simms, PRONI, T 1815; Madden, *United Irishmen,* vol. 3, pp. 178–79, 210.

45. McGee, *History of the Irish Settlers in America,* p. 95.

46. McGee, *History of the Irish Settlers in America,* pp. 15–16, 104–5, 188.

47. Emmet to Carey, April 22, 1819; Robert Johnson to Carey, December 23, 1820, Edward Carey Gardiner Collection, HSP; *Shamrock,* December 7, 1816.

Conclusion. The Tradition of All the Dead Generations

1. See Gwyn A. Williams, *Goya and the Impossible Revolution* (London, 1976), for a brilliant explication of Goya's art in the context of the "necessary but impossible revolution."

2. MacNeven, *Pieces of Irish History,* p. 305; Burke to Adrien-Jean-Francois Duport, March 29, 1790, in *The Correspondence of Edmund Burke,* ed. Thomas Copeland (Cambridge, 1967), vol. 6, p. 109.

3. Karl Marx, "The Eighteenth Brumaire of Louis Bonaparte," in Marx and Engels, *Selected Works* (London, 1970), p. 96.

4. Caldwell, "Particulars," p. 94.

5. Arthur O'Connor to William Tennent, n.d. [1801], Tennent Papers, PRONI, D 1748/A/1/238/1.

6. Caldwell, "Particulars," p. 94.

7. John Nevin to James Nevin, April 10, 1804, PRONI, T 3721/1. I thank Kerby Miller for supplying me with this reference.

8. W. T. W. Tone, *Life of Theobald Wolfe Tone,* vol. 1, p. 31.

9. See, for example, Birch, *Seemingly Experimental Religion,* p. 94; MacNeven, *Pieces of Irish History,* pp. 170–71, 197, 295.

Index

Adams, John, 1, 42, 43, 45, 52, 55, 105; attacked by Burk, 49, 50, 57
Adams, Samuel, 51
Adet, Pierre, 154
Adrain, Robert, 99
Albany (N.Y.), 84, 158
Alien and Sedition Acts (1798), 8, 11, 49, 50, 55, 57, 61, 85, 121–23; Irish reaction to, 35, 52
Alien Enemies Proclamation (1813), 87–89
Alien Friends Law (1798), 48; Irish reaction to, 31, 49, 51; move to repeal, 52–54
American Museum, The (literary journal), 99
American Patriot (Baltimore newspaper), 70, 104, 163, 176
American Philosophical Society, 96
American Revolution, 17, 39, 42, 68, 96, 100, 106, 178; Irish role in, 40, 47, 52; Irish view of, 5, 7, 14–16, 51–53, 57, 105, 115, 118, 129, 166; and millenarianism, 112, 113, 116, 123
American West, 39, 97, 127, Irish settlements in, 61, 156, 157
Amiens, Peace of (1802), 2
Antrim, Battle of (1798), 30, 32, 159
Antrim, County, 14, 17, 115; Rising of 1798 in, 30, 32, 33, 84
Armagh, County, 19, 22, 27
Armstrong, John, 84
Atalanta (Royal Navy sloop), 80
Augusta (Ga.), 61, 111
Augusta Chronicle (newspaper), 61, 70, 136
Aurora (Philadelphia newspaper), 41, 42, 51, 56, 73, 143

Bache, Benjamin Franklin, 42
Bacon's Rebellion (1676), 101, 102
Baldwin, Ebenezer, 112
Ballinamuck, Battle of (1798), 31
Ballymena, Rising of 1798 in, 32, 84
Ballymoney, 15, 17, 32
Ballynahinch, Battle of (1798), 5, 30, 33, 118
Baltimore, 71, 106, 147, 176; Irish in, 2, 40, 46, 59–61, 79, 84, 157, 159; Presbytery of, 121, 129, 131
Baltimore Hibernian Society, 158
Baltimore Irish Brigade (militia), 46
Bank of the United States, 92, 93, 149, 151
banking system, 3, 82, 151; and American politics, 89, 90, 92, 93
Bantry Bay, 25
Bastille Day, Irish celebration of, 34, 110
Behan, Brendan, 174
Belfast, 33, 115, 119, 134, 155; emigration from, 6, 33, 59, 60, 89, 97, 157; Presbytery of, 121; United Irish in, 12, 22, 23
Belfast Harpers' Festival (1792), 34, 110
Belfast Mercury (newspaper), 115
Belisarius incident (1811), 80
Belpre Island, 136

Berkeley, William, 101, 102
Beverley, Robert, 101
Bicheno, James, 113
Bingham, William, 41
Binns, Benjamin, 27, 28, 46, 173
Binns, John, 7, 11, 46, 60, 63, 64, 70, 72, 77–79, 82, 83, 90, 92–95, 113, 156, 161, 163, 170, 176, 177; and Duane, 73, 74; and Irish nationalism, 168, 169; and slavery, 136, 139, 140, 151; and United Irishmen, 26–28; in War of 1812, 84, 87–89
Birch, George, 119
Birch, Thomas Ledlie, 9, 61, 111, 113, 114, 131, 132, 134, 163, 164, 176–78; in County Down, 17, 115–17; emigration, 120, 121; ministry in America, 122–24; and revivalists, 125–30; in Rising of 1798, 33, 118, 119. Works: *Physicians Languishing Under Disease,* 117; *Letter from an Irish Emigrant,* 122; *Seemingly Experimental Religion,* 128
Birmingham (England), 6, 27
Black, John, 43, 44, 99
Blennerhassett, Harman, 61, 136, 151, 160
Blennerhassett, Margaret, 136
Bolivar, Simon, 61
Bond, Oliver, 23
Bond, Phineas, 166
Boston, 43, 104–6, 113, 178; Irish in, 24, 38, 49
Boston Polar Star (newspaper), 38, 147
Britain, 1, 96, 102, 136; American relations, 8, 10, 31, 39, 40, 73, 76, 78–80, 82, 83; as Antichrist, 122, 123; blockades of France by, 25, 77; and Federalists, 51, 55–57, 106; immigration from, 49, 61, 87; Irish policy, 16, 17, 19; Irish view of, 9, 10, 177, 178; refusal to recognize American citizenship by, 86, 87; United Irish view of, 36, 37, 61, 62, 76, 80, 83, 165, 166; in War of 1812, 84–87, 89
British North America, see Canada
Brothers, Richard, 113
Brown, Andrew, 54
Bunker Hill, Battle of (1775): as dramatized by Burk, 103–6; Irish celebration of, 14
Burdett, Francis, 16
Burk, John Daly, 7, 13, 38–40, 43, 44, 46, 56, 57, 61, 72, 79, 100, 111, 133, 147, 155, 160, 163, 164, 173, 176–78; and cultural nationalism, 161, 162; deism of, 70, 71; dramatic works of, 103–11; and embargo, 81, 82; historical writings, 100–103; on Native Americans, 140–42, 151; on slavery, 135, 138; trial for sedition, 49, 50; and United Irish, 22–24; on women, 143, 144. Works: *Bethlem Gabor* (play), 108–10; *Bunker-Hill* (play), 103–8, 164, 176; "The Columbiad" (poem), 100; *Female Patriotism* (play), 106–9, 143, 164; *History of the Late War in Ireland,* 101, 102; *History of Virginia,* 100–103, 141, 142, 176
Burke, Edmund, 23, 72, 173
Burke, Thomas, 88
Burns, Robert, 110
Burr, Aaron, 49, 55, 61, 64, 136
Byrne, Patrick, 16

Cadore, Jean Baptiste Nompère de Champagny, duc de, 78
Caldwell family, 17, 32
Caldwell, John (father), 32
Caldwell, John (son), 13, 33, 44, 59, 64, 156, 158, 174, 175
Caldwell, Richard, 32, 84
Callender, James Thompson, 4, 43
Campbell, William, 33, 34
Canada, 80, 84, 93, 167, 170, 179
Cane Ridge (Ky.), 127
Canning, George, 158
Cannonsburg (Penn.), 127
Carey, James, 6, 11, 43, 44, 50, 161, 163, 164
Carey, Mathew, 11, 16, 24, 35, 41–44, 52, 54–56, 58, 60, 63, 72, 73, 78, 82, 90–92, 94, 97, 104, 111, 155, 156, 160, 177; and Irish nationalism, 168–70; and literature, 99, 100; and slavery, 138–40, 145, 151; and Volunteers, 17, 18; in War of 1812, 85, 86; on women, 145–47; writing of, 163, 165, 166. Works: *American Poetical Miscellany,* 160, 161; *Olive Branch,* 86; *Vindiciae Hibernica,* 163, 165, 166
Carey, William Paulet, 149
Carlisle, 29
Carlow, County, 30
Carnew, Battle of (1798), 5
Carpenter, Stephen Cullen, 67
Carrickfergus, 89
Carter, Edward, 44, 86, 100
Castlebar, Battle of (1798), 30
Castlereagh, Robert Stewart, Viscount, 32, 110, 121, 165
Catholic Committee, 15–18, 167
Catholic emancipation, 13, 14, 17–20,

Catholic emancipation (*contin.*) 115, 139, 155, 158, 163, 164; in 1829, 166–69
Catholic Irish, 24, 30, 58, 166; and American Revolution 15, 16; emigration of, 2, 90, 153, 157, 159; and Protestants, 15, 20, 34, 117; and United Irishmen, 20, 25, 115, 158, 174
Catholic Irish-Americans, 2, 54, 66, 76, 168; and discrimination, 69, 94, 95; and Federalists, 3, 40, 47, 53, 56
Catholic Relief Act (1793), 19, 20
Catholic Relief Act (1829), 168
Celtic Revival, United Irish role in, 97
Chambers, John, 5, 6, 18, 24, 35, 78–80, 89, 92, 93, 156–58, 160, 172; emigration of, 58–60
Charleston (S.C.), 2, 139, 178
Charleston Hibernian Society, 158
Chesapeake incident (1807), 79, 80
Church of Ireland, 69. *See also* Protestant Irish
citizenship, American, 48; British refusal to [illegible]
Clare, Lord, 29, 165
Clark, Daniel, 44
Clay, Henry, 91
Clinton, De Witt, 2, 64, 66, 84, 91, 92
Clintonian Republicans, in 1807 elections, 64–67; and United Irish, 59, 70, 71, 74, 91, 157
Cobbett, William, 85, 99, 174, 176; on Irish, 43–47, 49, Irish criticism of, 50–52
Cockayne, John, 21, 23
Coigly, James, 27, 28, 73
Coleman, William, 66
Coleraine, 32
Columbia College (New York), 99
Columbus, Christopher, 142
commerce, United Irish views on, 5, 6, 176
common law, Irish attitude to, 68, 69, 71, 111, 149, 150
Congress, U.S., 45, 48–50, 87, 91, 141; House of Representatives, 120; Senate, 55; United Irish lobbying of, 52, 91, 157
Congressional elections: of 1794, 40; of 1796, 42; of 1799, 55, 57
Connecticut, 5, 85, 112
Constitution, American, 39, 50, 87, 97
Constitutional Republicans, Society of (Quids), 63, 64, 73, 78
Continental Congress, 81
Cooper, Thomas, 62
Copenhagen Fields (London), 27
Cork (city), 5, 16, 23, 68, 176
Cork, County, 5, 61
Cornwallis, Lord, 178; in Rising of 1798, 31, 32
Coxe, Tench, 55, 56, 82
Crawford, William, 158
cultural nationalism, American, 96, 99, 100; Irish, 34, 161–63; and United Irishmen, 97, 103, 104, 110, 111
Cuming, George, 6, 60, 74, 76, 78, 88
Cuming, Samuel, 53, 54
Cunningham, Waddell, 134
Curragh, 30
Curran, John, 22
Curry, John, 166
Cushendall, 32
Cuxhaven, 154

Daignan, Luke, 23
Dallas, Alexander, 53
Danbury (Conn.), 112
[illegible] 53
Defender movement (Ireland), 19, 20, 22, 68; United Irish alliance with, 22–26, 172, 174
deism, 41, 62, 127, 173; in America, 69–71, 76
Democratic Party, 94, 159
Democratic Press (Phila. newspaper), 60, 73, 82, 89, 161
Democratic Societies (American), 40, 56
Derry, siege of (1689), 13
D'Evereux, John, 60, 61
Dickson, William Steel, 16, 115, 119, 120
Doheny, Michael, 179
Down, County, 17, 114, 115, 176; emigration from, 5, 33; Rising of 1798 in, 5, 30, 32, 33, 118
Downshire, Lord, 119
Drennan, William, 12–14, 19, 20, 44, 70, 72, 134, 174. Works: "Erin" (poem), 160
Driscol, Denis, 23, 46, 61, 62, 68, 79, 82, 106, 111, 113, 163, 174, 177, 178; and deism, 69–72; economic views of, 147, 148; on slavery, 135–37, 140
Driscoll, John, 5
Duane, William, 4, 11, 43, 46, 52–56, 60, 62–64, 70, 72, 76, 78, 79, 81–83, 90, 159, 163, 174, 176; on banking, 92, 93, 149; on common law, 68, 71, 149; on education, 97, 98; on Jay's Treaty, 41,

Duane, William (*contin.*)
42; on Native Americans, 140, 141; rivalry with Carey and Binns, 73, 74, 86; on slavery, 136, 137; in War of 1812, 84, 88; on women, 144, 145; and working class politics, 148–51. Works: *Epitome of the Arts and Sciences,* 98, 145
Dublin, 4, 7, 12, 16, 26, 30, 31, 44, 79, 80, 104, 110, 154, 155, 166, 167, 176; British repression in (1798), 29, 33, 60; emigration from, 5, 58, 60; United Irish in, 18–21, 23–25, 154; Volunteers in, 17, 19; workers' combinations in, 148, 149
Dublin Evening Post (newspaper), 23, 147, 165
Dundas, Henry, 77
Dungiven, 119
Dunlap, William, 106
Durey, Michael, 3–5

economic nationalism, and republicans, 3, 6; and United Irishmen, 81, 82, 91
Edinburgh Convention (1793), 70
education, republican, Irish influence on, 9, 95–99, 145, 175
egalitarianism, and United Irish, 10, 37, 38, 51, 52, 95, 105, 133, 134, 144, 150–52
elections. *See* Congressional elections; presidential elections
embargo on trade with Britain (1807), 78; Irish support for, 80–82
emigration and patriotic societies, Irish, 153, 155–58, 175
émigrés, Irish, 2–5, 8, 16, 17, 19, 21, 22, 24, 25, 32, 33, 38, 43, 44, 49, 155; first impressions of America, 36–39; flight to France and America, 37, 40, 58, 59; and Rufus King, 2, 65, 66
Emmet, Robert, 9, 65; insurrection led by (1803), 23, 34, 166
Emmet, Robert (son of Thomas), 84
Emmet, Thomas Addis, 11, 18, 24, 26, 29, 31, 34, 64–69, 79, 91, 94, 156–58, 166, 168, 170, 174, 177; emigration to America, 58, 59; on slavery, 135, 137, 139, 151; on trade unions, 149, 150; and United Irish, 20, 21; in War of 1812, 85, 88
England, 28, 29, 41, 162
evangelicalism, 71, 114; Irish, 34, 117. *See also* revivalism, American
Evening Post (New York newspaper), 65

factionalism, and United Irish, 38, 59, 76
Federalist Party, 7, 39, 43, 55, 78; decline after 1800, 8, 71, 76, 89; Irish support for, 3, 40, 155, 177–78; and United Irish, 10, 42, 50, 64, 67, 68, 73
Federalists, 1, 34, 44, 47, 64, 72, 83, 106, 108, 123, 130; and Britain, 51, 55–57; compared to Orangemen, 61, 76, 176; on immigration, 2, 66; and Presbyterianism, 120, 121, 125, 128, 129; removal from office after defeat of, 8, 10, 62; Republican clashes with, 49, 53; on United Irish, 7, 10, 45–48, 51, 53, 55–57; on War of 1812, 85, 86
Fenian Brotherhood, 179
Fenno, John Ward, 52, 55, 176; on United Irish, 43–48, 54
Fitzgerald, Edward, 26, 29
Fitzsimons, Thomas, 40, 47, 155
Fitzwilliam, Earl of, 20
Flood, Henry, 14
Florida, acquisition of, 93
Ford, Patrick, 159
Forkhill, 13
Fort George (Scotland), 58, 139
Fort Greene (New York), 85
Foster, John, 18
Foster, Roy, 30
France, 15, 40, 49, 50, 58, 65, 77, 78, 85, 107, 167; American relations with, 43–45, 55, 57, 60, 108; entry into American war by (1778), 16, 24; invasion attempts in Ireland, 1, 25, 30, 31, 154; United Irish in, 2, 31, 38, 50, 59; United Irish relations with, 17–22, 24–26, 28, 37, 118, 136, 153, 154, 172, 174. *See also* French Revolution; Quasi-War with France
Franklin, Benjamin, 17, 97
Frazer, James, 88
freedom of expression, 51, 53, 173
Freeman's Journal (newspaper), 17
freemasonry, 115; and United Irishmen, 1, 44
French Revolution, 70, 108; to Americans, 39, 40, 121; to Irish, 6, 7, 12–14, 18, 37, 44; and millenarianism, 113, 115, 116, 123; and theater, 103, 104, 106; and United Irishmen, 19, 22, 24, 105
Friendly Sons of St. Patrick (Phila. Irish organization), 155
Friendly Sons of St. Patrick (N.Y. Irish organization), 158
Friends of Ireland (N.Y. Irish organization), 168, 169

Friends of Ireland Society (Phila. Irish organization), 168
Fries Rebellion (1799), 54

Gaelic (language), 48, 162
Gaine, Hugh, 47
Gallagher, James, 54
Gazette of the United States (Federalist newspaper), 47, 62
Genet, Edmund, 40, 56
genocide, English accused of, 80, 166
George III, 120, attack upon (1795), 27, 46
Georgia, 139,141; Irish in, 61, 88, 135
German Americans, 36; in Pennsylvania elections, 55, 63, 74
Germany, 31, 99, 154
Giles, William Branch, 70
Gillespy, Edward, 80
Glasgow University, 32, 95, 114, 134
Glendy, Rev. John, 120, 177
Glorious Revolution (1688), 13
Gloucester jail (England), 60, 77
[illegible], William, 100, 10[illegible]
Gordon Riots (1780), 49
Gowdy, Robert, 120
Goya, Francisco, 172
Grattan, Henry, 16, 20
Great Famine, The (1846–51), 9, 80, 81, 153, 179
Greenwich Village (N.Y. City), Irish community in, 157
Grégoire, Henri, 136

Hamilton, Alexander, 39, 40, 55
Hammond, George, 41
Hancock, John, 51
Harcourt, Lord, 15
Harper, Joseph, 118
Harvey, Bagenal, 23
Henry, Alexander, 121
Hibernian Provident Society (N.Y. Irish organization), 64, 66, 67, 83, 87, 131, 134, 135, 157, 159
Hibernian Society (Phila. United Irish organization), 42, 43, 155, 169
Hopkinson, Francis, 53, 54
Huntingdon, Presbytery of, 126

Illinois, 156, 157
impressment, 37, 123, 137; and America, 77–80; and Britain, 83, 87
Incorporated Benevolent Society of St. Patrick (Phila. Irish organization), 159
indentured servitude, Irish, 44
Industrial Revolution, in America, 6, 82, 93, 150
informers, United Irish views on, 83
Irish administration (Dublin Castle), 16, 28, 32, 153, 160, 167; seizure plotted, 23, 26
Irish-American nationalism, 9, 10, 80, 153, 159, 169–71, 179; and cultural revival, 162, 163; and historical writing, 164–66; in patriotic clubs, 157–58
Irish Americans, 40, 52, 80, 87, 88; leadership of, 3, 4, 9, 10, 68, 175; political divisions within, 45, 47, 56, 67, 155
Irish history, mythical Golden Age of, 102; United Irish writing on, 163–66
Irish immigrants, 4, 38, 43, 48, 52, 66, 70, 80, 90, 92, 94, 122, 125, 128, 159, 167; Catholic, 153, 157; class origins, 3–5, 151; cultural nationalism, 96; loyalism among, 47, 67; patterns of settlement, 2, 3, 5; and Republicans, 2, 9, 40, 56; in War of 1812, 86–89; and Washington, [illegible]
Irish immigration, encouragement of, 155, 156; phases of, 8, 9; post-Famine, 159, 179
Irish nationalism, 159, 166; music and poetry, 160, 161; revolutionary vs. constitutional, 9, 10
Irish Parliament, 19, 20; House of Commons, 17, 18; and Protestants, 16, 17
Irish republicanism, 5, 6, 8, 113, 144, 159; and revolution, 7, 42; and social conservatism, 3, 9, 133; transplanted to America, 3, 8
Irish vote, 48, 155; in 1794 elections, 40; in 1796 elections, 42, 43; in 1800 elections, 55, 56; United Irish struggle for control, 73, 74
Islandmagee, 159
Israel, Israel, 43

Jackson, Andrew, 89, 90, 92, 131, 158; and Jacksonianism, 150, 151; and United Irish, 93, 94
Jackson, Francis James, 158
Jackson, Henry, 29, 60, 64, 66; and United Irish, 19, 25
Jackson, William, 21, 22
Jacobins, 37, 39, 113; republicans characterized as, 4, 6, 7, 10, 22, 27, 45, 46, 53, 66, 122
Jay, John, 40, 41
Jay's Treaty (1795), 40–42, 56

Jefferson, Thomas, 2, 39, 62, 91, 98–100, 120, 136, 137, 140, 141, 159, 165; in 1796 election, 42, 43; in 1800 election, 55–57. Works: *Notes on the State of Virginia,* 140
Jews, American, 69
Joan d'Arc, as dramatized by Burk, 107, 108, 143, 144
Johnson, Robert, 170
Jones, John Gale, 27
journalism, Irish-American, 153, 163, 168, 175–76
Juvenile Sons of Erin (N.Y. Irish organization), 135

Kelburn, Sinclair, 121
Kentucky, 127, 141
Kildare, County, 29, 30
Kilmainham jail, 121
Kinderhook Academy, 98
King, Rufus, 1, 2, 8, 31, 32, 60, 68; in 1807 election, 64–67
Kingsborough, Lord, 164
Kingston Academy (New York), 98, 145
Know-Nothing Party, 95
Knox, Samuel, 97, 129

labor movement. *See* trade unions
Lake Champlain (N.Y), in War of 1812, 84, 89
Lake, General, 155
Larne, 155
Lawler, William, 23
Leib, Michael, 63, 73, 74
Leinster Directory (United Irish organization), 26, 29
Lewis, Morgan, 64, 66, 67
Limerick, 16
Limerick, Treaty of (1691), 40
Lisburn, in Rising of 1798, 118, 119, 129
literature, American, Irish influence on, 9, 95, 99, 100
Livingston, Edward, 40, 49, 64, 66, 67
Locke, John, 97, 106
London, 40, 49, 59, 110, 113; United Irish in, 7, 11, 26–28
London Company (Va. colonizers), 102, 103
London Corresponding Society, 11, 27, 28, 41, 63
Londonderry, 22, 41. *See also* Derry
Londonderry, Lord, 119
Louisiana Purchase, 93
Louth, County, Defenders in, 19, 20
loyalists, Irish, 15, 25, 30, 47; 51, 130, 139, 155, 166; in Rising of 1798, 117–19. *See also* Orange Order
Lurgan, 121, 129
Lyon, Matthew, 44

Macdonough, Thomas, 89
MacNeven, William James, 18, 29, 31, 44, 81, 83, 85, 91, 92, 151, 156–58, 160, 173, 177; emigration to America, 58, 59; and France, 24, 26; historical writing of, 163, 165; on O'Connell, 167–69. Works: *Pieces of Irish History,* 165
Macomb, Alexander, 89
Macpherson, James, 161, 162
Madden, Richard R., 10
Madison, James, 39, 74, 78, 120, 166; in War of 1812, 86, 87
Madoc, Prince, 97
Maidstone, trials for treason at, 28
Manchester, 6, 28, 155
manufacturing, 81, 82, 138; and United Irish, 3, 5, 6, 82, 90–92
Manumission Society (N.Y. abolitionist organization), 135
martial law (Ireland), declaration in Ulster of (1797), 25, 29
Marx, Karl, 165, 173
Maryland, 135
Mayo, County, Rising of 1798 in, 30
McCabe, Thomas, and slavery, 134
McClelland, William, 158, 159
McClenachan, Blair, 41, 42
McClintock, John, 88
McCracken, Henry Joy, 22
McCreery, John, 61, 110, 111, 162, 176. Works: "The American Star" (song), 111, 176
McCurtin, Daniel, 52
McGee, Thomas D'Arcy, 170, 178. Works: *History of the Irish Settlers in America,* 170
McGready, James, 127
McKean, Thomas, 1, 53; as Pennsylvania governor, 62, 63; 1805 re-election, 64, 73
McKee, Hugh, 118
McMillan, John, 125–29
McNally, Leonard, 26, 153, 154, 167
McTier, Martha, 21, 34
Melish, John, 110
Menin, Jeremiah, 5
mermaid, capture of, 159
Methodists, American, 71, 72
Mifflin, Thomas, 154
militia, American, 111; and Irish, 46, 56,

militia, American (*contin.*)
87, 88; and United Irishmen, 79, 83, 84
militia, Irish, 25, 164
Millar, John, 32, 114, 134
millenarianism, 3, 9, 34, 111–13, 131, 173; in America, 121–24, 130; in Ireland, 114, 115, 123, 129, 177; secular, 113
Miller, Samuel, 121
Millerites, 124
Mingo Creek, 130
Mississippi Territory, 136
Mitchel, John, 179
Monroe, James, 154
Montgomery, Richard, 79; United Irish admiration of, 50–52
Moore, Robert, 53, 54
Moore, Thomas, 111, 161
Morris, Andrew, 66, 67
Muir, James, 120
Munro, Henry, 33, 118
music, Irish influence on American, 9, 95, 110, 111, 176; Irish nationalist, 160

Napoleon, 28, 58, 77–79, 83, 167, 174
Native Americans, 9, 40, 97, 101, 103, 178; and United Irishmen, 134, 140–43, 151, 175
nativism, American, 79, 175, 178; in 1807 elections, 66, 67; origins of, 47, 53, 54, 57; post-1815, 90, 94, 95
Naturalization Law (1798), 48, 52, 128
naturalization laws, effort to liberalize, 8, 48, 63, 76
Neilson, Samuel, 22, 31, 58–60, 113
New England, 122, 138, opposition to War of 1812 in, 85, 86, 94
New Orleans, Battle of (1815), 90, 131
New Ross, Battle of (1798), 61
New School Democrats (Penn. Republican party), 74
New York (state), 55, 68, 84, 111; and common law, 68–69; elections of 1807, 64–67; Republicans in, 59, 62, 70
New York City, 50, 70, 74, 80, 84, 98, 99, 121, 122, 131, 149, 151, 170, 177, 178; Irish in, 2, 11, 17, 18, 22, 32, 33, 41, 58, 59, 61, 66, 79, 83, 84, 135, 137, 157–59; Irish immigration to, 39, 43; Irish vote in, 40, 55, 56; United Irish in, 42, 43, 49, 50, 56, 64, 66–68, 71, 87, 91, 166–68
New-York Gazette (Federalist newspaper), 106
New York Irish Emigrant Society, 157
New York Society for the Promotion of Domestic Manufactures, 91
New York St. Patrick Society, 47
Newgate Prison (Dublin), 18, 21, 37, 60
Newton, Isaac, 142
Newtownards Peninsula, 32
Niles, Hezekiah, 91
Non-Importation Act (1807), 78; and Irish, 81, 82
Non-Intercourse Act (1809), 78
Northern Liberties (Philadelphia district), 73, 74; class politics in, 150, 151; and Republicans, 39, 43, 55
Northern Star (newspaper), 25, 31, 60, 113
Northumberland (Penn.), 60
Northwest, American, 40
Nugent, Maj. Gen. 33, 118

O'Connell, Daniel, 10, 140, 157, 158, 165; and Catholic emancipation, 167–70
O'Connor, Arthur, 29, 73, 74, 174, 177; and French invasion, 26–28
O'Connor, Thomas, 91, 156, 159, 170
Ohio, Presbytery of, 125–28
Old School Democrats (Penn. Republican party), 74, 84, 151
O'Mahony, John, 179
Opechancanough, 142
Oporto, 59
Orange Order, 22, 48, 61, 62, 74, 76, 95, 119, 157, 176
Orr, Robert, 164
Ossian, 161, 162
O'Sullivan, John, 176
Oswald, Eleazor, 21
Otis, Harrison Gray, 48

Paddy's Resource (democratic song collection), 160
Paine, Thomas, 68, 90, 113, 128, 150; deism of, 69–71. Works: *Age of Reason,* 70; *Rights of Man,* 68, 113
Palmer, Elihu, deist philosophy of, 69
Paris, 45, 60, 78, 103; United Irishmen in, 17, 25, 27, 37, 59, 154
Parks, James, 32
Patriot Party (Ireland), 16
patronage, and American politics, 63, 72–74, 76, 81, 90
Patterson, Robert, 99
Penal Laws (Ireland), 15
Pennsylvania, 1, 2, 36, 43, 54, 63, 64, 68, 74, 84, 114, 122, 124–27, 129, 131, 176; elections of 1799 and 1800, 55, 56;

Pennsylvania (*contin.*)
Irish immigration, 5, 43; Irish in, 60, 61, 178; Republican divisions in, 62–64, 72–74; United Irishmen in, 71, 76, 154, 158
Pennsylvania, University of, 99
Pestalozzi system, of education, 98
Petersburg (Va.), 100, 108, 110; Irish in, 61, 79, 82
Philadelphia, 36, 39, 46, 70, 74, 82, 93, 94, 98, 99, 103, 122, 149, 170, 177; Germans in, 63, 74; Irish in, 2, 9, 17, 18, 20, 25, 59–61, 67, 79, 87, 88, 136, 158, 159, 168, 169; Irish vote in, 40, 47, 56; Republicans in, 41, 42, 53; United Irish in, 37, 38, 42–44, 48, 53–56, 62–64, 72, 73, 90, 154–57, 166, 167
Philadelphia Gazette (Federalist newspaper), 54
Philadelphia riots (1844), 94
Philadelphia Society for the Promotion of National Industry, 91
Philanthropic and Telegraphic Societies, 23, 44, 109
Pickering, Timothy, 46, 49, 50, 51, 55
Pitt (the Younger), William, 63
Pittsburgh, Irish community in, 158
Playfair, William, 46
poetry, United Irish influence on, 100; Irish nationalist, 34, 160, 161
Portaferry, 129
Porter, James, 32, 120, 129
Portland, Duke of, 2
Portugal, 31, 59
Postlethwaite (prison ship), 33, 119
Powhatan, 142
Presbyterian Americans, 71, 120–22, 124–29
Presbyterian Irish, 9, 33, 61, 97, 111, 114, 115, 117, 130, 131, 134; among immigrants, 2, 5, 43, 47, 120, 121, 158; and millenarianism, 113, 116, 177; in Rising of 1798, 30, 32, 119
presidential elections, of 1796, 42, 43; of 1800, 1, 2, 8, 55, 57, 59
Prevost, Sir George, 89
Price, Richard, 113
Priestley, Joseph, 60, 113
Prince Edward Island (St. John's Island), 80
Prince Regent, in War of 1812, 86, 87
prison reform, and United Irishmen, 151
prisoners of war, status of, 86, 87
Privy Council (British), 27, 28
productive classes, United Irishmen and, 98, 133, 148, 150
protectionism and protective tariffs, 3; and American politics, 90–92; and United Irishmen, 82, 92, 93
Protestant Ascendancy, 154
Protestant Irish (Church of Ireland), 15, 20, 28, 30, 34, 40, 46, 54, 56, 70, 139, 166
Protestant Irish Americans, and Catholics, 157, 168

Quakers, 36
Quasi-War with France (1798), 1, 85, 121; and Federalist fortunes, 55, 57; origins of, 45, 46
Quebec City, 87; Siege of (1775), 51
Quids. *See* Constitutional Republicans, Society of

Reform Bill, defeat of (1794), 20
Reid, Thomas, 114
Reign of Terror (French), 30, 37, 49, 81. *See also* French Revolution
religious freedom, 34, 69, 71, 76; in colonial Virginia, 103, 132; United Irishmen and, 8, 10, 53, 95
religious tensions, 10, 67, 94, 136, 168, 172, 174
Republican Argus (Penn. newspaper), 60
Republican Greens (Phila. militia), 46, 55, 79, 159
Republican Greens (N.Y. militia), 79, 84
Republican Party, 1, 2, 39, 45, 99, 122, 124, 148; divisions after 1800, 8, 9, 62–64, 66, 71, 76, 78, 89; in election of 1796, 42, 43; in election of 1800, 55, 56, 58; and Irish immigrants, 2, 4, 8, 40, 155, 158
Republicans, 1, 41, 49, 51, 56, 67, 85, 89, 128, 143; and patronage, 72–74; and Presbyterians, 120, 125; religious background, 70, 71
republican thought, 98, 175; classical tradition, 5, 6, 107; Paineite tradition, 3, 5, 6, 64, 69, 70, 92, 150
revivalism, American (Second Great Awakening), 114, 124, 125, 127–31, 176
Reynolds, James, 37, 38, 40, 43, 44, 60, 62, 64, 70, 154, 164, 177; attacks on Washington, 42, 57; on Jay's Treaty, 41, 42; in St. Mary's riot, 53, 54; and United Irishmen, 20–23
Reynolds, Thomas, 24
Rhees, Morgan John, 96
Richmond (Va.), 136

Rising of 1798, 9, 23, 29–33, 51, 56, 57, 69, 76, 84, 88, 105, 113, 118, 119, 120, 129, 142, 154, 163, 172, 178; emigration following, 5, 8, 17, 32, 33, 59, 158; United Irish view of, 101–3, 164–66
Robespierre, Maximilien-François-Marie-Isodore de, 49, 97
Robinson, Thomas, 29, 61, 111, 164
Rochambeau, Count, 24
Rockite movement, 34
Rodgers, Peter, 5
Ross, James, 55, 128
Rousseau, Jean-Jacques, 93, 107, 143
Rowan, Archibald Hamilton, 6, 14, 15, 17, 37, 38, 41, 44, 51, 174; on Native Americans, 141, 151; return to Europe, 154–56; and United Irishmen, 18–23
Rowan, Sarah, 20, 21, 38, 51
Rowson, Susanna, 143
Royal Navy, 40; and impressment, 77–80
Rush, Benjamin, 96, 104, 110
Rush, Richard, 87, 89
Rushton, Edward, 160, 161
[illegible]

Saint Domingue (Haiti), 138
Saintfield (County Down), 33, 115, 117–19, 127; emigration from, 122, 124
Saintfield, Battle of (1798), 99, 118
Sampson, William, 11, 22, 29, 31, 59, 69, 79, 86, 91, 92, 157, 160, 162, 167–69, 177, 178; on common law, 68, 71, 111; historical writing of, 163–65; on trade unions, 149, 150; in War of 1812, 85, 88; on women, 146, 147, 151. Works: *Memoirs,* 164, 165
Savannah (Ga.), 88
Scotland, 28, 32, 98, 134; immigration from, 43, 87, 96; and Ireland, 161, 162, 170
Scrabo Hill, 32
Scullabogue, 30
Seceders (Irish Presbyterian sect), 117, 124, 127, 128, 130, 176
seditious libel, 68; trials of United Irishmen for, 49, 50, 55
Seneca Falls, 147
Shakespeare, William, 107
Shamrock (N.Y. Irish newspaper), 79, 80, 89, 91, 134, 135, 137, 156, 163
Shamrock Friendly Society, 91, 92, 156, 157
Sheares brothers (Henry and John), 23
Simms, Robert, 22, 110, 174
Simpson, James, 119
Sinclair, William, 17, 119, 174
slave ownership, 42, 43; among Irish, 9, 136, 151, 175
slavery, 9, 103, 178; and United Irishmen, 9, 134–40, 151, 175
Smith, Adam, 90, 91
Smith, Dr. James, 49, 50
Smith, James Morton, 50
Smith, John, 142
Snyder, Simon, 2, 74, 84; alliance with Binns, 63, 64, 73; Irish support for, 158
Society of United Irishmen. *See* United Irishmen, Society of (Ireland)
South Carolina, 43, 94, 139
Southwark (Philadelphia district), 73, 74, 150; and Republicans, 39, 43, 55
Spain, 15, 141; New World colonies of, 61, 93
Spenser, Edmund, 170
standing armies, Irish opposition to, 51, 81
Stanton, Elizabeth Cady, 147
states' rights, 89, 90, 94, 138
Steele, Robert, 119
[illegible]
St. Mary's Church (Philadelphia), riot at (1799), 53, 54, 56
Storey, Thomas, 60
St. Patrick's Benevolent Society (Phila. United Irish organization), 73
St. Patrick's Day, parades on, 159, 160
Strugglers, 23, 44
Sunday School Association, 97
Swanwick, John, 40
Swift, Jonathan, 50

Talleyrand, Charles Maurice de, 45
Tammany Society (New York), 121
Tandy, Napper, 17, 26, 38, 154; and United Irishmen, 18, 19, 22
tariff bill of 1824 (American), 91
Taylor, William, 164
Temple of Reason (N.Y. deist newspaper), 69, 70
theater, Irish impact on American, 9, 95, 100, 103–6
Theophilanthropic Society (N.Y. deist organization), 69, 70
Thomas, Antoine L., 98
Thornton, William, 96
Time-Piece (N.Y. Republican newspaper), 49, 50, 56, 100, 160
Tompkins, Daniel, 64, 67, 111
Tone, Theobald Wolfe, 12–14, 19, 46, 154, 158, 173, 177, 178; on America, 36–38; and Rising of 1798, 21, 22, 25

Tooke, Horne, 27, 165
Townshend, Lord, 80
Tracy, Uriah, 1, 2
trade unions, 159; and United Irishmen, 9, 134, 148–51
transportation improvements, United Irishmen support for, 82, 92
Trenor, Thomas (Thomas Traynor), 60
Trinity College (Dublin), 23, 29, 61, 140
Twomey, Richard, 3–6
Tyler, John, Jr., 100
Tyrone, County, 20, 44, 113

Ulster, 13, 14, 17, 25, 29, 113, 154; emigration from, 2, 43, 60, 158; Presbyterianism in, 114, 115, 117
Union, Act of (1801), 34, 81, 154, 165; movement to repeal, 140, 168, 169
Union Greens (Baltimore militia), 79
United Britons, 60; formation of, 27, 28
United Irish and Scotch Benevolent Society (Albany organization), 158
United Irishmen, American Society of, 44, 56, 57, 64, 66, 67, 70, 158; and Federalists, 45, 48, 50, 51; founding of (1797), 8, 11, 43
United Irishmen, Society of, 11, 12, 23, 27, 68, 95, 101, 102, 110, 114, 115, 118, 119, 134, 149; call for uprising by (1798), 29, 30; dealings with French, 2, 20–22, 24, 25, 46, 58; divisions within, 26–29, 176–77; early years in Dublin, 18–21; flight of members to America, 32–35; ideology, 172–75; imprisonment of leaders, 1, 37, 121; recruitment of Defenders, 19, 22–25; release of leaders after 1802, 2, 8; suppression of (1797–98), 26, 28, 29, 43, 60
United Irishmen in the United States, 44, 63, 69, 79, 90, 94, 95, 108, 109, 113, 120, 122, 129, 138, 155, 157, 163, 175; Anglophobia of, 9, 76, 174; and bank reform, 92, 93; class composition, 3, 44; and common law, 68, 69; cultural contributions, 100, 105, 106; divisions within, 71–74, 76–78; and economic policy, 81, 82; and education, 97–99; effect on American politics, 7–10; effect of Jefferson's victory on, 57–59, 61; and Federalists, 44–49, 51–53, 55–57, 65–67; immigrant support for, 45, 54, 56; and music, 110, 111, 160, 161; and nationalism, 153, 154, 166, 167; and Native Americans, 140–43; and O'Connell, 168, 169; and Republicans, 40–43, 56, 64; and slavery, 9, 134–40; and social policy, 133–34, 147, 148, 150–52; and trade sanctions against Britain, 80, 81; view of America, 8, 34, 35, 51–53, 57, 133, 170; in War of 1812, 83–89; and women, 9, 143–46
United States Recorder (Republican newspaper), 50

Vallencey, Charles, 162
Valmy, Battle of (1792), 115
Van Buren, Martin, 98
Vinegar Hill, 30, 164
Virginia, 70, 100–103, 110, 125, 127, 138, 142, 143; Irish in, 50, 61, 135
Volney, Constantin-François de Chasseboeuf, Comte de, 69
Volunteer companies (American), 84, 87
Volunteer Convention (1783), 17
Volunteer movement (Ireland), 16–19, 82, 115, 121, 134
Volunteers Journal (Dublin newspaper), 17, 82

Wales, 59; emigration from, 96–97
War of 1812, 6, 9, 76, 84, 87, 90, 92, 136, 141; causes of, 78–80, 82; opposition to, 85, 86, 94; songs of, 111, 176
Warden, David Bailie, 6, 7, 69, 76, 78, 80, 82, 90, 93–95, 119, 120, 134, 136, 138, 140, 141, 165, 169, 177; on America, 134; on education, 97–99; emigration, 59, 60; in Rising of 1798, 32, 33; on women, 144–46, 151
Warren, General, as dramatized by Burk, 104–6
Warwick, Archibald, 120
Washburn, Wilcomb, 102
Washington (D.C.), 97; Irish in, 2, 5, 79
Washington, George, 51, 97, 115, 118, 124, 158, 178; Irish attacks on, 42, 57
Washington (Penn.), 129–31; Irish settlement in, 122, 124–26
Washington (Penn.) College, 130
Washington Reporter (Penn. newspaper), 130
Watson, Bishop, 71
Webster, Noah, 96, 110
Wellington, Arthur Wellesley, Duke of, 158
West Indies, 134
western expansion, and American politics, 90, 93, 94
Wexford bridge, massacre at (1798), 30
Wexford, County, 61, Rising of 1798 in, 5, 30, 164
Whig Party (American), 159

Whig Party (British), 59
White, John Campbell, 60, 158
Whiteboys, 15
Wicklow, County, 29, 30
Wollstonecraft, Mary, 143
women, Irish views on rights of, 9, 134, 143, 144–46, 149, 151
working class, Irish-American, 149, 151, 159
Working Men's Party, 150, 151
Wylie, Samuel, 44, 99

XYZ affair (1798), 44, 45, 108

Yorkshire Fencibles, 118
Yorktown, Battle of (1781), 31
Young Ireland, 10, 34, 169–70

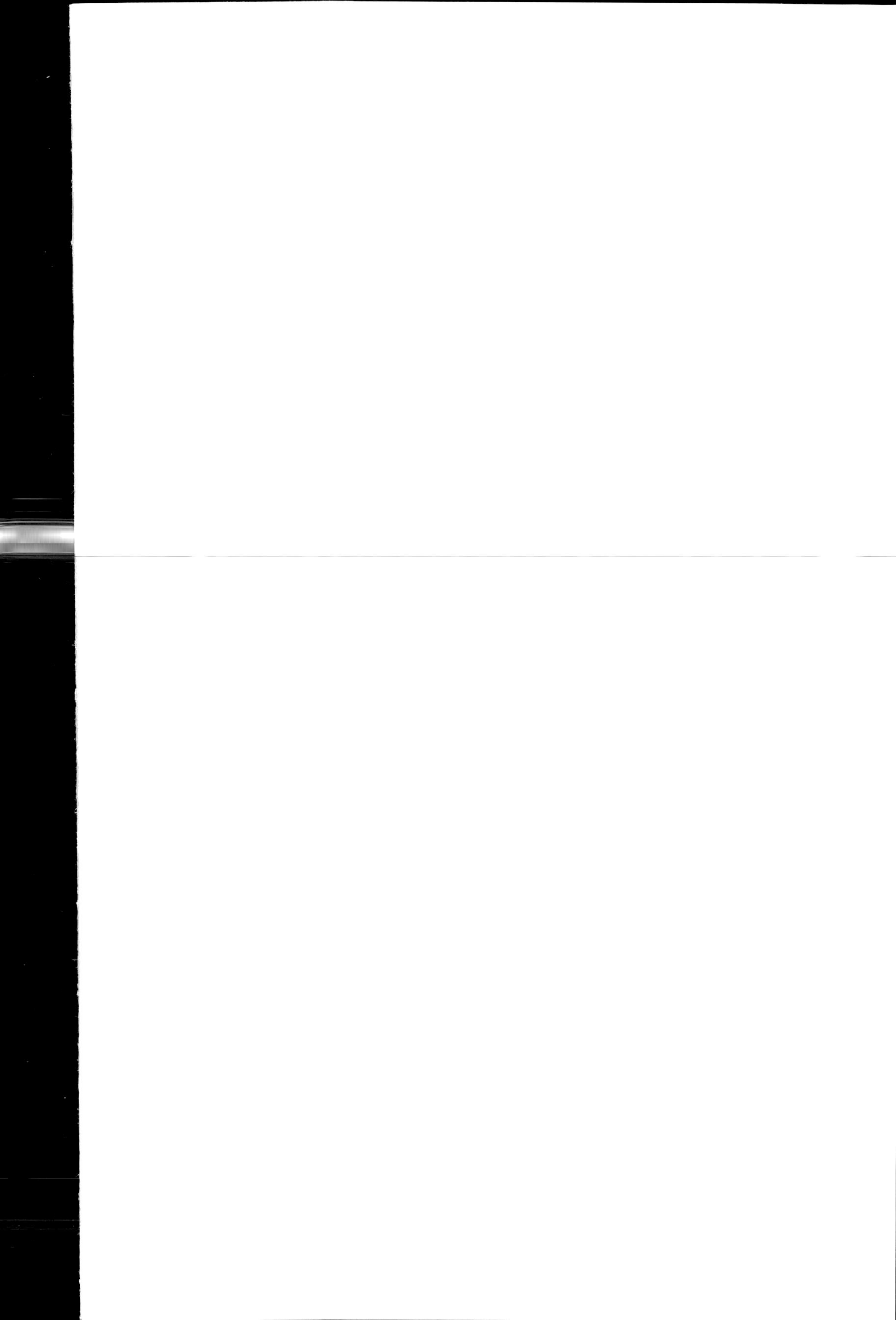